WRITING WILD

WRITING
WILD

WOMEN POETS, RAMBLERS, and MAVERICKS Who Shape How We See THE NATURAL WORLD

KATHRYN AALTO

TIMBER PRESS
PORTLAND, OREGON

With love for
Helen, Joan, and Tess
My grandmother, mother, and daughter

Published in 2020 by Timber Press, Inc.
The Haseltine Building
133 S.W. Second Avenue, Suite 450
Portland, Oregon 97204-3527
timberpress.com

Printed in China

Text design by Laura Shaw Design
Cover illustration by Gisela Goppel

ISBN 978-1-60469-927-2

Catalog records for this book are available from the Library of Congress
and the British Library.

DOROTHY WORDSWORTH

17

SUSAN FENIMORE COOPER

27

GENE STRATTON-PORTER

39

MARY AUSTIN

48

VITA SACKVILLE-WEST

58

NAN SHEPHERD

69

RACHEL CARSON

80

MARY OLIVER

90

CAROLYN MERCHANT

100

**ANNIE
DILLARD**

109

**GRETEL
EHRLICH**

117

**LESLIE
MARMON SILKO**

125

**DIANE
ACKERMAN**

132

**ROBIN WALL
KIMMERER**

142

**LAURET
SAVOY**

150

**REBECCA
SOLNIT**

158

**KATHLEEN
JAMIE**

167

**CAROLYN
FINNEY**

176

What do we wish for? To be whole. To be complete. Wildness reminds us what it means to be human, what we are connected to rather than what we are separate from.

TERRY TEMPEST WILLIAMS,
RED: PASSION AND PATIENCE IN THE DESERT (2001)

Isn't it queer: there are only two or three human stories, and they go on repeating themselves as fiercely as if they had never happened before; like the larks in this country, that have been singing the same five notes over for thousands of years.

WILLA CATHER,
O PIONEERS! (1913)

I hope you love Birds too. It is economical.
It saves going to Heaven.

EMILY DICKINSON,
LETTER TO EUGENIA HALL (1885)

INTRODUCTION

WHEN I WAS A CHILD, I ran away from home a lot.

Over my shoulder, I slung a knapsack fashioned from a red handkerchief pulled from my costume trunk of gowns, hats, and heels. Before spearing it with an almond tree branch, I filled that pack with provisions: my toothbrush, a box of raisins, my small silk blanket, and bread pilfered from the kitchen when my mother wasn't looking.

"This is goodbye," I would lisp-whisper to my parents.

"Okay, Honey," they'd say, watching five-year-old me flounce out the back door—1940s earrings clipped to my ears, mangy fur stole around my neck—and into the cornfields and peach orchards of our home on Lemon Avenue.

There was never any reason to leave. Ours was a happy home. The culprits for inspiring my wanderlust were books. The whimsical per-ambulations of the trickster Br'er Rabbit from *The Tales of Uncle Remus* tickled my imagination. I read and reread the blissful over-land and underland adventures of Mole, Toad, Rat, and Badger from *The Wind in the Willows* and pined for the storybook landscapes of England. The darkness of "Hansel and Gretel" by the Brothers Grimm inspired the trail of breadcrumbs I dropped in the powdery dirt of California's San Joaquin Valley as I made what, to me, felt like epic odysseys. You never know when you might encounter a cannibalistic witch.

Decades have passed, and the appeal of journeys on foot remains. At university, I read an account by the great naturalist John Muir of walking from San Francisco to Yosemite National Park through the valley where I grew up. It instilled a lifelong interest in narrative nonfiction, nature writing, and the essay. I pieced together nature writing like a puzzle to understand who and what came before and after Muir.

In the Pacific Northwest during our twenties and thirties, my other half pursued graduate studies in sediment while I studied sentiment. He became a geology professor; I taught American literature of nature and place. We renovated a turn-of-the-century farm. Looking back on those years of rewilding a salmon spawning stream, interlacing footpaths through our meadows and woods, and planting sequoias that will outlive our great-great-great grandchildren, I can identify a few key ideas that led to me writing this book.

For one thing, I'd gotten the feeling that nature writing and environmentalism was a club for white men, even in the late twentieth century. Anthologies of thirty years ago reflect this. Voices were missing. Ear to the ground, I have long listened for the footfalls of others.

For another, on our farm, I began to feel like the ballerina of my childhood jewelry box who, upon opening the lid, twirls and spins in one place. America has stunning national and state parks, but trespassing laws confine folks to their fiefdoms within rural and suburban geographies. Walking the circuitous paths of the farm as the sun glinted off the backs of coho salmon in October, I wished I could ramble along the stream from source to sea. I could not. I wished I could walk into town. With logging trucks whizzing past, I couldn't without putting my life at risk. Though we could travel by car, and did, I felt I was living on an island.

And then, we moved to a real island—England.

Here in Britain, the ramble, the through-hike, and the literary pilgrimage are delicious pastimes protected by "right to roam" laws. My strong desire to stride is quenched. There is an athletic lyricism in any movement—dance, basketball, running, skiing—that seduces my heart, mind, and spirit (I can spend hours in Hyde Park watching people move), and Britain's ancient footpaths invite us to move in ways humans were designed for. It's blissful to pass in and out of history and holloways, to picnic and prospect on green hilltops. The pace of walking is ideal for the sensual intake of fragrance, birdsong, and cloud watching. The tempo of the artful amble appeals to the writer in me. Where walking and writing intersect is the personal essay—the beating heart of the nature-writing genre.

So when *Outside* magazine published an article they called "Essential Books for the Well-Read Explorer," I noted with some interest that twenty-two of the twenty-five books were by white men. "Hold your horses," I said, wedging my foot in the door, and wrote a rebuttal. That article—part of a conversation academics have been having for decades about who has access to and writes about nature—buzzed and hummed online, with readers wanting more stories about the lives and literature of women who have written about the natural world, some of whom—*sigh*—did not get credit, wrote anonymously, or were maligned for being female. This book emerged from that curiosity and clamor.

I should say that, although I have done my best to summon the spirit and language of classic, overlooked, and new nature writing over two centuries, this book is not a definitive anthology. Some of your own favorite writers might not be included, but it is only for lack of space that I could not include everyone. Think of these pages as a glance backward and a look forward, as well as a celebration of women who bring a different dimension to nature writing, rather than a compendium of every woman who ever wrote about the natural world. I love the work of Terry Tempest Williams—especially her shimmering 1991 book *Refuge: An Unnatural History of*

Family and Place. However, Gretel Ehrlich's 1985 book, *The Solace of Open Spaces*, came earlier in the subgenre of Western American writing and was pivotal in opening a gate to that particular field. In Britain, Melissa Harrison is a brilliant novelist of nature writing, and Australian Aboriginal poet Oodgeroo Noonuccal and Australian memoirist and fiction writer Inga Simpson are well worth exploring. To shine light on as many writers as possible, at the end of many essays are side paths, which invite further exploration.

As a personal essayist, I weave my own voice in and out of the narrative, but I want you to hear the voices of these women. They are the stars. As we journey together, I am merely pointing up to their constellations—highlighting what they have written, their historical significance, and, where relevant, the barriers, biases, and bullying they overcame to write.

I also liberally use the term "nature writing" to include many categories: natural history, environmental philosophy, country life, scientific writing, garden arts, memoirs, and meditations. All these writers are concerned with an essential wildness. Some write about being in the wild. Some mourn the vanishing wild—from ecosystems to native peoples. Some write about inhabiting the idea of wildness— which sometimes can mean an uncultivated part of themselves. As a wordsmith who often has a foot in academia, I am conscientious about the nuanced differences between "nature," "wild," "place," and "landscape"—but here in these pages, I am relaxed about it.

Gender, race, and physical abilities are also important prisms through which to understand how people access and experience the natural world. If you are white, for example, a poplar tree in a park may look innocuous—an innocent object of beauty. Imagine though that you are unable to reach it over a rocky trail. If you are differently abled and cannot access its shade or touch its leaves, how might your relationship to the tree change? If you are black, that same tree may have a more sinister feel, perhaps a symbol of lynching's legacy. Think of jazz star Billie Holiday's haunting rendition of the song "Strange Fruit." Within a musical landscape of minor chords, Holiday transports us to the "gallant" South and a lynching scene where bodies swing like fruit from trees—leaves and roots soaked in blood. It's a vivid example of how perspective colors experience. If we don't give diverse narratives, first, the opportunity to exist, and second, recognition and legitimacy, it can appear that able-bodied white guys have, in the words of comedian Hannah Gadsby, "a monopoly on the human experience."

While it's time to turn up the volume on narratives by women, it's never a time to knock what anyone—man or woman—has done well. In no way do I dismiss the important contributions of men in the genre. I can no more easily dislodge my hero Henry David Thoreau from my thinking than I can heartthrob Andy Gibb from my preteen memories. Indeed, hanging in my office is a reproduction of Caspar David Friedrich's painting "Wanderer Above the Sea of Fog." Two hundred years ago, this, in the words of poet Kathleen Jamie, "lone enraptured male"—hair tousled, topcoat billowing in the wind atop a mountain as he gazes over a valley of fog— embodied the Romantic view of nature and the rapture of sublime experiences. Though iconic, it is but one of infinite experiences in nature. On this warming flipside of the Industrial Revolution, the tenor and urgency of nature writing has shifted beyond our individual emotions. Poles are melting, sea levels rising, coral reefs dying. Biodiversity is plummeting, and weather systems grow ever more erratic. Those who write about the natural world can harness science and reason with the personal and poetic to heighten awareness, influence policy, and stir the soul. Today's ecopoetics, dystopian fiction, cli-fi, and solar punk invite us to consider catastrophic as well as hopeful futures for life in this Anthropocene. Some say this is "new nature writing," but it is not new. Susan Fenimore Cooper's 1850 *Rural Hours* and Elizabeth Rush's 2018 *Rising* are part of the same urgent tradition.

Much of this book was researched and penned outside—mountain climbing, mudlarking, canoeing, beachcombing, gardening, hiking, and birdwatching. I retraced the footsteps of those who have passed on, some of whom wrote anonymously or were chastised for daring to venture off without male chaperones. I walked and talked with living authors. I read original nineteenth-century journals, letters, essays, and books. I held tangible personal objects. I searched the faces in old photographs. I listened to historians, archivists, and experts. I attended live author readings and listened to recordings. I passed through two hundred years of women's history through nature writing.

The women I met are authentic and remarkable. Ramblers, scholars, and spiritual seekers. Conservationists, scientists, explorers. Historians, poets, and novelists. Heroines, mavericks, and swashbuckling trailblazers. They defy broad categorization beyond their grit to sidestep any pesky No Trespassing signs in their way.

May they inspire you to do the same. Be bold. Dive deep. Map your own way with new coordinates. Whether you take a suitcase, backpack, or handkerchief knapsack, remember a notebook—and don't forget a pencil.

DOROTHY WORDSWORTH

I left my sole companion-friend
To wander out alone.
Lured by a little winding path,
I quitted soon the public road,
A smooth and tempting path it was,
By sheep and shepherds trod.

"GRASMERE – A FRAGMENT"

OUR JOURNEY BEGINS in Wasdale, one of the most remote valleys in England's Lake District. In the pink predawn light of midsummer, I set out on a narrow lane lined in drystone walls overflowing in fragrant wild honeysuckle and mustard lichen. I pass St. Olaf's, possibly England's smallest church, a stone structure set amid a grove of yews in ancient Viking fields.

I lift the latch at a path marked Scafell Pike, step through the gate, and hear the metallic *clink* break the morning silence. I cross a pasture toward a wooden bridge and onto a narrow ascending gravel trail. The way is up, but Scafell Pike—the peak I'm aiming for and England's tallest—is hidden for the moment by Goat Crag. I walk through Brackenclose then rise along the rocky cascades of Lingmell Gill and higher, through alpine meadows of purple saxifrage and carpets of moss along Brown Tongue. Above me is Black Crag, a peak shorter than my destination, and I stop here to appreciate the pleasures of total silence. When I begin hiking again, I can hear my breath, and my feet crunching in the gravel. Somewhere in the clear air above me, a ring ouzel calls, pauses, then sings a warbled song that sounds like marbles in hand. An hour passes, 1,500 feet climbed. Higher up at Lingmell Col, the saddle between Broad Crag and Scafell Pike, Herdwick sheep rest in boulder shadows, where they leave tufts of black and white wool in the parsley fern. Above me, a sharp *ping, ping, ping* of a buzzard against the fingernail moon. The sun is rising, and soon it will be hot. My legs are strong and I travel light. I don't mean to overtake two sets of highly kitted men—but I do. And I wink at them.

I reach a large debris field of scree and shattered rock and look for cairns to lead me in the final steep climb. I leap across rocks and boulders. There are some final steps onto a platform, and I'm finally standing at the 3,209-foot summit. For a little while, before less-early risers make their way up, I am alone on one of the world's most rapturous stages. I take a deep breath, surrounded by a study in blues.

Dark blue lakes. Indigo mountain shadows. Robin-egg sky. It's seven in the morning, and the sun is spreading golden light into these blue hues. I see Helvellyn and Skiddaw and can just make out the Mourne Mountains across the Irish Sea and Snowdonia in Wales to the south. Somewhere in the hills below me is Grasmere, the home of England's most famous poet.

Here on top of Scafell Pike, it's easy to understand why few landscapes are more steeped in literary history than this. It's a place celebrated over two hundred years ago by the enraptured band of brothers known as the Lake Poets—Robert Southey, Samuel Taylor Coleridge, and William Wordsworth—who all walked and wrote among these hills and vales. In their landmark 1798 *Lyrical Ballads*, Wordsworth and Coleridge sought to overturn the pompous epic poetry that came before them. They were their generation's Sex Pistols and Dead Kennedys, and this was poetry's punk moment. Old subjects were thrown out—sensations were celebrated. In ordinary language and in folk-ballad form, these poets celebrated their *own* memories, their *own* emotions, and their *own* experiences in nature. Their work represents the start of what is known as English Romanticism, the artistic celebration of the individual, nature, and the past that extended from the late 1700s to the early 1800s. It was a reaction to the Industrial Revolution and the new faith in reason, science, and mathematics embodied by the Enlightenment. Romantics sought a return to individual experiences like awe, horror, and fear, as a way to cultivate mystery and wonder in an increasingly mechanistic society. In simple terms, you could say that a Romantic preferred to wake to a cockerel than to a clock.

Squinting in the direction of Grasmere, I think of Glencoyne Bay near Ullswater, where Wordsworth and his younger sister Dorothy often walked together. I haven't climbed all this way to celebrate him—170 years after his death, he still has his fame, and rightly so. Instead, I'm thinking of Dorothy.

She was born in 1771 in Cockermouth, a market town on the western edge of the Lake District, the middle child and only girl of the five Wordsworth children. Tall and slender, radiating intelligence and kindness, Dorothy's natural disposition and sensibilities mirrored the wild and emotive traits the Romantics esteemed. As a little girl, she wept at first sight of the sea—as an adult, contrasts of color and texture in fields also moved her deeply. Their mother and father died when the Wordsworth children were young, and the four brothers bounced between relatives, while Dorothy was sent to Yorkshire to live with her mother's cousin. There was "life before," with her family. And there was "life after," a time that cut into her well-being and caused a deep sense of abandonment and rejection. Though only 100 miles separated her from them, Dorothy did not see her brothers for ten years. When at last she did, she and William discovered they shared an especially close poetic companionability. They began to walk great distances together, and she became his sensitive sounding board, inspiration, and eventual amanuensis.

One immortal walk took place in the green hills near Ullswater on 15 April 1802. As they strolled around Glencoyne Bay, they encountered a scene of wild English daffodils flouncing with effervescence in the wind along the water. After stopping to marvel at it in the manner of true Romantics, they continued to Dove Cottage, their rose-covered home surrounded with wild strawberries, primroses, dandelions, and foxgloves, all collected by Dorothy on walks in nearby woods. That evening, Dorothy recorded the scene in her journal:

> When we were in the woods beyond Gowbarrow park we saw a
> few daffodils close to the water side, we fancied that the lake had
> floated the seed ashore and that the little colony had so sprung
> up—But as we went along there were more and yet more and at
> last under the boughs of the trees, we saw that there was a long
> belt of them along the shore, about the breadth of a country

turnpike road. I never saw daffodils so beautiful they grew among the mossy stones about and about them, some rested their heads upon these stones as on a pillow for weariness and the rest tossed and reeled and danced and seemed as if they verily laughed with the wind that blew upon them over the Lake, they looked so gay ever glancing ever changing.

Known today as *The Grasmere Journal*, this collection is one of four small diaries that captured Dorothy's own lyrical voice and acute observations of the natural world from 1800 to 1803. And yet, two years later, William Wordsworth wrote "Daffodils," arguably one of the most famous poems in the English language:

> I wandered lonely as a cloud
> That floats on high o'er vales and hills,
> When all at once I saw a crowd,
> A host, of golden daffodils;
> Beside the lake, beneath the trees,
> Fluttering and dancing in the breeze.

In twenty-four breezy lines, the future poet laureate praises the purity and beauty of nature, reflecting the gospel of Romanticism that "all good poetry is the spontaneous overflow of powerful feelings." Beloved around the world, "Daffodils" captures the essence of the Romantic era—but it doesn't entirely belong to him. How this came to be reveals much about what has changed from the Wordsworths' time to now.

William's Cambridge University education was out of the question for Dorothy as a woman, but her talent and urge to create would not be stifled. She penned poetry, kept journals, and wrote thousands of letters, including 700 we can still read today, which are marked by an acute and cultivated power of observation equal to the many formally educated men who visited Dove Cottage. She wrote so well that both her brother and Coleridge are known to have lifted phrases from her journals, but Dorothy was more than the wind beneath their wings, and her own work deserves to be celebrated as distinct from her famous brother and his peers.

Dorothy's poetic sensibilities flow throughout her unpretentious journals—both the experimental, sublunary *Alfoxden Journal* and the more revealing *Grasmere Journal*. Neither were intended for publication. Rather, she wrote pieces to share with family and friends about walks and travel to Scotland, the Alps, the Isle of Man, and more. Ernest de Selincourt, one of her earliest posthumous editors and biographers, remarked that Dorothy was "probably the most remarkable and the most distinguished of English prose writers who never wrote a line for the general public." But more people have read her uncredited work than they know. In a revision of his book *A Guide through the District of the Lakes*, William Wordsworth includes a letter Dorothy wrote to a friend about her 1818 ascent of Scafell Pike, now considered one of the most notable ascents of a mountain by a woman during the Romantic era. However, he didn't attribute the letter to Dorothy, giving the appearance that it was his own climb and he wrote the piece.

Call it what you will—plagiarism, borrowing, lifting—what *was* Mr. Wordsworth thinking? But we must give some thought to circumstance. Casting a glance back to that time, my guess is that Dorothy simply did not mind—maybe she considered the experiences she wrote about to be mutual. She never sought out notoriety or pursued publication, and brother and sister had a long, respectful, and loving sibling relationship. But, as many Romantic scholars have done, we can mind for her now and make sure she gets credit where it is due. Her essay enticed me to climb Scafell myself, to see what she saw, and I believe Harriet Martineau, Victorian feminist icon and Britain's first sociologist, would have wanted to know that the ascent, which she republished in her famous 1855 *A Complete Guide to the English Lakes*—the book that eclipsed Wordsworth's as the seminal Lake District walking book—belonged not to William, but Dorothy.

From the village of Rosthwaite, Dorothy set out with her friend, painter and poet Mary Barker, along with Barker's maid, a hired porter, and a Borrowdale shepherd to act as guide, to ascend the mountain. In her signature picturesque and phenomenological style, she observed and recorded the hike as it unfolded in the moment:

> Cushions or tufts of moss, parched and brown, appear between the blocks and stones that lie in heaps on all sides to a great distance, like skeletons or bones of the earth not needed at the creation, and there left to be covered with never-dying lichens, which the clouds and dews nourish and adorn with colors of vivid and exquisite beauty.

On reaching the summit, she burst with delight, "But how shall I speak of the deliciousness of the . . . prospect! At this time, that was most favored by sunshine and shade. The green Vale of Esk—deep and green, with its glittering serpent stream, lay below us. . . . We were far above the reach of the cataracts of Scaw Fell; and not an insect there was to hum in the air." In the delicious silence, her group begins a conversation about what they see in the distance. Dorothy's effervescent wonder is contagious.

> While we were gazing around, "Look," I exclaimed, "at yon ship upon the glittering sea!" "Is it a ship?" replied our shepherd-guide. "It can be nothing else," interposed my companion; "I cannot be mistaken, I am so accustomed to the appearance of ships at sea." The guide dropped the argument; but, before a minute was gone, he quietly said, "Now look at your ship; it is changed into a horse." So indeed it was; – a horse with a gallant neck and head. We laughed heartily; and I hope, when again inclined to be

positive, I may remember the ship and the horse upon the glittering sea; and the calm confidence, yet submissiveness, of our wise Man of the Mountains, who certainly had more knowledge of clouds than we, whatever might be our knowledge of ships.

After my own summit of Scafell, I stay a few days at an inn near Wasdale then travel on to Dove Cottage. In one of the front rooms, I notice the small 1806 silhouette of Dorothy. Like that illusory ship, which turned out to be something else entirely, this portrait feels indistinct, an ironic representation for a woman who was, in fact, at her critical and poetic peak and in her strongest body. Hoping to see beyond the illusion, I read her original letters, sitting in the sunshine, in the garden she tended.

I think how Dorothy was an outlier among women for climbing the tallest mountain in England, but she was not alone. Women explored in the company of mothers, aunts, and sisters, as well as husbands, fathers, uncles, and brothers. Some climbed with a guide because they felt threatened, were subject to verbal abuse, and could experience "reputational anxiety" about walking alone and what that conveyed to others. Dorothy herself received a steady stream of letters from a disapproving aunt and grandmother reprimanding her for her daring habit of walking in the moonlight and at twilight. Women of this era were often trapped by marriage and society into states of dependency, but Dorothy seemed to escape this fate, at least until the end of her long life.

In my visit to Rydal Mount, the house where Dorothy lived with William and his wife and children, I am finally able to shake off the gauzy veil of passing time and sort of lock eyes with this remarkable woman. An oil painting shows Dorothy in her early sixties, seated in a vibrant orange chair with a white terrier at her feet, a scenic lake and mountain just over her shoulder. Her gray-blue eyes are lively. Like many women who spent decades walking, Dorothy lived long, to age eighty-three, and though she was not without health problems, her eyes retain their twinkle. On her lap is a paper notebook, to her side a collection of inkwells and perhaps a canister of opium. She looks vibrant and alive. This woman treaded and recorded our literary landscapes before they were iconic, and she helped make them so. Far more than "the poet's sister," she is a woman worth her *own* words: Dorothy Wordsworth, "mountaineer, diarist, poet."

MORE ON MOUNTAINS

DOROTHY PILLEY

Pilley (1894–1986) attended the exclusive boarding school Queenswood, outside London, but turned rebellious at the prospect of life as a housewife, a trait she brought to mountaineering. She became a journalist for the British Women's Patriotic League, an early feminist group, and climbed mountains, first in Wales then Europe. She cofounded the Pinnacle Club, the world's first climbing club for women, and captured her swashbuckling mountain adventures in *Climbing Days*, her 1935 memoir.

HELEN MORT

Helen Mort is a dazzling British poet. A five-time winner of the Foyle Young Poets of the Year Award, she was the youngest-ever poet-in-residence at the Wordsworth Trust in 2010. Her second collection, *No Map Could Show Them* (2016), is a precise and feisty response to what one review called "the chauvinism faced by the earliest female mountaineers." She edited *Waymaking: An Anthology of Women's Adventure Writing, Poetry and Art* in 2018, and her debut novel, *Black Car Burning* (2019), is about the climbing community of the Peak District around Sheffield.

CHERYL STRAYED

A new classic in wilderness writing and modern feminism, *Wild: From Lost to Found on the Pacific Crest Trail* (2012) by Cheryl Strayed recounts a blistered and breathtaking 1100-mile solo trek on the PCT, which the author embarked upon at age twenty-six. The book tells two difficult parallel narratives: Strayed's life challenges before stepping foot on the trail, precipitated by her mother's death at the age of forty-five, and the trials and insights from her long journey.

SUSAN FENIMORE COOPER

A thunder-shower last night, by way of keeping the equinox, and this morning, to the joy of the whole community, the arrival of the robins is proclaimed. It is one of the great events of the year for us, the return of the robins; we have been on the watch for them these ten days, as they generally come between the fifteenth and twenty-first of the month, and now most persons you meet, old and young, great and small, have something to say about them.

RURAL HOURS

ACROSS THE ATLANTIC from the Lake District, the towering Manhattan skyscrapers and nineteenth-century mansions along the Hudson River recede as I leave New York City and pass through the Adirondacks, a pastoral landscape of apple orchards, farms, and dairies. Reminders of past rural life dot the landscape. Draft-kiln hop houses left over from American-grown hop fever. Painted and peeling barns built by English, German, and Dutch farmers. Sugar maples tapped for syrup.

I arrive in the leafy village of Cooperstown, set amid the rolling hills and river valleys of central upstate New York. The country roads that brought me here have the narrow, horse-and-cart width I know from my home in ye olde Devon—but the National Baseball Hall of Fame on Main Street reminds me I'm standing in twenty-first-century America.

When politician and judge William Cooper bought 10,000 acres here in 1785, true wilderness was already gone, and it was the new American frontier. Nestled on the south shore of Otsego Lake (from the Iroquois word *ote-sa-ga*), his namesake town has held a population of 2,000 for generations. It's where William's son, James Fenimore Cooper, perhaps America's first internationally known novelist, sometimes set his iconic Leatherstocking Tales (though the most famous of these, *The Last of the Mohicans*, 1826, takes place nearby).

I have traveled to Cooperstown to dip my toe into history and find a spot where I might for a few moments imagine the area in 1850, the year Susan Fenimore Cooper, James's daughter, wrote *Rural Hours*. As I retrace Susan's footsteps along a streambank dotted with Jack-in-the-pulpit and raccoon imprints in the mud, I muse to my hiking companion, Jessie, "I wish I had a boat to go out on the lake."

Jessie, an experienced hiker, paddler, and former book editor who knows the landscape of *Rural Hours* better than anyone, volunteers her canoe. Though I am a better cyclist and runner than paddler, at six o'clock the next morning, we are both on the lake, a shimmering mirror of clear blue sky that James Fenimore Cooper nicknamed "the Glimmerglass."

Surrounded by reflections of the low forested hills on the water, we pause in our paddling. I know from Susan's writing that an array of birds—bluebird, osprey, bald eagle, great blue heron, great white egret, northern shoveler, and warblers—called the area home. This morning I see ducks chuntering along the muddy shore and hear a solitary woodpecker drumming into a tree. Rising and swirling in the green water below us are walleye and spotted brown trout. A veil of morning fog disguises the ribbon of road circling the lake, along with the boats at the dock and the Federal- and Greek revival–style houses on shore. In this moment I can easily imagine the landscape as Susan saw it, when she became America's first nature writer—before her name and work faded into the mist of time.

Given his iconic status, most people assume the first book of American nature writing was Henry David Thoreau's 1854 *Walden*. But this is inaccurate. *Rural Hours* was published four years earlier. Scholars of nineteenth-century American literature know this, but the general public, less so. "Cooper is often designated the first American nature writer," says my friend Rochelle Johnson, an English professor who co-edited several important books of Cooper's work including *Susan Fenimore Cooper: New Essays on Rural Hours and Other Works* (2001), *Rural Hours and Essays on Nature and Landscape* (2002), and *Passions for Nature: Nineteenth-Century America's Aesthetics of Alienation* (2009). "She was the first American we know of to publish a book-length portrait of her home place—focusing on its inhabitants (both human and nonhuman), the recent changes to its landscape, and the small details of its seasons."

With early botanical knowledge passed down from three women—her grandmother, aunt, and mother—Cooper developed an early love for nature, an affinity on full display in her eloquent journal, which takes place over a year in Cooperstown. *Rural Hours* has been likened to *The Natural History and Antiquities of Selborne*

(1789), a series of simple, refined letters written by parson-naturalist Gilbert White about the natural history of his village in the hills of Hampshire, England. Like White's book, *Rural Hours* wasn't overlooked in its day—far from it. Widely and favorably received, the book was in print for nearly forty years, its detailed history of this pocket of America fascinating prominent naturalists of the time, including Charles Darwin. In a letter to Asa Gray on 6 November 1862, Darwin wrote:

> Talking of Books, I am in middle of one which pleases me ... viz "Miss Cooper's Journal of Naturalist". Who is she? She seems a very clever woman & gives a capital account of the battle between our & your weeds. Does it not hurt your Yankee pride that we thrash you so confoundedly?

The book is a delightful mix of detailed personal impressions alongside astute philosophical meditations. Inspired by her daily perambulations in the woods and village, Cooper writes with an artless spontaneity about everything from violets to vistas, observing local natural history, contemplating the meditative qualities of lakes, and conveying early conservation ideas. The reader is given a glimpse into life in a mid-nineteenth-century village—the excitement people felt upon the return of robins each spring, the bemusement an Irish farmer gives people when he buys buckets and taps for sap but learns it doesn't rise all year, and the sadness Cooper feels for dwindling stands of old-growth trees. We understand what it feels like to live in a place that rapidly transformed from wilderness to frontier to a cultivated landscape of small farms and dairies.

On 18 May, she records new spring blossoms:

> A pretty habit this, with many of our early flowers, growing in little sisterhoods, as it were; we rarely think of the violets singly, as

of the rose, or the lily; we always fancy them together, one lending a grace to another, amid their tufted leaves.

On 9 June, the soothing effects of water capture her attention:

> Even in a limited water-view, there is a flow of life, a ceaseless variety, which becomes a perpetual source of delight; every passing hour throws over the transparent countenance of the lake, or river, some fresh tint of coloring, calls up some new play of expression beneath the changing influences of the sun, the winds, the clouds, and we are all but cheated into the belief that the waters know something of the sorrows and joys of our hearts; we turn to them with more than admiration—with the partiality with which we turn to the face of a friend.

Born in 1813, Cooper, like Dorothy Wordsworth, lived in the shadow of a literary giant. For much of her life she acted as copyist for her famous father. She was well educated, having lived in France with her family from ages thirteen to twenty, and, like the heroine of her nearly forgotten, semi-autobiographical, 1846 novel *Elinor Wyllys,* she was single—though it may not have been from choice. Today asking a father for woman's hand in marriage is a fading formality, but in Cooper's time, it was strict protocol. At least one European gentleman who sought Susan Cooper's hand was rebuffed. Her father wrote to a friend, "I had proposals for Susan last week coming from a Frenchman of good fortune, noble family and very fair hopes, but the thing would not do. We mean to continue as Americans." No evidence survives to suggest her feelings about being unwed. Nonetheless, as a woman free of a husband and children, she had more time to pursue interests outside the home (including founding an orphanage and hospital) and to record what she saw and thought about nature and human impact on it.

Well read, she kept abreast of publications in natural history, including books by Darwin and early ecologist Alexander von Humboldt.

Rural Hours is notable for Cooper's early "think globally, act locally" philosophy, on display in a 28 July entry where she writes about the importance of trees beyond their economic value:

> Independently of their market price in dollars and cents, the trees have other values: they are connected in many ways with the civilization of a country; they have their importance in an intellectual and in a moral sense. After the first rude stage of progress is past in a new country—when shelter and food have been provided—people begin to collect the conveniences and pleasures of a permanent home about their dwellings, and then the farmer generally sets out a few trees before his door. This is very desirable, but it is only the first step in the track; something more is needed; the preservation of fine trees, already standing, marks a farther progress, and this point we have not yet reached. It frequently happens that the same man who yesterday planted some half dozen branchless saplings before his door, will to-day cut down a noble elm, or oak, only a few rods from his house, an object which was in itself a hundred-fold more beautiful than any other in his possession. In very truth, a fine tree near a house is a much greater embellishment than the thickest coat of paint that could be put on its walls, or a whole row of wooden columns to adorn its front; nay, a large shady tree in a door-yard is much more desirable than the most expensive mahogany and velvet sofa in the parlor.

It is impossible to resist comparing *Rural Hours* with *Walden*. Though they differ in style, intent, and impact, both are close observational diaries of a year in one place, written only a few years apart, which had the effect of raising awareness of the rapidly changing American environment. Side by side, the two books also reveal fascinating differences in the ways men and women could voice their thoughts in mid-nineteenth-century America. Thoreau does something considered commonplace now, which made him unusual then—in nearly every paragraph, on every page, his prose is punctuated by the first-person singular pronoun *I*.

In our current Age of the Selfie, it may be hard to imagine a time when speaking declaratively of oneself could be considered immodest and vain. But as Phillip Lopate, author of *The Art of the Personal Essay: An Anthology from the Classical Era to the Present* (1994), describes it, too much "first person" in essays risked the writer becoming known for "the stench of ego." Some writers of that time used it but knew they had to do so with charm, so as to not appear arrogant.

Today that first-person singular pronoun, used judiciously, is a common and compelling hallmark of creative nonfiction. Me, myself, and I make the small loom large and the personal universal, and most nature writers employ it to different degrees as a conversational approach. In Thoreau's writing, readers feel less like they are listening to a sermon and more like they're on a walk with him as he declares his intention "to front only the essential facts of life." He writes, "When I first took up my abode in the woods . . ." and "Wherever I sat, there I might live . . ." And his consistent zesty presence gives his writing punch and pop. Women did not, for the most part, speak to their readers with such intimacy.

A product of her times, Cooper avoids the whole situation and writes with the impersonal first-person plural *we*. This formality in *Rural Hours* can convey a sense of being one step removed from the narrative. But then, in Cooper's time, writing was a complicated act filled with extremes. At best, it was one of the few respectable ways a woman could make a living. At worst, women who wrote could be seen as prostituting themselves. Cooper may not have been inclined to experiment with form when she was already pushing boundaries. However, while her voice may read as less personal than Thoreau's, her innovative ecological thinking and the vivid picture she paints of mid-nineteenth-century Cooperstown life in the is in no way less vital.

Thoreau also had the uncomplicated luxury of putting his name on his writing. Female writers with a byline risked being called out as a "scribbling dame," "female quill-driver," or "half man." Many women wrote anonymously, like Aphra Behn, the English poet, playwright, fiction writer, and translator, who earned her own living writing poems and novels under a pseudonym, to become one of the most prolific authors of the Restoration. Others adopted the modest moniker "By a Lady." Though she initially used this discreet convention, Cooper was widely known to be the author of *Rural Hours* and was treated with respect. She dropped the pretense in later editions—those and other works show her full name resplendently printed as "Susan Fenimore Cooper."

After paddling around the lake with Jessie, I find breakfast in the village and wind my way over to the Fenimore Art Museum. Among Fenimore memorabilia—letters, portraits, a suit belonging to her father—I find the most famous image of Susan, a tiny black-and-white carte-de-visite circa 1855. The limits of still photography and class conventions preclude any sense of her personality—no Mona Lisa twinkle in her eyes nor sly smile at the corner of her mouth.

I wonder why Susan passed from popular memory. Rochelle Johnson later tells me, "It's partly because she lacked children, a devoted editor, or an intact archive bequest to ensure her literary legacy. But the fact that she was a woman no doubt also played a role: her era would come to be known as that of Emerson, Hawthorne, Thoreau, Melville, and Whitman, rather than of Margaret Fuller, Lydia Maria Child, Susan Fenimore Cooper, Catherine Sedgwick, and Emily Dickinson. Given a different cultural moment, things could have been different."

Though it's her most famous and impactful work, *Rural Hours* was composed early in Susan's writing career. She wrote it, in part, as a way to persuade Americans to develop a sense of stewardship for their new nation. Environmental history and the impact of humans on the natural world would remain her lifelong focus.

In 1854, a curious book called *Rural Rambles; or, Some Chapters on Flowers, Birds, and Insects* was published "By a Lady." A six-chapter volume, scholars say it mirrors Susan's signature fusion of personal observation, natural history, and lyrical prose—and while nothing survives to confirm this now-rare book is definitively Cooper's, she is assumed to be the author. In 1855, she wrote *The Rhyme and Reason of Country Life*, a collection of poems about rural life and the natural world. Her introduction to this book teems with insights into the hive of her environmental mind. Nature writing, she asserts, is a vital force in shaping attitudes and actions toward nature in the new American nation. She elevates rural American nature writers to a high cultural position as influencers. In her 1853 introduction to *Country Rambles in England*, the American edition of John Leonard Knapp's *Journal of a Naturalist* (1829), she again writes that Americans should make their new nation the subject of their writing.

Cooper's long writing career included articles, essays, and letters (and keeping her father's novels in the spotlight with new editions). Her most curiously polemical piece, "Female Suffrage: A Letter to the Christian Women of America," was published in *Harper's New Weekly Magazine* in 1870. It was an argument against female suffrage, written when Cooper, a devout Episcopalian, was in her late fifties. Divine powers, Cooper reasoned, subordinated women to men, physically and intellectually. "The great mass of women," she wrote, "can never be made to take a deep, a sincere, a discriminating, a lasting interest in the thousand political questions ever arising to be settled by the vote."

From my modern vantage point, I search Susan's eyes for something I just cannot put my finger on—perhaps a hint of how she could write so progressively about the natural world yet be on the wrong side of history with the vote. But her face gives nothing away, not even a contradiction.

Humanity's myriad relationships with nature in the "New" World would become a distinguishing literary aesthetic in the first half of the nineteenth century—especially with the writing of Emerson, Thoreau, Whitman, and Melville. Cooper's contribution to this American renaissance is as fresh as ever, and, thankfully, no longer overlooked. While her feeling that a woman's voice would never be vital enough to shape the landscape of the new nation through voting seems impossibly distant from where we stand today, I don't judge her. I simply wonder what it must have been like to walk in her shoes, fifty years before the Nineteenth Amendment was ratified in August 1920.

MORE EARLY AMERICAN VOICES

CAROLINE LOCKHART

Lockhart was a firecracker. The first female reporter for the *Boston Post*, she traveled to Cody, Wyoming, when she was thirty-three to write a newspaper story about Blackfoot Indians. And then she never left. Lockhart (1871–1962) loved horses, open ranges, and the Old West. In the 1920s, she was one of the most famous women west of the Mississippi. She wrote seven Western novels known for their universality of characters, geographical descriptions, and Western vernacular, which were turned into two major films. She was the first woman to cross Swiftcurrent Pass in Glacier National Park. She may also have been the first to descend the Middle Fork of the Salmon River in Idaho, an experience she drew upon for *The Man from the Bitter Roots* (1915). While *The Fighting Shepherdess* (1919) addressed issues of feminism and conformity in frontier towns, some of its scenes should be criticized for their racial insensitivities.

WILLA CATHER

In a 1915 letter, Cather (1873–1947) thanked a critic for suggesting that the "cow-puncher's experience of the West was not the only experience possible there." Indeed, characters in her novels often undermined gender conventions and were alternatives to popular Western male mythology. Raised in windswept Nebraska, Cather had immense sympathy for and wrote masterful descriptions of the natural world. Prairies were places to be nurtured, it seems, rather than territories seized. Cather wrote a number of prairie rhapsodies with unforgettable heroines. *O Pioneers!* (1913) features Alexandra, a strong girl with "Amazonian fierceness" who domesticates and enlarges the family property after a series of tragedies. In *The Song of the Lark* (1915), Thea is the talented daughter of a miner in a small Colorado town trying to understand her place in the world. An

American classic about immigrants in a new landscape, *My Ántonia* (1918) is an elegiac novel about home and homesickness. Cather received the Pulitzer Prize in 1923 for *One of Ours*.

LAURA INGALLS WILDER

Little House in the Big Woods was first published in 1932. It was followed by six more nostalgic stories of a pioneer family who struggled to make their home on the plains in the late nineteenth century. The semi-autobiographic *Little House* books—including *Farmer Boy* (1933), *On the Banks of Plum Creek* (1937), and *These Happy Golden Years* (1943)—along with the immensely popular television series, helped shape the myth of the West. At the same time, they downplayed the power of nature in curtailing, if not destroying, some settlers' dreams. The books are valuable windows into native flora and fauna of the plains. However, Wilder (1867–1957) has been criticized for sanitizing the dark realities of pioneer life and sentimentalizing the encroachment of settlers on the land of Native Americans.

GENE
STRATTON-PORTER

Graceful maiden-hair ferns tossed their tresses from wiry stems. Bleached mandrake umbrellas, that would later unfurl shades of green to shelter cups of wax and gold, pushed stoutly through the sod. Half the corners were filled with the whiteness of wild plum and service-berry; the others were budding the coming snow of alder and the blush of wild rose.

FRIENDS IN FEATHERS

MORE THAN A CENTURY AGO, there was another kind of J. K. Rowling, one whose bestselling books were set not in a school of witchcraft and wizardry, but in an Indiana swamp. The Limberlost, a 13,000-acre hardwood forest and wetland, with streams that flowed into eastern Indiana's Wabash River, was the setting for these romance novels, nature books, and films. The author, Gene Stratton-Porter, is a fascinating figure at the nexus of early twentieth-century changes in conservation and gender roles. Wife and mother, yes. Maverick, too. A gun-toting, bird-loving, moth-chasing, free-spirited filmmaker and artist, who opened new territory for women and influenced American environmental ethics. Some have said her impact on conservation was as influential as President Theodore Roosevelt's.

Because of her name, many young readers assumed the bestselling author was a man, but Stratton-Porter was a self-made woman. She wrote twenty-eight books—including internationally popular novels, nature studies, poetry collections, and children's books—which have been adapted into twenty-three films, a number of them produced by Gene Stratton-Porter Productions, one of the first film production companies owned by an American woman.

In her books for young adults, Stratton-Porter combined compelling characters with detailed knowledge of the natural world to help her readers understand how activities like logging were affecting the environment, what the impact of those changes could be, and how to listen to the life around them. Her popular *Freckles* (1904), a coming-of-age story of love, bravery, and devotion, is set in the Limberlost, as is her best-known book, the one that brought her worldwide recognition, *A Girl of the Limberlost* (1909). This Cinderella story stars Stratton-Porter's best-drawn character, Elnora Comstock, a self-reliant teenage heroine who funds her own education, against the wishes of her mother, by collecting butterflies and moths from the swamps near her home.

Three years had changed Elnora from the girl of sixteen to the very verge of womanhood. She had grown tall, round, and her face had the loveliness of perfect complexion, beautiful eyes and hair and an added touch from within that might have been called comprehension. It was a compound of self-reliance, hard knocks, heart hunger, unceasing work, and generosity. There was no form of suffering with which the girl could not sympathize, no work she was afraid to attempt, no subject she had investigated she did not understand. These things combined to produce a breadth and depth of character altogether unusual. She was so absorbed in her classes and her music that she had not been able to gather many specimens. When she realized this and hunted assiduously, she soon found that the changing natural conditions had affected such work. Men all around were clearing available land. The trees fell wherever corn would grow. The swamp was broken by several gravel roads, dotted in places around the edge with little frame houses, and the machinery of oil wells . . . Wherever the trees fell the moisture dried, the creeks ceased to flow, the river ran low, and at times the bed was dry. With unbroken sweep the winds of the west came, gathering force with every mile and howled and raved; threatening to tear the shingles from the roof, blowing the surface from the soil in clouds of fine dust and rapidly changing everything. From coming in with two or three dozen rare moths in a day, in three years' time Elnora had grown to be delighted with finding two or three. Big pursy caterpillars could not be picked from their favorite bushes, when there were no bushes. Dragonflies would not hover over dry places, and butterflies became scarce in proportion to the flowers, while no land yields over three crops of Indian relics.

Born Geneva Grace Stratton on a Wabash farm in 1863, Stratton-Porter witnessed firsthand the extraction and exploitation of the

Limberlost. Named after a local man, Limber Jim, who got lost hunting in its treacherous waters and woods (when news spread, the cry went out, "Limber's lost!"), the wetlands sat on the largest oil and gas field in the state and were coveted by Standard Oil for drilling and by European-American settlers for farming. In 1888, the draining began with steam-powered dredges. Despite Stratton-Porter's advocacy for the Limberlost through her books and speaking, all 13,000 acres of this valuable ecosystem were gone by 1913. And with it went its rich, biodiverse habitat, a resting place for birds such as cardinals, vultures, king rail, great blue herons, purple martins, cuckoos, robins, blue jays, shrikes, and more. Stratton-Porter saw it disappearing and presciently captured its flora and fauna in books and photographs, before the interlocking forests of oak, hickory, walnut, and cherry became furniture in Michigan factories.

As with many people, Gene's love of nature had roots in her childhood. She was the last of twelve children, born to older parents who had already passed on the family's baby clothes. She was fortunate to have a free-range childhood, exploring the forest and swamp of the Limberlost with, according to biographer Eugene Francis Saxton, only this obligation: "If she reported promptly three times a day when the bell rang at meal time, with enough clothing to constitute a decent covering, nothing more was asked until the Sabbath."

When she learned that workers on the family farm were killing songbirds, she became so distressed that her father offered her a gift and an opportunity. "I give you ownership of each bird that makes its home on my land," he told her. Gene became the tender guardian of more than sixty-four nests—larks, swallows, hummingbirds, doves, thrushes, catbirds, bluebirds, vireos, and hawks. This upbringing developed into a lifelong passion for birds, moths, butterflies, and plants.

Gene's semi-autobiographical novel *Laddie* (1913) shows how the natural world can be a child's inspirational playground, emotional refuge, and place of deep knowing. The story spans the course of a year and is filled with her sensitive observations of nonhuman and human worlds, especially the relationship between a brother and a sister. A portrait of a small American family farm, in which the father weaves baskets from soaked hickory strips while the children, especially Little Sister, Gene's alter ego, identify beech, hollyhock, tasseled lady slipper, catalpa, and other plants on sight, the book captures a snapshot of a time when children entertained themselves hunting snakes, fishing in creeks, wandering far, and building moss houses in the forest. Gene writes:

> The orchard and the birds were behind me; on one hand was the broad, grassy meadow with the creek running so swiftly, I could hear it, and the breath of the cowslips came up the hill. Straight in front was the lane running down the barn, crossing the creek and spreading into the woods pasture, where the water ran wider and yet swifter, big forest trees grew, and bushes of berries, pawpaw, willow, and everything ever found in an Indiana thicket; grass and wild flowers and ferns wherever the cattle and horses didn't trample them, and bigger, wilder birds, having names I didn't know.

In 1886, Gene married Charles Porter, a successful druggist and businessman thirteen years her senior. In the 1926 book *Gene Stratton-Porter: A Little Story of the Life and Work and Ideals of "The Bird Woman,"* Eugene Francis Saxton recounts how Stratton-Porter took pride in maintaining a house of fourteen rooms without a maid, making her daughter's clothes, keeping a conservatory of hundreds of bulbs and a menagerie of pets, cooking three times a day, and washing up, all while learning to master photography to such an extent that the supplier of the print paper she used came to her house to learn how she handled the paper in her darkroom—which turned out to be the family bathroom and the kitchen. These photographs are remarkable. Had she not been a self-taught woman, more attention certainly would have been paid to her skills and talent.

Drawing on a "deep love for, and comprehension of, wild things [that] runs through the thread of [her] disposition," Stratton-Porter's young adult romances weave romance and hardship with memorable characters who draw on the natural world for sustenance, solace, and strength. Some of these plots and characters can be saccharine or sentimental, but they are of their time and give glimpses into the wildlife and ecosystem of the Limberlost. Certain critics have likened Porter's stories of young people collecting butterflies and moths to a "capitalist pastorale" that somehow equates harmonious human foraging in nature with the wholesale natural resource extraction practiced by timber and oil corporations. Such witty but flawed parallels can be dismissed: small-scale human foraging does not destroy entire ecosystems as Standard Oil did. *The Harvester*, published in 1911, can be read as a refutation of such arguments. The story of a young man who grows medicinal herbs and finds the girl of his dreams, its characters live in harmony with the natural world.

Stratton-Porter's Limberlost romances were hugely popular, and, though not necessarily her true calling, gave her financial freedom on her own terms through her tenacity and creativity. One of her earliest book signings took place in Fort Wayne, Indiana, at Lehman Book & News, a store owned by three enterprising friends of Porter's named Eugenia Lehman, Alice Habecker, and Laura Detzer. Detzer's son Karl recalled a story of the women sitting in the shade of elms during a visit at their home and having the following exchange:

> "What's the name of your new book, Gene?"
> "*Freckles*," replied Porter.
> "Oh yes, I tried to read it," replied Laura, who was more
>   interested in Porter's bird books.
> "Don't try," Porter said. "You just wouldn't like it, Laura.
>   I didn't write it for you."
> "How many copies have you sold?"

"Half a million so far," Porter replied. "I sometimes think they must use them for paving bricks."

Though her nature books sold much slower than her romances, they were Stratton-Porter's passion and are my personal favorites. Her intrepid research methods and use of photography cut a portrait of an adventurous American writer who understood the urgency of what was happening in real time to the landscape she loved. Written long before creative nonfiction was the established literary genre it is now, *Moths of the Limberlost* (1912) includes Stratton-Porter's photographs of moths in the wild. Her vivid, often comedic, first-person field guides make readers feel present with her in the Limberlost and read, at times, like adventure novels. My favorite of her books, *What I Have Done with Birds* (1907), is an early work she wrote before the Limberlost was completely "shorn, branded and tamed." It's filled with the author's presence—her daring and hilarious mishaps and keen observations of flora and fauna. We see her bumping along forested trails. We read about her recalcitrant horse, Patience, who sabotages the work by backing a carriage of expensive camera equipment into the swamp. "[We scrambled and] unreined the horse and it was well we did, for half the way across the carriage was floating, we were up on the seat holding the camera, and Patience swam several rods." We picture her in waist-high waders, trudging through swamp water in search of vultures and in fields pursuing killdeer, "bathed in perspiration, crimson in our faces, breathless, our hats lost, our clothing torn on the bushes." We learn her methods, the way she approaches birds, and how she gains their confidence. It's lively nonfiction, showing Stratton-Porter's mettle and strength, the challenges she faced in capturing shots, her eye for beauty, and her ear for lyricism in writing about bird plumage, nests, and behaviors.

At the end of *Friends in Feathers* (1917), a revision of *What I Have Done with Birds*, she writes about an exchange with a male editor who questioned whether her profession was suitable "women's work." Her response illustrates her comfort navigating gender roles.

> In its hardships, in wading, swimming, climbing, in hidden dangers suddenly to be confronted, in abrupt changes from heat to cold, and from light to dark, field photography is not women's work. But in the matter of finesse in approaching the birds, in limitless patience in awaiting the exact moment for the best exposure, in the tedious and delicate processes of the dark room, in the art of winning bird babies and parents, it is not a man's work. No man has ever had the patience to remain with a bird until he secured a real character study of it. A human mother is best fitted to understand and deal with a bird mother.

Whatever her approach with birds and books, it was golden. Or maybe green. In a state where, as literary historian R. E. Banta put it, "literature grows as naturally and as luxuriantly as the horseweed along the banks of the quiet Indiana streams," Stratton-Porter remains a popular Hoosier, and one of its most commercially successful authors. More than this, she educated millions of children and adults around the world and immortalized the vanishing Limberlost watershed through her writing. A trailblazer in fashion as well, she made strong pleas for the abolishment of all feathers and wings from ladies' hats.

In 1924, Stratton-Porter died from injuries sustained in a car accident less than a mile from her new home in Bel-Air, California, where she moved for warmer weather and to be closer to Hollywood. Neither a politician nor a forester, Stratton-Porter's nature writing, black-and-white photography, coming-of-age films, and novels helped foster a growing awareness for conserving the natural heritage of a still nascent nation.

WORKS BY GENE STRATTON-PORTER

NOVELS AND NATURE STUDIES

The Song of the Cardinal (1903)

Freckles (1904)

At the Foot of the Rainbow (1907)

What I Have Done with Birds (1907,
revised as *Friends in Feathers* in 1917)

A Girl of the Limberlost (1909)

Birds of the Bible (1909)

Music of the Wild (1910)

The Harvester (1911)

Moths of the Limberlost (1912)

Laddie (1913)

Michael O'Halloran (1915)

A Daughter of the Land (1918)

Her Father's Daughter (1921)

The White Flag (1923)

The Keeper of the Bees (1925)

The Magic Garden (1927)

POETRY, CHILDREN'S BOOKS, AND ESSAY COLLECTIONS

The Fire Bird (1922)

Jesus of the Emerald (1923)

After the Flood (1911)

Morning Face (1916)

Let Us Highly Resolve (1927)

Field o' My Dreams: The Poetry of Gene Stratton-Porter,
edited by Mary DeJong Obuchowski (2007)

MARY AUSTIN

What women have to stand on squarely is not their ability to see the world in the way men see it, but the importance and validity of their seeing it in some other way.

CACTUS THORN

N THE SMALL CALIFORNIA farm town where I grew up, streets were named after one of three things: fruits, grapes, or women. We lived on Lemon Avenue. Friends lived on Deborah Circle. My newspaper route wound along Zinfandel Drive. Our town planners unwittingly instilled in me the childhood belief that places were feminine and fertile in name and nature.

When I was young, I wove my candy-apple-red bike down the center yellow lines on Lemon Avenue past the heady blossoms of almond orchards in spring and ripening peaches in summer. To the west, I saw undulating Coast Ranges. To the east, the long spine of the Sierra Nevada. As I grew up and explored beyond the confines of home, I was miffed to learn most geographical features—mountains and rivers, valleys and counties, gulches and creeks—were named for the European male geologists, surveyors, homesteaders, and military officers who measured, climbed, and claimed them. Tranquil lakes and cascading waterfalls, embodiments of idealized feminine virtues, seemed the only exceptions. However, while climbing mountains in my twenties, I discovered another: 150 miles south of Yosemite's granite cliffs, among Mount Whitney, Mount Muir, and Mount Humphreys, one peak stands out for more than its 13,057 feet of elevation.

It's Mount Mary Austin.

Well known in her time, less so now, Mary Hunter Austin was not a geologist, scientist, or soldier, but an explorer of new terrain: an ethnographer and feminist, activist and mystic, speaker and writer, whose life still haunts and inspires me decades after I first read her debut title, *The Land of Little Rain* (1903). Austin found an enthusiastic audience for her first authorial effort, a collection of fourteen vivid and meditative essays detailing the landscape and diverse inhabitants of the Owens Valley. She experienced spiritual transcendence and liberation in the sagebrush wilderness there— and in its alkali meadows, broad bajadas, and riparian forests. She herself was a force of nature and overcame great personal trials to make a name for herself. Austin's story is dizzying, a personal trajectory carved from an audacious determination to claim authorship of her own life and become one of America's great writers.

She was born in 1868 in Carlinville, Illnois, the fourth of six children. In her 1932 autobiography, *Earth Horizon*, Austin describes her charming eighteen-year-old self as "under the average height, not well filled out, with the slightly sallow pallor of the malaria country." With slightly more charity, she says her tawny hair was "brown with coppery glints, thick and springy, falling below her knees when loosed, and difficult to get under any sort of hat suitable to her years." She studied natural science at Blackburn College and was named class poet by fellow students. An aspiring suitor there informed her she had the very good fortune of meeting all *his* requirements for a preacher's wife; soon, he said, she should expect a marriage proposal! In her head, she said she would rather be dead—and she politely declined.

In 1888, Mary's family traveled west from Illinois to settle in the Owens Valley, a high-desert region of California in the shadow of the Sierra Nevada. Pioneer life was never easy, no matter where the homestead, but building a life from the ground up was excruciating in this unyielding desert. Mary suffered from malnourishment and a nervous breakdown from abrupt life changes. It was harsh and unfamiliar, and she had no sense of place nor understanding of the region's seasons, migrations, people, plants, and animals. Though dislocated, she saw beauty everywhere and yearned to learn the natural and human history of her new home, becoming an acute observer of flora and fauna and befriending Paiute and Shoshone who lived in the valley. She was fascinated by their deep knowledge of native foods and animal husbandry, which had been nearly wiped out by the Spanish Franciscans whose missions dotted the California coast and the introduced livestock that had replaced wild herds.

By the time she married the irresponsible, Berkeley-educated spendthrift Stafford Wallace Austin in 1891, she was teaching art and literature in local Owens Valley schools and had committed herself to the idea that she would write about the West. She describes her early writing life in *Earth Horizon*.

> [My] interior energies were set on sorting [my] really voluminous notes about strange growths and unfamiliar creatures, flocks, herders, vaqueros, Henry Miller, pelicans dancing on Buena Vista, Indians, phylloxera, and a vast dim valley between great swinging ranges . . . collections of colloquial phrases, Spanish folklore, intensively pondered adjectives for the color and form of natural things, the exact word for a mule's cry—"maimed noises"—the difference between the sound of ripe figs dropping and the patter of olives shaken down by the wind.

In marrying, a person hopes for stability and security, but for Mary, life just seemed to get harder. Her twenties and thirties were one agonizing trial after another. The couple's one child, Ruth, was born developmentally disabled. Family blamed Mary for Ruth's condition. For ten years, on the shoestring salary of a teacher and artist, she pulled Stafford out of debt and near-bankruptcy from ill-planned dreams. In *Earth Horizon*, she wrote that despite her attempts to support him, he had "no well-defined way of life to which she could tender a confirming devotion." Family also criticized her for questioning his financial schemes. Mary's life could be described as a whirlwind and dust devil: finding work for her husband, paying off his debts, taking care of their daughter, maintaining a home, and teaching others. She eventually left Stafford and institutionalized their daughter, who died in 1914.

In the midst of this pressure, Austin did something remarkable. She began writing. Her novel *Outland* (1910) is probably an account of her unfortunate marriage. Her *Can Prayer Be Answered?* (1934) is a slim visionary book that begins during this difficult personal time, in which she explored the nature of prayer—from Paiute Indian traditions to those in Italy, where she traveled and studied Greek and Roman invocations and the lives of early Christian saints. It might also be said that writing, an act of creation for herself, gave her peace of mind. An amateur naturalist, she walked and watched and talked to people of the valley. She submitted her writing for publication, too, landing the articles that would become *The Land of Little Rain* in the *Atlantic Monthly*. Her audience was urban readers who knew little about desert biodiversity, but Austin was a highly visual writer who conveyed a well-sculpted sense of place, as she wrote of "hills, rounded, blunt, burned, squeezed up out of chaos, chrome and vermilion painted" and "the rainbow hills, the tender bluish mists, the luminous radiance of the spring . . . the lotus charm." As the city of Los Angeles surreptitiously bought land in the Owens Valley to divert the Owens River—a time known as the California Water Wars, made famous by the film *Chinatown*—Austin captured, with nuance and wit, the desert ecology and cultural traditions of both settlers and native people before the collapse of the valley's economy.

> It is the proper destiny of every considerable stream in the west to become an irrigating ditch. It would seem the streams are willing. They go as far as they can, or dare, toward the tillable lands of their own boulder fenced gullies—but how much farther in the man-made waterways. It is difficult to come into intimate relations with appropriated waters; like very busy people they have no time to reveal themselves. One needs to have known an irrigating ditch when it was a brook, and to have lived by it, to mark the morning and evening tone of its crooning, rising and falling to the excess of snow water; to have watched far across the valley, south to the Eclipse and north to the Twisted

Dyke, the shining wall of the village water gate; to see still blue herons stalking the little glinting weirs across the field.

Perhaps to get into the mood of the waterways one needs to have seen old Amos Judson asquat on the headgate with his gun, guarding his water-right toward the end of a dry summer. Amos owned the half of Tule Creek and the other half pertained to the neighboring Greenfields ranch. Years of a "short water crop," that is, when too little snow fell on the high pine ridges, or falling, melted too early, Amos held that it took all the water that came down to make his half, and maintained it with a Winchester and a deadly aim. Jesus Montaña, first proprietor of Greenfields—you can see at once that Judson had the racial advantage—contesting the right with him, walked into five of Judson's bullets and his eternal possessions on the same occasion. That was the Homeric age of settlement and passed into tradition. Twelve years later one of the Clarks, holding Greenfields, not so very green by now, shot one of the Judsons. Perhaps he hoped that also might become classic, but the jury found for manslaughter.

Austin's early defense of Spanish Americans and Native Americans and their rights to their land and their livelihoods set her apart from other Western writers, who too often and too easily saw these groups as impediments to "progress." It is a theme in many of Austin's books, including *California: Land of the Sun* (1914), which opens: "For a graphic and memorable report of the contours of any country, see always the aboriginal account of its making." She emphasizes the value of this way of understanding geography, and her detailed prose (whether in this book or in passages like the following from *The Land of Little Rain*) expresses the deep-felt sesnse of place that infuses all her writing.

With the water runs a certain following of thirsty herbs and shrubs. The willows go as far as the stream goes, and a bit farther on the slightest provocation. They will strike root in the leak of a flume, or the dribble of an overfull bank, coaxing the water beyond its appointed bounds. Given a new waterway in a barren land, and in three years the willows have fringed all its miles of banks; three years more and they will touch tops across it. It is perhaps due to the early usurpation of the willows that so little else finds growing-room along the large canals. . . .

Wild fowl, quacking hordes of them, nest in the tulares. Any day's venture will raise from open shallows the great blue heron on his hollow wings. Chill evenings the mallard drakes cry continually from the glassy pools, the bittern's hollow boom rolls along the water paths. Strange and far-flown fowl drop down against the saffron, autumn sky. All day wings beat above it hazy with speed; long flights of cranes glimmer in the twilight. By night one wakes to hear the clanging geese go over. One wishes for, but gets no nearer speech from those the reedy fens have swallowed up. What they do there, how fare, what find, is the secret of the tulares.

A prolific author, Austin wrote about more than physical landscapes: she composed poetry about the metaphysical and the mystic, essays and novels about women's rights, plays and children's literature about Native Americans, and science fiction about utopian societies. Her 1912 novel, *A Woman of Genius*, drawn from her own life, is about a talented actress in the socially restrictive Midwest, who leaves her dull husband to pursue a life in theater. Her most popular play, *The Arrow Maker*, a three-act piece about Paiute life in the Sierras, was produced in New York in 1911. Her 1918 political monograph, *The Young Woman Citizen*, stood out by asserting gender equality through women's intellects—rather than through virtue, as advocated by mainstream suffragettes. She travelled throughout the world giving lectures and cultivated friendships with a roster of notable modern-era Americans: President Theodore Roosevelt, conservationist John Muir, writer Willa Cather, dancer Isadora Duncan, anarchist Emma Goldman, painter Georgia O'Keeffe, photographer Ansel Adams, and countless other movers and shakers. She died in Santa Fe, New Mexico, in 1934.

Today, the trailhead to Mount Mary Austin begins in the eastern Sierras on the high and dry desert floor at an elevation of 6,000 feet. The first steps are a sharp ascent up a former cattle trail through rocks and sagebrush. Terrain is dusty and rough, the trail unmaintained. Obstacles complicate the way. Slippery, burnt, and fallen trees—remnants of the Inyo Complex Fire of 2007—crisscross a stream like a game of pick-up sticks. It is prickly, dry, dangerous— full of thorns, nettles, and rattlesnakes. At 10,000 feet, there's an open area to camp in view of Diamond Peak. If you look closely, you can see bighorn sheep settling into rocky perches for the night. In the morning, there's a field of rubble to traverse and an upward scramble across rocks. Climbing higher into the bluer-than-blue sky, you take a few more breaths in the thin air, and arrive, finally, at the summit of this California mountain named for one of early America's first female nature writers. The view across the valley is sweetly ironic—there's the little town where she lived for her first seventeen years in California—a place she left behind for good in 1905 yet always wanted to be.

Its name? Independence.

WORKS BY MARY AUSTIN

NONFICTION

The Land of Little Rain (1903)

California: Land of the Sun (1914)

The Young Woman Citizen (1918)

*The American Rhythm: Studies and Reëxpressions
of Amerindian Songs* (1923)

The Land of Journeys' Ending (1924)

Everyman's Genius (1925)

Taos Pueblo (1930), photography by Ansel Adams

Experiences Facing Death (1931)

Earth Horizon (1932)

Can Prayer Be Answered? (1934)

Beyond Borders: The Selected Essays of Mary Austin (1996)

NOVELS

Isidro (1905)

The Flock (1906)

Santa Lucia: A Common Story (1908)

Lost Borders (1909)

A Woman of Genius (1912)

The Ford (1917)

No. 26 Jayne Street (1920)

Cactus Thorn (1927)

Starry Adventure (1931)

DRAMA, FOLKTALES, AND CHILDREN'S BOOKS

The Arrow Maker: A Drama in Three Acts (1911)

Fire: A Drama in Three Acts (1914)

One-Smoke Stories (1934)

The Basket Woman: A Book of Indian Tales for Children (1904)

The Trail Book (1918)

VITA
SACKVILLE-WEST

I worshipped dead men for their strength,
Forgetting I was strong.

"MCMXIII"

L IKE MANY PASSIONATE gardeners, I was smitten with Sissinghurst Castle Garden long before I set foot there. Less than a century old, but old-world atmospheric, the garden entices from afar and lingers with you long after you leave. Elizabethan ruins crumble in an ancient hunting ground, surrounded on two sides by a moat, and a spiral staircase up a fairy-tale tower invites breathtaking views of the gentle Weald of Kent and insights into how its creator, Vita Sackville-West, liked to be "surrounded by evidence of time."

My first visit to Sissinghurst was a long time in coming—a full decade after moving to England. It was an afternoon stop on a July road trip with my sons, August and Stellan, then nineteen and thirteen. After a morning journey from Devon to Kent, we left the motorway for narrow country roads, then even slimmer country lanes. As soon as we walked through the arch of the brick house, the boys broke off together. Strolling in the Yew Walk and Rose Garden, I would occasionally glimpse them diminishing down long evergreen corridors. Leaving them to their own adventures, I turned to Vita's library, study, and gardens to learn as much as I could about this intriguing woman.

Victoria Mary Sackville-West was an English poet, novelist, travel writer, and gardener. She was born in 1892 and published more than a dozen collections of poetry, ten nonfiction books of travel and biography, and thirteen novels, including her 1930 bestselling *The Edwardians* and her 1931 *All Passion Spent*. In 1913, she married author, diarist, politician, and diplomat Sir Harold Nicolson, six years her senior. Theirs was famously not a traditional romance. They were peripheral members of the counterculture Bloomsbury Group of artists, writers, and philosophers, and their fifty-year union was complex and kind—an open marriage allowing both to pursue discreet (yet occasionally and accidentally, not-so-discreet) same-sex lovers while maintaining an aristocratic mirage of tradition. Vita would become known for her passionate relationships with dozens of women, including writers Violet Trefusis and Virginia Woolf, whose 1928 feminist classic *Orlando*, about a gender-shifting poet who lives for centuries, was based on Vita and her family history.

And, of course, in time Vita would be known for her exquisite creation at Sissinghurst.

But her passion for landscape and place had tragic roots. As a Sackville, one of England's oldest families and brothers-in-arms to William the Conqueror (the Wests came later), Vita grew up in her family's magnificent ancestral home of Knole, possibly England's first "calendar house," with its 7 courtyards, 52 staircases, and 365 rooms that sprawled across four acres in a sweeping thousand-acre deer park in Sevenoaks. She was the only child of Baron Lionel Edward Sackville-West and his cousin Victoria, and male-to-male primogeniture rules prevented her from inheriting Knole. Instead, upon the death of her father in 1928, Vita watched this treasured home and estate, along with the title of baron, go to her Uncle Charlie.

If only she had been a *he*.

Her attachment to Knole was the strongest bond of her life, and its loss was acute. Beyond the opulence of material treasures—lush tapestries, silver tables with matching candlesticks and mirrors, Jacobean staircases, detailed headboards on curtained four-poster beds—Knole held her family history. It was where she could see her own deeply hooded blue eyes in portraits of her ancestors. Knole's wilderness was the setting of her childhood—where she wandered widely, climbed trees with abandon, played in leaves, and collected bird eggs. Knole, she felt deeply, was a living, breathing family member. She wrote, "I knew thy soul, benign and grave and kind / To me, a morsel of mortality."

Losing Knole was Vita's greatest life sorrow.

Her sex had cast her from her kingdom—the connection between this lost landscape and Vita's rejection of conventional gender roles in her writing has ofen been made. Her novels are filled with male protagonists who give up sexual appetites and dominant roles. She lived decades before the Sexual Offenses Act of 1967 decriminalized homosexuality in England—during a time when men and women who sought the intimate company of their own sex could be imprisoned under gross indecency laws. Nevertheless, Vita broke free of the gender binary and, in 1918, swapped feminine skirts, smock blouses, and ribboned hats for mannish breeches and leather gaiters. Being tomboyish brought her intense freedom, not just for practical movement in her gardens but also through wildly subversive gender reinvention in her love affairs. Her lover Violet remarked that Vita was like "the wild hawk and the windswept sky . . . splendid and dauntless, a wanderer in strange lands."

Vita's confident androgyny would be her trademark and an outward link to the lost past, where she could "stride like any Sackville squire from the previous five or six centuries" and take up residence in her *own* castle tower. This unconventional life was the subject of her compelling *Portrait of a Marriage*, a book published by her son Nigel Nicolson in 1973, with context added by him and occasional insights from Harold.

Whatever their personal tumult as a complex married couple, creating Sissinghurst and raising their two sons, Benedict and Nigel, were stable, joint ventures for Vita and Harold. When they bought the derelict estate in 1930, they were already experienced and knowledgeable gardeners, and their two boys were sixteen and twelve. Overgrown with weeds and scattered with chicken coops, garbage pits, broken windows, and rusty bedframes floating in the moat, Sissinghurst must have been a squalid sight, the least likely place to become the substitute ancestral mansion denied Vita. But together the couple would make it "Sleeping Beauty's castle with a vengeance," a place where, as she wrote in the opening of *The Garden* (1946), Vita could be "daring to find a world in a lost world, / A little world, a little perfect world."

I climbed the stairs in the tower, an old hunting lookout, to Vita's writing study, a room of faded elegance, with a floor-to-ceiling tapestry of a garden scene, a long wooden desk with leather-bound books, and two black-and-white portraits, one of Vita and one of Harold, positioned to face each other. From a window, I could see the expanse of the garden under blue skies and spotted my own sons as they brushed their hands on fragrant rosemary and roses then stretched on the shaded lawn, near the frothy Purple Border of salvias, dahlias, and sweet peas. With the heart of a poet, Stellan has an intuitive way of appreciating nature. Wanting few barriers between himself and sensations, he strips down to essentials; going shoeless and shirtless to feel grass underfoot and sunshine on his back are his barometers of beauty. True to character, Stellan was, as he would later describe it, "feeling summer in me." This, I thought to myself from the lookout, would have made Vita smile.

Harold and Vita wrote the Sissinghurst narrative together: he sketched plans on paper while her romantic plantings filled in the architectural framework with billowy, sensual, and complex plant combinations. The dreamy profusion of plants in the White Garden—*Echinacea purpurea* 'White Swan', *Veronicastrum virginicum* 'Album', *Delphinium* 'Snowgoose', *Anemone* ×*hybrida* 'Honorine Jobert', *Thymus* 'Silver Posie', and dozens more—feels like stepping into a frothy Cinderella gown. "I could have never done it myself," Vita wrote in 1953. "Fortunately, I had, through marriage, the ideal collaborator." Contemplating its entirety, it struck me that perhaps a reason for the garden's success is the duality and mutability, artistic and otherwise, of its gender-bending creators, who thought outside the boxes of their times to express their inner selves.

In her tower, Vita wrote commercially successful novels, popular gardening columns, prize-winning poetry, and voluminous letters and diaries—turning Sissinghurst and greater Kent into an indelible literary landscape. An excerpt from Vita's 1930 poem "Sissinghurst," written the year they bought their new home, illustrates the way nature and history intermingle to, at long last, restore the unsettled parts of herself left behind at Knole.

This husbandry, this castle, and this I
    Moving within the deeps,
Shall be content within our timeless spell,
Assembled fragments of an age gone by,
While still the sower sows, the reaper reaps,
Beneath the snowy mountains of the sky,
And meadows dimple to the village bell.
So plods the stallion up my evening lane
And fills me with a mindless deep repose,
    Wherein I find in chain
The castle, and the pasture, and the rose.

Beauty, and use, and beauty once again
Link up in my scattered heart, and shape a scheme
Commensurate with a frustrated dream.
The autumn bonfire smokes across the woods
And reddens in the water of the moat;
As red within the water burns the scythe,
And the moon dwindled to her gibbous tithe
    Follows the sunken sun afloat.
Green is the eastern sky and red the west;
The hop-kilns huddle under pallid hoods;
The wagon stupid stands with upright shaft,
As daily life accepts the night's arrest.
Night like a deeper sea engulfs the land,
The castle, and the meadows, and the farm;
Only the baying watch-dog looks for harm,
And shakes his chain towards the lunar brand.
In the high room where tall the shadows tilt
As candle-flames blow crooked in the draught,
The reddened sunset on the panes was spilt,
But now as black as any nomad's tent
The night-time and the night of time have blent

Their darkness, and waters doubly sleep.
Over my head the years and centuries sweep,
   The years of childhood flown
   The centuries unknown;
I dream; I do not weep.

This poem was printed by The Hogarth Press, Virginia and Leonard Woolf's famous publishing company. In a brilliant twist of history, one of the great hidden treasures at Sissinghurst is the publisher's original Cropper Minerva platen press—its cogs and large flywheel occupy a room just off the spiral staircase in Vita's tower. This machine printed some of the most important works of the twentieth century, including *Monday or Tuesday* (1921) by Virginia Woolf, the first UK edition of *The Waste Land* (1923) by T. S. Eliot, and Vita's own *Selected Poems* (1941).

Vita's writing career predates and anticipates Sissinghurst—she was an award-winning poet whose focus was rural life in Kent. In 1926, she published the epic poem *The Land* to considerable praise, winning the prestigious Hawthornden Prize and selling over 100,000 copies by 1971 in England alone. She won the prize again for *Collected Poems* in 1933. A love of gardening and nature permeates her epic poetry, but *The Land* is more than pastoral. A long, lyrical poem written in the Georgic tradition, it celebrates "the dignity of labor and the bond between mankind and the earth," and Vita's precise language and concrete rural imagery are "as rich and uneven as the landscape itself." After reading the poem, I feel like I need to check my boots for mud and my hair for loose weeds: I've spent a lot of time tromping about the forests in southern England, but *The Land* immersed me anew, instilling an unforgettable memory-record of postwar England:

   I sing the cycle of my country's year,
   I sing the tillage, and the reaping sing,
   Classic monotony, that modes and wars

Leave undisturbed, unbettered, for their best
Was born immediate, of expediency.
The sickle sought no art; the axe, the share
Draped no superfluous beauty round their steel;
The scythe desired no music for her stroke,
Her stroke is sufficed in music, as her blade
Laid low the swathes; the scythesman swept, nor cared
What crop had ripened, whether oats in Greece
Or oats in Kent; the shepherd on the ridge
Like his Boeotian forebear kept his flocks,
And still their outlines on our tenderer sky
Simple and classic rear their grave design
As once at Thebes, as once in Lombardy.
I sing once more;
The mild continuous epic of the soil,
Haysel and harvest, tilth and husbandry;
I tell of marl and dung, and of the means
That break the unkindly spirit of the clay;
I tell the things I know, the things I knew
Before I knew them, immemorially;
And as the fieldsman of unhurrying tread
Trudges with steady and unchanging gait,
Being born to clays that in the winter hold,
So my pedestrian measure gravely plods,
Telling a loutish life. I have refused
The easier uses of made poetry,
But no small ploy disdain to chronicle
And (like that pious yeoman laid to rest
Beneath the legend that told all his life
In five hard words: "He tilled the soil well")
Prune my ambition to the lowly prayer
That I may drive the furrow of my tale
Straight, through the lives and dignities I know.

Vita Sackville-West

Early reviewers praised the poem's "combination of accuracy of detail with almost mystical sensitivity." Vita captures country traditions grounded in timeless cycles and paints a countryside of rising sap, mating beasts, stirring bees, and constellations rising in autumn skies only to dip below the horizon at springtime. We readers feel we have inhaled ripening fruit and flowering grasses, and watched harvests gathered, stored, and stacked. She keeps delightful Kentish vernacular alive, including shrammed (numbed or paralyzed with cold), undern (the afternoon), and shippon (cattleshed). *The Land* is sumptuous and epic, entirely worthy of revival, and ought to be better remembered in the canon of regional nature writing.

When she turned her narrative and poetic crafts to garden writing and travel narratives in 1946, Vita produced what many consider her best works. Her storytelling, attention to language, and portraits of plants as characters elevates the genre of garden writing. For fifteen years she wrote a weekly column, In Your Garden, for the *Observer*, a Sunday British newspaper; the columns were later collected into four books. Her voice there was conversational and accessible, and she showed less interest in garden design than plant history, creating narratives about the plants themselves and often combining travel writing with garden writing.

> Many years ago, in the high mountains of Persia, I collected some seed pods off a mimosa which was most accountably growing there, some 5,000 feet above sea-level, and some hundred miles from any spot whence it could possibly be considered as a garden escape. I do not pretend to explain how it came there, in that cold, stony, snowy, desolate region; all I know is that there it was, and that I brought seeds home, and now have a tree of it growing out of doors in my garden and a vase full of it on my table, smelling not of the snows but of the warm South.

Rousing myself from this trip back in time to continue my own journey, I set out to find my boys. Stepping out of the tower, I entered the Cottage Garden, a riot of midsummer orange, red, and yellow blooms and stopped for a moment to watch a gardener dead-heading. "Would you like one?" he smiled, handing me an *Allium cristophii* flower head, a June-flowering garlic. Dried and spent, it looked like a Fourth of July sparkler or a magic wand from a fairy tale. I recalled Vita wrote about this very flower (as *A. albopilosum*) in a summery column about roses, thyme lawns, color planning, and growing peonies from seed, revealing her penchant, in a single sentence, for poetry, plants, and place.

> A native of Turkestan, it comes up in a large mop-sized head of numerous perfectly star-shaped flowers of sheeny lilac, each with a little green button at the center, on long thin stalks, so that the general effect is of a vast mauve-and-green cobweb, quivering with its own lightness and buoyancy.

My new prized possession, it would travel to Paris with us and back to Devon, where I would try to propagate its seeds into bulbs in my greenhouse. In early summer, when alliums burst forth into starry purple and pink fireworks atop towering stems, I recall memories of August and Stellan walking as young men, like Vita's own sons, through the dream of Sissinghurst that summer day. I'm also reminded of the woman who eschewed skirts for breeches, yet kept her long strands of pearls, to live life on her own terms. I remember the writer who channeled the loss of her ancestral home into a legacy of landscape and literature that celebrates the English countryside and, to this day, shapes in thought and practice how people imagine gardens. Vita was a sapphic rebel whose fluidity—through genres of literature, gender boundaries, and garden borders—makes her a fascinating figure and nature writer in twentieth-century Britain.

For a woman whose name means life, what better legacy to leave than a living one?

MORE CLASSIC GARDEN WRITERS

GERTRUDE JEKYLL

One of the most well-known horticulturalists and garden designers in the world, Jekyll was an influencer par excellence, and synonymous with fine British gardens. She was a plant breeder, artist, and photographer and wrote more than a thousand magazine articles as well as many books available in modern editions, including *Wood and Garden* (1899), *Home and Garden* (1900), *Wall and Water Gardens* (1902), *Colour in the Flower Garden* (1908), *Children and Gardens* (1908), and *Colour Schemes for the Flower Garden* (1919).

MARION CRAN

Living not far from Jekyll's home, Cran was a popular garden writer and the first female gardening broadcaster in Britain. She traveled widely and wrote many gardening books and novels. *The Garden of Ignorance: The Experiences of a Woman in a Garden* (1913), her most popular book, describes her journey from a complete horticultural ingénue to expert gardener. She was elected a Fellow of the Royal Horticultural Society in 1913, a rare honor for a woman at that time. Other well-known books include *The Story of My Ruin* (1924), *I Know a Garden* (1933), and *Gardens of Character* (1939).

CELIA THAXTER

One of America's favorite writers at the end of the nineteenth century, Thaxter's poetry appeared in the *Atlantic*, *Harper's*, *Scribner's*, and more. *Among the Shoals* (1878) and *An Island Garden* (1894) were two of her most popular books. She lived on Appledore Island, Maine, for much of her life, welcoming writers to the family's hotel salon, including Nathaniel Hawthorne, Sarah Orne Jewett, and

NAN SHEPHERD

Place and a mind may interpenetrate till the nature
of both is altered.

THE LIVING MOUNTAIN

WHAT THE KENT COUNTRYSIDE was for Vita Sackville-West and the Lake District for Dorothy Wordsworth, the Cairngorm mountains of eastern Scotland were for Anna "Nan" Shepherd. In the field of mountaineering literature, with hundreds of books chronicling glorious disasters and fatal ascents, Nan Shepherd, a writer active in the Scottish literary renaissance of the 1920s, is now recognized as one of its best. *The Living Mountain* is Nan's nonfiction masterpiece, a book written during World War II, when she often went *stravaiging*—a Scottish term for wandering—alone or with friends, in all seasons and all weather in the Cairngorms. Shepherd was a visionary who wrote about the mountains with a beautiful sensuality and Buddhist-infused sense of pilgrimage. This gentle feeling set *The Living Mountain* apart from its mountaineering contemporaries.

Long-distance walking was wildly popular across Britain in the early 1900s, and people joined rambling clubs for midnight walks — the kind so loved by the Wordsworths and other Romantics. Had I the chance, I would sleep under the stars in the Cairngorms too, but it's three days shy of a full moon when I meet my friend James in the lowlands. The February morning is so warm and bright, I nearly accept the illusion of spring's early arrival. (Winter would return the next week.)

James and I cross a bridge over the River Dee from Aboyne, the village where his family, the Littlejohns, have lived for seven generations. As we walk up the Fungle Road right-of-way, a rocky and saturated forest path, a buzzard flashes its ochre underside a few feet ahead of us and disappears over a fence. We come to a *rest and be thankful*, a centuries-old Scottish name for a collection of stones where travelers rest and refresh. We eat tangerines and sip water, and James describes how his great-granddad, James Young, was head keeper for the nearby Dunecht Estate and had planted most of the tall trees we were passing. As he tells me, there were many *dry steen dkykers*—drystone wallers—in his family as well, and I wonder, as wind blows through the pines, tossing blue moss branches with pinecones onto our path, if Nan Shepherd ever stopped to talk with his kinfolk as they stacked these stones or planted these trees.

Shepherd's book, *The Living Mountain,* is slender, yet it speaks volumes in precise and reverential prose poetry. Part memoir, part natural history and philosophical meditation, it captures a woman's singular, shimmering journey into these Cairngorms, named "the Red Mountains," or *Am Monadh Ruadh* in Gaelic, for their rosy-red pink granite. She spent decades walking through these mountains and honing her senses—her eye to *look,* her ear to *listen,* and her body to *feel* Cairngorm contours in all weather. A whisper of Tao oneness with peaks and plateaus, rivers and wildlife, rather than the testosterone-fueled spectacle of man versus nature so prevalent in mountaineering literature, *The Living Mountain* feels like a caress rather than a conquest. To Shepherd, the Cairngorms weren't adversaries but companionable allies. Walking *into* rather than *up* the mountains was her way. She wrote, "Often the mountain gives itself most completely when I have no destination but have gone out merely to be with the mountain as one visits a friend, with no intention but to be with him."

James, with his deep, generational knowledge of the Cairngorms, leads me on a ramble through lowland forests and breezy open heathlands, but he points out that the mountains earn their name as "the Arctic of Britain" higher up, where the highest, coldest, snowiest peaks meet the drama of avalanches, gale force winds, flash floods, and hard, blizzard-sculpted snowscape. Here, hardy plants and animals thrive: the native mountain hare and ptarmigan transform from dark fur and feather in summer to winter whites. Snow buntings, pine martens, and now-dwindling populations of capercaillie live on rocky hillsides and in native pinewoods. In summer, the alpine sow thistle shelters among boulders and trailing azalea blooms pink on windswept mountain ledges.

In reserved Scottish culture, Shepherd was unusual for writing with sensuality about her body in the world. She walked barefoot to feel the "delicious touch" of earth underfoot. She swam nude in luscious loch water and described how it "slides over the skin like shadow." She inhaled "rich fruity perfume rising from the mat of grass, moss, and wild berry bushes" on sultry midsummer days after rain. Reading her work, a portrait of a more intimate way of *being in a place* emerges: an independent woman walking through the wilderness in full possession of her own narrative—the written one and the one she lived. She is less interested in the "tang of heights" than in exploring her own inner landscape, pointedly writing, "I have been the instrument of my own discovering." She wrote how rousing from quiescence was the closest she could come to heightened consciousness and how experiencing the darker side of the Cairngorms without torch or flashlight sharpened other senses. She felt it was otherworldly.

> My one October night without a roof was bland as silk, with a late moon rising in the small hours and the mountains fluid as loch water under a silken dawn: a night of the purest witchery, to make one credit all the tales of *glamourie* that Scotland tries so hard to refute and cannot. I don't wonder. Anyone caught out of doors at four or five on such a morning would start spelling wrong. *Faerie* and *glamourie* and *witcherie* are not for men who lie in bed till eight. Find an October night warm enough to sleep out, and a dawn all mixed up with moonshine, and you will see that I am right. You too will be mis-spelled.

James and I step out of evergreen shade and into a shapely expanse of brown winter heather punctuated by wind-sculpted pines, a rain-shadowed slope that transforms into a rich autumnal tapestry of purple and pinks, every September. We stop to look four miles into the distance. He points out 3,789-foot Lochnagar and 3,927-foot Beinn a'Bhuird. Snow on these distant peaks reminds me of this passage from *The Living Mountain*: "The coming of snow is often from a sky of glittering blue. With serried battalions of solid white cumuli low on the horizon. One of them bellies out from the ranks, and from its edge thin shreds of snow, so fine one is hardly aware of their presence, eddy lightly in the blue sky."

Below me in the valley, I see a car pass silently between the roofs of conservative Scottish houses and think of how, emptied of people during the wars, the Cairngorms were a place where Nan mostly walked by herself. I wonder if the mountains made her feel less alone. From the valley floor to the peaks I see in the distance, she contemplated with keen attention the elemental—frost and snow, rocks and trees, water and lochs, and more—her sense of place illustrating how decades of observation as a localist leads to deep knowing.

Descended from Aberdeen farmers who tended sheep in rugged mountains, Shepherd's surname suggests hillwalking was in her blood. Born in 1893, she lived her entire life in Cults, a gray, granite, western suburb of Aberdeen, austere and industrial on sunless days, but a sparkling and infinite port of possibilities when the sun is out. Her life spanned dramatic cultural changes, from Queen Victoria through Ronald Reagan.

Shepherd's progressive parents ensured she was as educated as her older brother Frank, and in 1915, she was one of the first women to graduate from the University of Aberdeen. In her twenties, she saw Great Britain empty of men—drafted into World War I, with over 400,000 British soldiers perishing in the Battle of the Somme in 1916. People grieving the pointless loss of millions of lives walked for the solace and peace the natural world provided. "In that disturbed and uncertain world," Shepherd writes in her foreword to *The Living Mountain*, "it was my secret place of ease."

When some women gained the right to vote in 1918, the civil equality that had been held at bay by Queen Victoria's 1870 comment—"Let women be what God intended, a helpmate for man, but with totally different duties and vocations"—began to erode old mores, and women enjoyed more freedoms. For forty years, Shepherd was a lecturer in English at the teacher training college in Aberdeen. She was a popular, earthy teacher whose wit and warmth made her a favorite among her students. In her 2016 Shepherd biography, *Into the Mountain,* Charlotte Peacock writes about how Shepherd kept a revolving display of seasonal color on her desk, vases filled with saucer-shaped hellebores, bouquets of pastel primroses, and bright autumn leaves from her garden. Students remember how she arranged the classroom so sunlight cascading through the windows warmed her back and illuminated the faces of her students sitting at their desks.

A decade before she began her journeys in the Cairngorms, and around the time her brother died from tuberculosis in South Africa in 1917, Shepherd experienced an artistic and personal shift. She withdrew from the organized religion at Cults Free Kirk (the local name for the Free Church of Scotland), in which she'd been indoctrinated since childhood, and read the Eastern philosophy of Lafcadio Hearn, who wrote of life in Japan—including *Glimpses of Unfamiliar Japan* (1894) and *Kokoro: Hints and Echoes of Japanese Inner Life* (1896)—at a time when the country was still mysterious and exotic to Westerners. Through these readings, Shepherd began to lean toward the natural world as a source of spiritual energy. She was also influenced by the mystical and theosophical writings of author, critic, painter, and Irish nationalist George William Russell, who wrote under the pseudonym Æ. His theosophy teaches that the microcosm is the macrocosm, and diverse forms of life, both human and nonhuman, are one. This collapsing of boundaries between the seen and unseen would become an essential part of *The Living Mountain.*

So there I lie on the plateau, under me the central core of fire from which was thrust this grumbling grinding mass of plutonic rock, over me blue air, and between the fire of the rock and the fire of the sun, scree, soil and water, moss, grass, flower and tree, insect, bird and beast, wind, rain and snow—the total mountain. Slowly I have found my way in. If I had other senses, there are other things I should know. It is nonsense to suppose, when I have perceived the exquisite division of running water, or a flower, that my separate senses can make, that there would be nothing more to perceive were we endowed with other modes of perception. How could we imagine flavour, or perfume, without the senses of taste and smell? They are completely unimaginable. There must be many exciting properties of matter that we cannot know because we have no way to know them. Yet, what we have, what wealth! I add to it each time I go to the mountain—the eye sees what it didn't see before, or sees in a new way what it had already seen. So the ear, the other senses. It is an experience that grows; undistinguished days add their part, and now and then, unpredictable and unforgettable, come the hours when heaven and earth fall away and one sees a new creation. The many details—a stroke here, a stroke there—come for a moment into perfect focus, and one can read at last the word that has been from the beginning.

In her thirties, Shepherd wrote three semi-autobiographical novels—*The Quarry Wood* (1928), *The Weatherhouse* (1930), and *A Pass in the Grampians* (1933), as well as a volume of poetry, *In the Cairngorms* (1934), which established her reputation as one of the most highly respected members of the Scottish Modernist movement. So it is something of a mystery why, after she'd completed the 30,000-word manuscript that would become *The Living Mountain*, she put it in a drawer rather than publish it. How long did it sit there? One year? Two? A decade perhaps? For more than *thirty years* it languished in a dark drawer of her Cults home. Some have speculated her decision had something to do with post-WWII paper shortages in Britain, or a thyroid condition that sapped her energy and, she feared, her essential character, for a time. Others have suggested an initial rejection from a publisher (though for someone whose earlier publishing history suggests persistence and tenacity—her first book was published after thirteen rejections—it seems unlikely one negative response would discourage her).

To those who knew her well, the manuscript mystery was rooted in something more nuanced. Old family friends speculate she had mixed feelings about releasing a mystical piece of writing into the community of Cairngorm hillwalkers. She states her book's intentions clearly in passages like this one: "Summer on the high plateau can be as delectable as honey; it can also be a roaring scourge. To those who love the place, both are good, since both are part of its essential nature. And it is to know its essential nature that I am seeking here." Shepherd worried her sensual book about being and feeling in the mountains would be dismissed and shut down by the dominant culture of male climbers, data-driven scientists, and quest-obsessed mountaineers. *The Living Mountain* was radical because, as writer Robert Macfarlane has noted, "Shepherd was a woman writing out of a Highland Scottish culture in which cherishing of the body was not easily discussed."

Shepherd's fears would be borne out. Even as late as 2016, a voice of the old guard was trying to dismiss her work. Cairngorm scientist and mountaineer Adam Watson—an esteemed presence in his fields of study—used his book *Essays on Lone Trips, Mountain-Craft, and Other Hill Topics* to lampoon *The Living Mountain* as "fanciful, contrived, and fundamentally anthropomorphic." He wrote that the book was a good example of what some Aberdeen climbers in the 1950s called Salvationism, or "a way of gaining salvation for a person going to the hills or writing about them," and added, "[the Aberdeen climbers] spoke the term with sarcasm." His snide mansplaining feels like a cruel shot at someone who can no longer defend herself and denigrates Shepherd's interpretation of her own body in the landscape. This attitude is, I feel, the reason she kept *The Living Mountain* in a drawer.

Despite small-mindedness from some fading quarters, Shepherd's legacy only grows. The same year Watson trivialized her writing, the Royal Bank of Scotland stole wild hearts across Scotland by issuing an exquisite new £5 banknote featuring Shepherd. Her long braided hair is held by a bejeweled headband, and she looks with unbroken gaze into the distance, the Cairngorms outlined in the background. On the opposite side of the note, a quote from her first novel, *The Quarry Wood*—"It's a grand thing to get leave to live"—is suspended like clouds above faint mountain contours. Like George Washington on dollars and Queen Elizabeth on pounds, Shepherd will seep into British collective consciousness as a cultural cornerstone. On my own sojourns in Scotland, I made sure to keep these eye-catching blue notes when I received them as change. Now framed on my wall, they remind me that we own our voices and personal narratives. The relationships between our minds, bodies, spirits, and places are entirely our own experiences, and we need not hide them away in drawers or closets.

Remember Shepherd's words in *The Living Mountain*:

So my journey into experience began. It was a journey always for fun, with no motive beyond that I wanted it. But at first I was seeking only sensuous gratification—the sensation of height, the sensation of movement, the sensation of speed, the sensation of distance, the sensation of effort, the sensation of ease: the lust of the flesh, the lust of the eyes, the pride of life. I was not interested in the mountain for itself, but for its effect upon me, as puss caresses not the man but herself against the man's trouser leg. But as I grew older, and less self-sufficient, I began to discover the mountain in itself. Everything became good to me, its contours, its colours, its waters and rock, flowers and birds. This process has taken many years, and is not yet complete. Knowing another is endless. And I have discovered that man's experience of them

enlarges rock, flower and bird. The thing to be known grows with
the knowing.

I believe that I now understand in some small measure why the
Buddhist goes on pilgrimage to a mountain. The journey is itself
part of the technique by which the god is sought. It is a journey
into Being; for as I penetrate more deeply into the mountain's life,
I penetrate also into my own. For an hour I am beyond desire. It
is not ecstasy, that leap out of the self that makes man like a god.
I am not out of myself, but in myself. I am. To know Being, this is
the final grace accorded from the mountain.

The Living Mountain is a departure from mountaineering literature with overt displays of climaxing by men. It's the first book
of its kind in nature writing to be so intuitive and sensual, with a
Buddhist approach to pilgrimage—walking barefoot along a path
of pine needles, sleeping in heather in the sunshine, undressing for
a wild swim. Whether we are spiritual or sensual, Salvationist or
scientific, there should be no limitations imposed by others on the
ways we find meaning in the natural world. Shepherd went to the
mountains not to measure and quantify. Rather, she went to look.
To think. To feel. To be. In doing so, she captured the Cairngorms in
many dimensions and frequencies. *The Living Mountain* feels vital
and alive to this day, and as James and I make our way down the
mountain and over the River Dee to the pub in his village, it feels
like Shepherd is walking mindfully in step with us, as leaves quiver,
clouds pass, and rivers flow.

MORE MINDFUL WALKING

KATHARINE NORBURY

Following a miscarriage, a breast cancer diagnosis, and a letter from her birth mother, English writer and film editor Norbury set out on a journey: to follow rivers from sea to source on the Llŷn Peninsula of northwest Wales, in the company of her nine-year-old daughter. This lush and vivid walking journey, recounted in *The Fish Ladder: A Journey Upstream* (2015), became a profound reflection on the healing power of nature during times of grief and loss.

ANTONIA MALCHIK

Malchik's first book, *A Walking Life: Reclaiming Our Health and Our Freedom One Step at a Time* (2019) explores how walking relates to our health, creativity, and communities; how we have lost it through a century of car-centric design; how we can regain it; and more. It delves into the unanswered questions of our lives: Why are we so lonely? How can our technologies better serve us, rather than us serving them? How does living together build trust? *A Walking Life* reminds us that when we let our feet wander, our minds follow. A resident of Whitefish, Montana, Malchik has written essays for many publications, including *Aeon*, the *Atlantic*, *Orion*, and *High Country News*.

NATASHA CARTHEW

Carthew has written the first drafts of all her books outside, in the fields, coasts, or woods near near her home in Cornwall or in a cabin she built from scrap wood. This includes two books of poetry and three novels for young adults—*Winter Damage* (2013), *The Light That Gets Lost* (2015), and *Only the Ocean* (2018). *All Rivers Run Free* (2018), written entirely on the banks of the River Tamar, while walking it from source to sea, is her first novel for adults.

RACHEL CARSON

What has already silenced the voices of spring in countless towns in America? This book is an attempt to explain.

SILENT SPRING

T IS 1962. Rock-a-Stacks, Flintstone pedal cars, and Chatty Cathy dolls are the hit toys. John Glenn orbits Earth. Thalidomide is removed from the market. Soviets are building missile bases in Cuba. It is the height of the Cold War. The American mood is heavy with security concerns. And bird populations in the Western world are quietly plummeting.

At a press conference in late summer, President Kennedy is fielding questions about external military threats, when a reporter asks about a threat, not from abroad but on American soil. Captured on black-and-white film, it's a startling interaction.

4 PM 29 August 1962. US State Department Auditorium. Dressed in a dark, slim-notched lapel suit and white dress shirt with striped tie and white pocket square, President Kennedy stands at a wooden podium conducting a twenty-eight-minute press conference.

REPORTER, OFF-CAMERA: There appears to be growing concern among scientists of the possibility of dangerous long-range side effects from widespread use of DDT and other pesticides. Have you considered asking the Department of Agriculture or Public Health Service to take a closer look at this?

President Kennedy pivots left to address the reporter.

PRESIDENT KENNEDY: Yes, and I know that they already are. (*He stretches his right arm across the podium to emphasize his point.*) I think particularly, of course, since Miss Carson's book.

"Miss Carson's book" was none other than Rachel Carson's soon-to-be-monumental *Silent Spring*. And the threat? DDT—short for dichlorodiphenyltrichloroethane—a colorless chemical compound that became available in the United States in 1945 as an agricultural and household pesticide. With a title inspired by the last two lines of Keats's 1819 poem "La Belle Dame sans Merci" ("The sedge has withered from the lake, / And no birds sing."), *Silent Spring* explained to everyday Americans the devastating impact of DDT's widespread use. Carson challenged the practice of indiscriminate spraying in homes, neighborhoods, and the countryside, during a time when research into side effects was negligible to nonexistent. Her groundbreaking research with a team of female scientists persuasively linked DDT and other pesticides to cancer in humans and unnaturally high death rates in wildlife, particularly birds. Her book conveyed the idea that the world is an interconnected web of life that needs protection to a receptive public, an outraged chemical industry, and a mute government. Over the summer of 1962, *Silent Spring* was brilliantly serialized in the *New Yorker* ahead of its publication by Houghton Mifflin in September. Once published, it was a pop culture blockbuster. The first ecology book to have such a profound impact in the United States, it dramatically shifted the public's ecological consciousness.

In her time, Rachel Louise Carson was to ecology what, in our time, The Notorious Ruth Bader Ginsberg is to the judiciary: an unlikely rock star. Petite and soft-spoken, with a steely inner resolve, she was a whip-smart scientist with a poet's vision who understood the power of storytelling. Born in 1907, Carson earned a master's in zoology from Johns Hopkins University in 1932. She planned to continue studying for a doctorate, but the Depression forced her to drop out of school and find work to support her family. She worked for the federal government, eventually becoming editor in chief of all U.S. Fish and Wildlife Service publications. The success of her sea trilogy—its second installment, *The Sea Around Us* (1951), spent eighty-one weeks on the *New York Times* bestseller list—gave her the financial freedom to write full-time. A year later, it also won both the Burroughs Medal for nature writing and the National Book Award for nonfiction. A documentary of the book won an Oscar.

It may be hard to imagine now, but until *Silent Spring*, few people—not the public, not the government, not even the scientific community—understood the links between toxicity and pesticides. But when songbirds began turning up dead in a friend's garden, Carson started researching and felt called to open the public's eyes and take on the chemical industry. Before *Silent Spring*, DDT was actually celebrated in the media—a 1947 advertisement in *Time* magazine claimed, "DDT is good for *mee-e-e!*" In television commercials, housewives in festive floral party dresses, hair pinned in victory rolls, sashayed through their homes to rapturous orchestral music while spraying the "miracle" product under sofa cushions and inside pianos. DuPont's slogan, "Better Things for Better Living . . . Through Chemistry," was the tune of the day—until *Silent Spring* exposed the downside.

In language anyone could understand, Carson explained how profligate use of synthetic chemical pesticides after World War II upset the delicate balance of ecosystems. She connected plummeting bird populations—brown and white pelicans, peregrine falcons, and golden and bald eagles—to the way DDT altered the birds' calcium metabolism, resulting in thin eggshells. Because the shells couldn't support the weight of an incubating bird, nests turned into omelets. Poisons that washed into waterways traveled up the food chain in ever-greater concentrations, affecting worms, insects, fish, birds, soil, and ultimately humans, Carson wrote. Her opening chapter, "A Fable for Tomorrow," vividly frames the stakes.

> There was once a town in the heart of America where all life
> seemed to be in harmony with its surroundings. The town lay in
> the midst of a checkerboard of prosperous farms, with fields of
> grain and hillsides of orchards where, in spring, white clouds of
> bloom drifted above the green fields. In autumn, oak and maple
> and birch set up a blaze of color that flamed and flickered across a

backdrop of pines. Then foxes barked in the hills and deer silently crossed the fields, half hidden in the mists of the fall mornings.

Along the roads, laurel, viburnum, and alder, great ferns and wild flowers delighted the traveler's eye through much of the year. Even in winter the roadsides were places of beauty, where countless birds came to feed on the berries and on the seed heads of the dried weeds rising above the snow. The countryside was, in fact, famous for the abundance and variety of its bird life, and when the flood of migrants was pouring through in spring and fall people traveled from great distances to observe them. Others came to fish the streams, which flowed clear and cold out of the hills and contained shady pools where trout lay. So it had been from the days many years ago when the first settlers raised their houses, sank their wells, and built their barns.

Then a strange blight crept over the area and everything began to change. Some evil spell had settled on the community: mysterious maladies swept the flocks of chickens; the cattle and sheep sickened and died. Everywhere was a shadow of death. The farmers told of much illness among their families. In the town the doctors were becoming more and more puzzled by new kinds of sickness that had appeared among their patients. There had been several sudden and unexplained deaths, not only among the adults but also among the children, who would be stricken while they were at play and die within a few hours.

There was a strange stillness. The birds, for example—where had they gone? Many people spoke of them, puzzled and disturbed. The feeding stations in the backyards were deserted. The few birds seen anywhere were moribund; they trembled violently and could not fly. It was a spring without voices. On the mornings which had once throbbed with the dawn chorus of robins, catbirds, doves, jays, wrens, and scores of other bird voices there was now no sound; only silence lay over the fields and woods and marsh.

On the farms, the hens brooded, but no chicks hatched. The farmers complained that they were unable to raise any pigs— the litters were small and the young survived only a few days. The apple trees were coming into bloom but no bees droned among the blossoms, so there was no pollination and there would be no fruit.

The roadsides, once so attractive, were now lined with brown and withered vegetation as though swept by fire. These, too, were silent, deserted by all living things. Even the streams were lifeless. Anglers no longer visited them, for all the fish had died.

In the gutters under the eaves and between the shingles of the roofs, a white granular powder still showed a few patches; some weeks before it had fallen like snow upon the roofs and lawns, the fields and streams.

No witchcraft, no enemy action had silenced the rebirth of new life in this stricken world. The people had done it themselves.

Though a fable, this passage resonated with people, and it illustrates Carson's gift for simplifying complex scientific information and for lyrical storytelling. "Nature has introduced great variety into the landscape," she wrote in the *New Yorker*. "But man has displayed a passion for simplifying it. Thus he undoes the built-in checks and balances by which nature holds the species within bounds." Her writing emotionally invigorated people and raised public consciousness about chemical pollution in a way that had never been done. "Know the facts," she urged readers, while backing up her own research in *Silent Spring* with a whopping fifty-five pages of scientific references.

The public, Carson felt, acquiesced to the use of pesticides simply because lack of research on the subject seemed to indicate all was okay. It was not. She encouraged readers to become proactive consumers and citizen scientists. "We urgently need an end to these false assurances, to the sugarcoating of unpalatable facts. It is the public that is being asked to assume the risks that the insect controllers calculate. The public must decide whether it wishes to continue on the present road, and it can do so only when in full possession of the facts." For the first time, Americans questioned the government and the scientists who reassured them there were no toxic links between pesticides and health—while children played in billowing clouds of DDT pumped by trucks through American neighborhoods and climbed fruit trees to wave as crop dusters sprayed chemicals on orchards.

Gardeners and farmers were unaware that when they sprayed their homes and land for gypsy moths or mosquitoes, it upset a larger web of life. "The problem I dealt with in *Silent Spring* is not an isolated one," she wrote in the *New York Times* in 1962.

> The excessive and ill-advised use of chemical pesticides is merely one part of a sorry whole—the reckless pollution of our living world with harmful and dangerous substances. Until very recently, the average citizen assumed that "Someone" was looking after these matters and that some little understood but confidently relied upon safeguards stood like shields between his person and any harm. Now he has experienced, from several different directions, a rather rude shattering of these beliefs.

While President Kennedy was receptive—he established a presidential advisory committee on the subject—the old boys' club and the chemical industry went to war with Carson, leveling personal attacks on her gender, marital status, and "hysterical" character as a woman—to say nothing of her science. The Department of Agriculture refused to speak to her. She was accused of being a communist, a fanatic, and—horrors!—a hippie. The chemical industry was concerned about her effect on homemakers who might think twice before buying bug bombs. "If man were to faithfully follow the teachings of Miss Carson, we would return to the Dark Ages, and the insects and diseases and vermin would once again inherit the earth," said Robert White-Stevens, a former biochemist, assistant director of the agricultural research division of American Cyanamid, and spokesman for the biochemical industry in the 1960s.

Said another critic: "*Silent Spring*. It kept reminding me of trying to win an argument with a woman. It can't be done."

And yet another: "We can live without birds and animals, but we cannot live without business."

Nevertheless, she persisted.

Carson biographer Linda Lear writes about how women were, in fact, *Silent Spring*'s most receptive audience. "Women were concerned with a spectrum of pollution and contamination issues: fluoride in water, food additives, thalidomide, radioactive fallout, government secrecy, and corporate deception. They linked their concern with their primary roles as housewives and mothers and with the protection of future generations. Their outlook was not so much economic as humane."

Eventually, Kennedy's science advisory committee report, "The Uses of Pesticides," concluded that Carson's evidence was stronger than her critics admitted. The *Saturday Review* wrote:

> *Silent Spring*, winner of eight awards, is the history-making best-seller that stunned the world with its terrifying revelation about our contaminated planet. No science-fiction nightmare can equal the power of this authentic and chilling portrait of the unseen destroyers which have already begun to change the shape of life as we know it.
>
> *Silent Spring* is the devastating attack on human carelessness, greed and irresponsibility. It should be read by every American who does not want it to be the epitaph of a world not very far behind us in time.

Many people attending Kennedy's 1962 press conference would later see President Nixon heed *Silent Spring*'s warnings and establish the Environmental Protection Agency in 1970. It wouldn't be Kennedy, and it wouldn't be Carson. Within twenty months of that remarkable moment, both history makers would be dead—the charismatic president assassinated at the age of forty-six, the biologist claimed by breast cancer at fifty-six. In 1972, DDT was banned, and this, combined with the Endangered Species Act, is a major reason bald eagles and peregrine falcons rebounded from near-extinction.

Silent Spring would go on to be celebrated by *Discover* magazine as one of the top twenty-five science books ever written, and Carson named one of *Time* magazine's "100 Most Influential People of the Twentieth Century." Her book remains one of the most prominent pieces of literature on industrial malpractice and is credited with birthing the modern environmental movement in the United States and Europe.

The Notorious RLC changed the world.

MORE ON FIGHTING POLLUTION

SANDRA STEINGRABER

Recipient of the Rachel Carson Leadership Award, Steingraber is an American ecologist, author, and cancer survivor who has written several books exploring links between human rights and the environment. She is best known for *Living Downstream: An Ecologist's Personal Investigation of Cancer and the Environment* (1997) and *Raising Elijah: Protecting Our Children in an Age of Environmental Crisis* (2011). She has been named woman of the year by *Ms.* magazine and one of twenty-five "Visionaries Who Are Changing Your World" by the *Utne Reader*.

SVETLANA ALEXIEVICH

Winner of the 2015 Nobel Prize in Literature, Alexievich is a Belarusian investigative journalist, essayist, and writer of documentary literature. Her beautifully crafted monologues of war and disaster create unforgettable impressions of the Russian soul. Published in Russian in 1997 and English in 2005, *Voices from Chernobyl: The Oral History of a Nuclear Disaster* is a deeply touching, first-person, polyphonic collage of voices from those who survived the 1986 nuclear catastrophe.

REBECCA ALTMAN

A writer and environmental sociologist, Altman's essays and her TEDx Talk explore the social history of plastics, pollution, and chemistry and what is passed on from one generation to the next. Her essays, including "Time Bombing the Future," "American Petro-topia," and "How the Benzene Tree Polluted the World," have appeared in the *Atlantic*, *Aeon*, *Orion*, *Terrain*, and more. She is working on a nonfiction book about a personal history of plastics that includes a biography of her father, who worked for Union Carbide—the plastic company that touted manufacturing a billion pounds of plastic in one year in the 1960s.

MARY OLIVER

Attention is the
beginning of devotion.

"UPSTREAM"

CAPE COD, MASSACHUSETTS, is a hook-shaped apostrophe of dune beaches and marshes, tidepools and lighthouses punctuating the North Atlantic. Sculpted by waves, wind, and winter storms, this eastern outpost is the place Pulitzer Prize–winning poet Mary Oliver once called home. In the weather-beaten landscape, she wrote poetry and prose inspired by the world around her.

On a balmy weekend in September, I set out from Boston and loop around Cape Cod to Provincetown, the spot where the Pilgrims first landed and Oliver lived for more than forty years. A former fishing village, it's now a rakish arts colony of worn brick sidewalks and picket fences. Intense sunlight has long attracted painters here from around the world. Rainbow flags on porch posts rise and fall in the ocean breeze.

I fill my canvas handbag with Oliver's poetry, along with a thermos of tea and chocolate biscuits, and hop on a bike. It's mid-morning, and I'm cycling a little north to Blackwater Pond, in the Cape Cod National Seashore. I find the trailhead to the Beech Forest Walk, a sandy, circular path through tupelo, sassafras, pines, and oaks. There are blackbirds, bluebirds, nuthatches, and orioles overhead, and, as I cross a wooden bridge, I see a mosh pit of silver water bugs rippling the water below.

Never without a notebook, Oliver cultivated her sense of wonder through her daily practice of rising early in the morning—a time she felt the soul most receptive to insights—and walking these beaches, ponds, and forests. As I follow in her footsteps, I remember a more furtive habit of hers. As she wanted no thought to go unrecorded, she would hide pencils on her rambles so she would always have one handy. For someone like me, who loves mudlarking, this is such an exciting opportunity that my eyes dart among nooks and crannies in trees and rocks, searching for a Mary Oliver pencil—something I would treasure forever. In combing, I discover other things—gossamer spiderwebs stretching between branches, fly agaric mushrooms with their white-speckled red caps, and solitude.

At the edge of the pond, I find a rock surrounded by bright goldenrod and white asters and sit down in the sun. I search my bag for a poem. Oliver always said poetry should be read aloud and heard. I'm alone today, and easily amused, so I take a sip of tea, clear my throat, and imagine the poet, at that moment living in Florida, also charmed by this audience of birds, frogs, and dragonflies.

AT BLACKWATER POND

At Blackwater Pond the tossed waters have settled
after a night of rain.
I dip my cupped hands. I drink
a long time. It tastes
like stone, leaves, fire. It falls cold
into my body, waking the bones. I hear them
deep inside me, whispering
oh what is that beautiful thing
that just happened?

That wonder—a fusion of mystery, prayer, and presence—is at the heart of all Oliver's poetry and prose. A gateway to a sacred place. A mixture of transcendental, Buddhist, and Christian thought. Joyful and simple, Oliver's words sit with me as I look out on the lily pads and unpeel the poem's final question. Then I listen to a recording of Oliver reading "At Blackwater Pond" herself, and her inflections and pauses add more layers. Mindful of the warblers overhead and swirling pools of dappled light around me, I think about how the "beautiful thing" of poetry came into Oliver's own life.

Mary Oliver was born in Maple Heights, Ohio, in 1935. As a girl, she packed books by Walt Whitman and Ralph Waldo Emerson into her knapsack and escaped to neighborhood woods to read litera-ture and write poetry. The woods were a place for wonderment, but they were also far more—they provided safety and solace during a time of childhood sexual abuse—an experience she obliquely writes about in "Staying Alive," from *Upstream: Selected Essays* (2016). Her collection *Dream Work* (1986) also includes personal poems about these challenging early years.

Through the trees on the other side of the pond, I see a family with children hopping on rocks, and I cringe, imagining a little girl feeling she had to flee her own home for the safety of wild places. It is a more natural order to be the inverse. In the few interviews she granted, Oliver, a private person, said her strength came from finding salvation in nature—a place where she could talk to herself through writing and rebuild herself through literature. The joy and prayers she found there were instructive and extended throughout her life.

"Lord knows when I started writing poetry it was rotten," she once said in a voice both graceful and gravelly. "I was ten, eleven, twelve years old. But I kept at it, kept at it, kept at it. I used to say that with my pencil, I traveled to the moon probably a few times. I kept at it every day, and finally you learn things."

She left home the day after her high school graduation. She visited Steepletop in Austerlitz, New York, home of poet and play-wright Edna St. Vincent Millay, the third woman to win the Pulitzer Prize for poetry, in 1923. There she struck up a friendship with the late poet's sister, Norma, and took a position organizing the estate's papers, a job she had for years while attending Vassar College and Ohio State University. Steepletop is also where, in 1958, she met the love of her life, Molly Malone Cook, a photographer, gallerist, and Oliver's future literary agent, whom she followed to Cape Cod. In 1963, at twenty-eight, she published her first volume of poetry, *No Voyage and Other Poems*. More than twenty books of poetry and prose followed over her nearly sixty-year career—many of them dedicated to Cook.

After sauntering around Blackwater Pond, I return to my bike and head for the beach. I cycle past pink salt spray roses along the dunes of the bike trail to the Race Point Lighthouse. Tossing the bike in beachgrass, I kick off my shoes to feel sand between my toes. The sky is cloudless, and the wind is picking up. I look out at the blue sea. Grain by grain, season by season, nature is sculpting this far-flung edge of America. These elemental forces shaped the terrain of Oliver's inner life as well. I sit on the beach, and, with gulls, gannets, and terns flying overhead and diving into the Atlantic, I search my bag for Oliver's most anthologized poem, "Wild Geese," from *Dream Work*. I don't really need the paper copy. I can recite it by heart and, appropriately, it always gives me goosebumps. After awhile, on the sand in the sunshine, I listen to a recording of Oliver reading, and it sounds like a prayer.

WILD GEESE

You do not have to be good.
You do not have to walk on your knees
for a hundred miles through the desert, repenting.
You only have to let the soft animal of your body
　　love what it loves.
Tell me about despair, yours, and I will tell you mine.
Meanwhile the world goes on.
Meanwhile the sun and the clear pebbles of the rain
are moving across the landscapes,
over the prairies and the deep trees,
the mountains and the rivers.
Meanwhile the wild geese, high in the clean blue air,
are heading home again.
Whoever you are, no matter how lonely,
the world offers itself to your imagination,
calls to you like the wild geese, harsh and exciting—
over and over announcing your place
in the family of things.

Communion, interconnection, transcendence. Simple, deep, and elegant, "Wild Geese" is a rapturous ode to awakening, acceptance, and *attention*—to ourselves and to the world around us. In no small way, this poem has saved lives by assuaging personal anguish. Looking at the ocean horizon, I recall the soft gasps I heard when I read it aloud at a nature writing workshop in the Lake District. Line by line, emotion builds like energy in waves crashing ashore.

When she writes, "You only have to let the soft animal of your body / love what it loves," her warm reassurance resonates in people struggling with life's transitions or conflicts—perhaps we feel lonely or different, perhaps our sexual or gender orientation is in conflict with ourselves or others, perhaps we feel guilty for not living up to others' expectations. Acceptance flows through Oliver's body of work, offering comfort by blurring boundaries between ourselves and the natural world. In plain language, she describes a wild creature calling us into a larger community.

Oliver never expresses postmodern cynicism or conveys ideas in inscrutable imagery. Inspired by what she encountered and felt on her morning walks, her writing has a deep sense of place: whale bones on beaches, honeysuckle growing in a garden, green snow crickets, and blacksnakes; clams, mussels, moon snails, and barnacles; owls, clouds, and marsh hawks. The world, she once wrote, was "frisky." As were her many dogs, with whom she shared a joyful and inspirational bond celebrated in her book *Dog Songs* (2015).

Though America's bestselling poet, she never considered herself a poet at all. "I consider myself kind of a reporter," she said, "one who uses words that are more like music and that have a choreography." Oliver's poems are like songs or prayers to hold close and recite in times of need. Throughout her difficult childhood, she always attended Sunday school, where she developed an interest in religion and spirituality. In her later years, she read the short poetry of the Persian mystic Rumi. This sense of the sacred permeates her poetry.

I cycle back to Herring Cove Beach near Provincetown, where kids send jaunty kites into the early autumn sky. Looking toward the village, I imagine the real-life encounter in a neighbor's garden where Oliver, attending a birthday party, watched as a grasshopper ate frosting from the cake on her plate. Billy Collins, US poet laureate from 2001 to 2003, included the resulting poem, "The Summer Day," in the first edition of the digital anthology *Poetry 180: A Poem a Day for American High Schools*. A generation of American kids were raised on this beautiful meditation on a grasshopper.

In the poem, Oliver delves into the nature of prayer while collapsing boundaries between herself and nature. She questions the nature of three creatures: a white swan that floats on water and flies in skies, a dark-coated predator that roams forests, and a short-lived insect that hops through grass. The bird is a symbol of grace and beauty, sacred to Venus, Roman goddess of love, while the bear is a sharp-toothed totem of strength, independence, and tenacity. The grasshopper's life is short—perhaps, Oliver suggests, all our lives are—yet miraculous all the same. The woman and grasshopper gaze at each other in mirrored states of wonder.

At the end, she asks a question that, paired with the wild animals, prompts us to take stock: "What is it you plan to do with your one wild and precious life?"

To that very question, Oliver once replied in an interview, "I used up a lot of pencils."

I feel blue leaving the Cape a few days later. When you appreciate Oliver's poetry and spend a waning summer weekend in the place that so deeply inspired it, departing feels like leaving a friend. I never did find a Mary Oliver pencil. Instead, I pressed fragrant wild roses, goldenrod, and asters between pages of her poetry. That was treasure enough.

Four months after my visit to Cape Cod, on 17 January 2019, Mary Oliver died at the age of eighty-three. Her partner, Molly, preceded her by fourteen years. I like to imagine them both still there—in streams, in sky, in sea.

THE SUMMER DAY

Who made the world?
Who made the swan, and the black bear?
Who made the grasshopper?
This grasshopper, I mean—
the one who has flung herself out of the grass,
the one who is eating sugar out of my hand,
who is moving her jaws back and forth instead of up and down—
who is gazing around with her enormous and complicated eyes.
Now she lifts her pale forearms and thoroughly washes her face.
Now she snaps her wings open, and floats away.
I don't know exactly what a prayer is.
I do know how to pay attention, how to fall down
into the grass, how to kneel down in the grass,
how to be idle and blessed, how to stroll through the fields,
which is what I have been doing all day.
Tell me, what else should I have done?
Doesn't everything die at last, and too soon?
Tell me, what is it you plan to do
with your one wild and precious life?

Mary Oliver

WORKS BY MARY OLIVER

POETRY AND ESSAY COLLECTIONS

No Voyage and Other Poems (1963)

The River Styx, Ohio, and Other Poems (1972)

The Night Traveler (1978)

Twelve Moons (1978)

Sleeping in the Forest (1979)

American Primitive (1983)

Dream Work (1986)

Provincetown (1987)

House of Light (1990)

New and Selected Poems, Volume One (1992)

White Pine: Poems and Prose Poems (1994)

Blue Pastures (1995)

West Wind: Poems and Prose Poems (1997)

Winter Hours: Prose, Prose Poems, and Poems (1999)

The Leaf and the Cloud (2000)

What Do We Know (2002)

Owls and Other Fantasies: Poems and Essays (2003)

Why I Wake Early (2004)

Blue Iris: Poems and Essays (2004)

Wild Geese: Selected Poems (2004)

Long Life: Essays and Other Writings (2004)

New and Selected Poems, Volume Two (2005)

At Blackwater Pond: Mary Oliver Reads Mary Oliver
(audio cd) (2006)

Thirst: Poems (2006)

Our World (with photographer Molly Malone Cook) (2007)

The Truro Bear and Other Adventures:
Poems and Essays (2008)

Red Bird (2008)

Evidence (2009)

Swan: Poems and Prose Poems (2010)

A Thousand Mornings (2012)

Dog Songs (2013)

Blue Horses (2014)

Felicity (2015)

Upstream: Selected Essays (2016)

Devotions: The Selected Poems of Mary Oliver (2017)

NONFICTION AND OTHER BOOKS

A Poetry Handbook (1994)

Rules for the Dance: A Handbook for Writing and
Reading Metrical Verse (1998)

CAROLYN
MERCHANT

The Renaissance philosophy of nature was one of a living organism. It was a projection of the human body onto the cosmos. The cosmos, like the human being, had body, soul, and spirit. The earth also was alive and conceptualized as a nurturing mother which had systems like the human being: circulation, reproduction, and even elimination systems. Earthquakes were said to be the earth breaking wind.

"ENVIRONMENTALISM: FROM THE CONTROL
OF NATURE TO PARTNERSHIP"

I T WAS AUGUST 1989, and I sat across from the kindly but skeptical chairman of Berkeley's English department. In my hand was a flyer I'd plucked from a post in Sproul Plaza, advertising an unusual course entitled "Nature Writers." I was in his office to plead for his signature permitting me to enroll. The cards were stacked against me. First, the course was well outside the English department's domain in the College of Letters and Sciences—it was in the College of Natural Resources, where landscapes, not literature, were studied. Second, it was student-led, with no professor to pace a cavernous lecture hall. Third, it was interdisciplinary, focused on science, history, ethics, and philosophy rather than arts and humanities. Lastly, it would entail modern creative nonfiction rather than the classics, epics, and poetry the English department was naturally steeped in. As I described why it was important to me, I imagined the chairman saw "Nature Writers" as a ruse for weekly New Age sage-burnings. This was, after all, the late 1980s, before terms like "ecocriticism" and "ecopoetics" were common parlance in English departments.

I pushed the flyer across his desk. He studied it. "I see," he said, looking at me above his glasses, furrows easing in his brow, "that Carolyn Merchant is the advisor."

With that, he signed the papers.

The next day I was sitting cross-legged on grass with young foresters in an outdoor classroom of soft light under eucalyptus and live oaks. I didn't yet know who Carolyn Merchant was, but her name alone had cut an important new path for me. There were just twenty-five of us, and we had the spirited feeling of revolutionaries roaming edgelands in search of relevant and rapturous new narratives about the natural world. A professor of environmental history, philosophy, and ethics in Berkeley's Department of Environmental Science, Policy, and Management, Merchant had compiled a nature-writing reader for us to discuss over the term. She would occasionally drop by to listen to our discussions from the sidelines, and when she did, there was a palpable flurry. Once, a classmate leaned over and whispered what we were all thinking: "Rock star."

Impressive as she was to us, her impact on the field of environmental history—the study of how humans and nature interact and respond to each other over time—changed the landscape. One of the most influential ecofeminist philosophers and science historians of all time, Merchant is responsible for work considered both ground-breaking and foundational. Her classic 1980 book, *The Death of Nature: Women, Ecology, and the Scientific Revolution,* is one of the most important feminist books ever written. In analyzing the ways "humans have used, abused, and conserved nature, and how nature has changed ecologically," Merchant focuses on how the acceleration of commercial development and technological changes during the sixteenth and seventeenth centuries overrode the then-prominent organic mindset of people who conceived of nature as female and a nurturing mother—ideas they had long projected onto the cosmos.

If this sounds intimidating, don't despair. Think of it this way: the book you now hold in your hands is a field guide to twenty-five individual trees in a forest of voices. Merchant's work explains how the forest itself came to be. For this reason, if you are inclined toward The Big Historical Picture, I recommend *The Death of Nature* as the place to begin your journey. It offers opportunities to understand and question how the past has profoundly shaped us—from conceptions of ourselves as men and women to how we live now in society and nature. Readers can reflect on what it means to have a just relationship with the natural world and find hope for leading us out of the Anthropocene and into the Age of Sustainability, Merchant's name for the time when wind, water, and solar are better harnessed and we live in harmony with our surroundings.

Just as Rachel Carson's *Silent Spring* revealed the detriments of toxic chemicals, *The Death of Nature* challenged a "grand narrative" that had been built up over the last several centuries.

Merchant herself later wrote that it questioned the notion of "the Scientific Revolution as progress" and "undermined the valorization of the most revered fathers of modern science—such as Harvey, Bacon, Descartes, and Newton." These were the mathematicians, philosophers, and scientists who advocated control over nature and mechanical order over organic patterns. Merchant analyzes environmental history to frame the relationship between the natural world and humanity, particularly gender and the environment. She demonstrates how sexism and domination are connected to ecological devastation, while raising questions about the ways nature has been viewed in eras past. She opens *The Death of Nature* by explaining the old dynamic:

The world we have lost was organic. From the obscure origins of our species, human beings have lived in daily, immediate, organic relation with the natural order for their sustenance. In 1500, the daily interaction with nature was still structured for most Europeans, as it was for other peoples, by close-knit, cooperative, organic communities.

Thus it is not surprising that for sixteenth-century Europeans the root metaphor binding together the self, society, and the cosmos was that of an organism. As a projection of the way people experienced daily life, organismic theory emphasized interdependence among the parts of the human body, subordination of individual to communal purposes in family, community, and state, and vital life permeating the cosmos to the lowliest stone.

The book's twelve chapters include topics such as "Nature as Female," "Farm, Fen, and Forest: European Ecology in Transition," "The Mechanical Order," and "The Management of Nature." Otherworldly images of sixteenth- and seventeenth-century engravings and sculpture punctuate the narrative, along with riveting excerpts from historical texts of the era. The 1661 illustration

The Earth-Centered Hierarchical Cosmos from Andreas Cellarius's *Harmonia Macrocosmica* in the chapter "The World an Organism," for example, situates Merchant's discussion of the rise of lyrical nature writing—as we remember from Dorothy Wordsworth's story—to have been a reaction by the Romantics in the early nineteenth century against the Scientific Revolution and the Enlightenment. It was an attempt to return to what she called "organismic principles" that bound the world together holistically in people's minds. She synthesizes literature, art, and history and discusses how American transcendentalists such as Emerson "looked toward wildness as a source of spiritual insight, while Thoreau found evidence of a vital life permeating the rocks, ponds, and mountains in pagan and American Indian animism."

An especially provocative chapter is "Nature as Disorder: Women and Witches," which analyzes the two-sided association of women as both the nurturing Mother Earth figure celebrated by the courtly Renaissance lover *and* the figure burned at the stake by inquisitors for her wild uncontrollable nature. It's a heady and mind-expanding read, in clear, approachable prose. In this passage, she describes the time when a shift in attitudes toward subduing nature began:

> Sixteenth- and seventeenth-century writers exhibit a growing tendency to view both nature and society as wilderness and to advocate over the forces and fates dealt by nature. For Niccolò Machiavelli (1479–1527) society appeared as a wilderness, and fortune, like nature, was unpredictable, violent, and must be subdued.
>
> > [To Machiavelli] fortune is the ruler of half our actions. . . . I would compare her to an impetuous river that when turbulent, inundates the plains, casts down trees and buildings, removes earth from this side and places it on the other; everyone flees before it and everything yields to its fury

without being able to oppose it; and yet . . . when it is quiet, men can make provision against it by dikes and banks, so that when it rises it will either go down a canal or its rush will not be so wild and dangerous. So it is with fortune which shows her power where no measures have been taken to resist her, and directs her fury where she knows that no dikes or barriers have been made to hold her.

But the potential of violence of fortune could be mastered by aggression,

for fortune is a woman and it is necessary if you wish to master her, to conquer her by force; and it can be seen that she lets herself be overcome by the bold rather than by those who proceed coldly, and therefore like a woman, she is always a friend to the young because they are less cautious, fiercer, and master her with greater audacity.

By adopting animal-like cunning and manipulative methods, a prince could meet the enemy on its own terms. "A prince being thus obliged to know well how to act as a beast must imitate the fox and the lion, for the lion cannot protect himself from traps, and the fox cannot defend himself from wolves. One must there-fore be a fox to recognize traps, and a lion to frighten wolves."

Reading environmental history helps us understand connections between our past and present and deepens our understanding of being human now. Merchant's work traverses previously unexplored territory and the forces that inform how societies function and our roles within them. In and out of academia, *The Death of Nature* is a critique of modernism as well as the mechanistic science of the Enlightenment's progress and optimism on the planet. As ecofem-inism—a feminist approach to understanding ecology—gained attention in the 1980s and 90s, it embraced Merchant's book as an account of the relationship between women and nature. Her work also provided a way to reassess the ethical relationship of humans with nature, by moving toward what Merchant calls a "new dynamic partnership between people and their environment"—emphasizing empathy and collaboration with Earth's systems.

Merchant's impactful career is inspirational for young women interested in science, history, or both. In the article "The Death of Nature: A Retrospective," Merchant reflected on this and said, "The influences on my life and their intersections with history seem an odd coupling of chance occurrences, mundane events, and strange flashes of understanding." In 1954, as a senior in high school, Merchant was a Top Ten Finalist for the Westinghouse (now Regeneron) Science Talent Search. At Vassar College, she studied chemistry. "During the 1960s and 1970s," she writes, "the women's movement sparked by Betty Friedan's *The Feminine Mystique* (1963), the environmental movement propelled by Rachel Carson's *Silent Spring* (1962), and the social upheavals of the civil rights and antiwar movements formed my nascent social consciousness." Within this context, raising two sons "sensitized [her] to the problems of housewife and career." She became one of the first women to be awarded the E. B. Fred Fellowship to support women with children in pursuit of their graduate degrees at the University of Wisconsin–Madison, where she earned her PhD in the history of science. She is a fellow of numerous scientific organizations, including the American Council of Learned Societies and the American Association for the Advancement of Science.

The Death of Nature is just a fraction of Merchant's body of work; she has written more than a dozen subsequent environmental history books and hundreds of articles in magazines and journals. Of note is *Reinventing Eden: The Fate of Nature in Western Culture* (2003), which traces the European colonization of the North American continent as a Garden of Eden narrative and explores the ways this idea manifests today and could play out in the future.

Like *The Death of Nature*, *Reinventing Eden* focuses on creating partnerships with nature through progressive, non-linear "recovery narratives," an essential step toward a sustainable planet instead of a fractured ruin with only fenced-off parks and preserves. In finding a new story built on ecological partnerships, Merchant offers hope for the future of humans on Earth.

If a term like "ecofeminism" is new to you, or feels intimidating rolling off your tongue at, say, a cocktail party, it may be helpful to imagine it as a new word for ancient wisdom. Ecofeminism is about a nurturing approach to the natural world, a view we all—men and women—held in the past, but lost over time. Carolyn Merchant's writing will help reacquaint you with this approach and transport you to an immensely enlightened place that could change the way you perceive yourself, your relationships, your garden, your role in life, and, well . . . everything.

WORKS BY CAROLYN MERCHANT

WRITTEN BY

*The Death of Nature: Women, Ecology, and the
Scientific Revolution* (1980)

*Ecological Revolutions: Nature, Gender, and Science in
New England* (1989)

Radical Ecology: The Search for a Livable World (1992)

Earthcare: Women and the Environment (1996)

The Columbia Guide to American Environmental History (2002)

*Reinventing Eden: The Fate of Nature in
Western Culture* (2003)

American Environmental History: An Introduction (2007)

*Autonomous Nature: Problems of Prediction and Control from
Ancient Times to the Scientific Revolution* (2015)

*Spare the Birds!: George Bird Grinnell and the First
Audubon Society* (2016)

Science and Nature: Past, Present, and Future (2017)

EDITED BY

*Major Problems in American Environmental History:
Letters and Documents* (1993)

Ecology (Key Concepts in Critical Theory) (1994)

*Green Versus Gold: Sources in California's
Environmental History* (1998)

*Encyclopedia of World Environmental History,
Volumes 1–3* (2004)

ANNIE DILLARD

We must somehow take a wider view, look at the whole landscape, really see it, and describe what's going on here. Then we can at least wail the right question into the swaddling band of darkness, or, if it comes to that, choir the proper praise.

PILGRIM AT TINKER CREEK

A MOTH BURNING like a wick in a candle. A tomcat's bloody footprints painted like roses across a waking body. The dried jaws of a dead weasel clenching the neck of an eagle in flight. Annie Dillard's imagery lingers long after you've read her work, positing profound questions that, at some point in the future, may shake you awake with sudden insight. Through much of her work, Dillard has been in search of the answer to Thoreau's question of enlightenment: "With all your science can you tell how it is, and whence it is, that light comes into the soul?"

A self-described Christian mystic with a shimmering body of poetry, prose, and fiction spanning fifty years, she put this query in her very first book, *Tickets for a Prayer Wheel* (1974). It also appears in her second, *Pilgrim at Tinker Creek* (1974), the book that won her a Pulitzer Prize in 1975, when she was twenty-nine. *Pilgrim at Tinker Creek* has been described as a "great theological-pastoral-evolutionary-tragic-metaphysical-almanac." Part meditation and part "meteorological journal of [her] mind," it invites readers to travel with Dillard along two planes—the seen and unseen—into the soulful side of being human. Unlike Thoreau, Dillard doesn't give a lot of answers in her writing. In 2007, novelist Marilynne Robinson described Dillard's books as "like comets, like celestial events that remind us that the reality we inhabit is itself a celestial event, the business of eons and galaxies, however persistently we mistake its local manifestations for mere dust, mere sea, mere self, mere thought."

In "The Trouble with Wilderness, or Getting Back to the Wrong Nature," environmental historian William Cronon wrote, "The mythic frontier individualist was almost always masculine in gender." This stereotype has been a truism in contemporary nature writing. As late as the 1970s, far fewer women writing about nature were published than their male contemporaries. Dillard, in fact, lived with her husband in the Virginia suburbs when she wrote *Pilgrim at Tinker Creek* but left him out of the narrative completely as she ventured alone into the surrounding streams and fields. In "The Thoreau of the Suburbs," Diana Saverin describes how Dillard considered adopting a male, Thoreau-like persona and setting *Pilgrim at Tinker Creek* in a one-room cottage like Walden as a way of having her writing more accepted by a society who seemed to prefer the voice of a male narrator. "Dillard knew what American audiences wanted when she began working on her book," Saverin wrote. You can see this solitary individual connecting with a wild creature in "Living Like Weasels" from her early essay collection, *Teaching a Stone to Talk* (1982).

The sun had just set. I was relaxed on the tree trunk, ensconced in the lap of lichen, watching the lily pads at my feet tremble and part dreamily over the thrusting path of a carp. A yellow bird appeared to my right and flew behind me. It caught my eye; I swiveled around—and the next instant, inexplicably, I was look-ing down at a weasel, who was looking up at me.

Weasel! I'd never seen one before. He was ten inches long, thin as a curve, a muscled ribbon, brown as fruitwood, soft-furred, alert. His face was fierce, small and pointed as a lizard's; he would have made a good arrowhead. There was just a dot of chin, maybe two brown hairs' worth, and then the pure white fur began that spread down his underside. He had two black eyes I didn't see, any more than you see a window.

The weasel was stunned into stillness as he was emerging from beneath an enormous shaggy wild rose bush four feet away. I was stunned into stillness twisted backward on the tree trunk. Our eyes locked, and someone threw away the key.

Our look was as if two lovers, or deadly enemies, met unex-pectedly on an overgrown path when each had been thinking of something else: a clearing blow to the gut. It was also a bright blow to the brain, or a sudden beating of brains, with all the charge and intimate grate of rubbed balloons. It emptied our lungs. It felled the forest, moved the fields, and drained the pond; the world dismantled and tumbled into that black hole of eyes. If you and I looked at each other that way, our skulls would split and drop to our shoulders. But we don't. We keep our skulls. So.

He disappeared. This was only last week, and already I don't remember what shattered the enchantment. I think I blinked, I think I retrieved my brain from the weasel's brain, and tried to memorize what I was seeing, and the weasel felt the yank of separation, the careening splashdown into real life and the urgent current of instinct. He vanished under the wild rose. I waited motionless, my mind suddenly full of data and my spirit with pleadings, but he didn't return.

Please do not tell me about "approach-avoidance conflicts." I tell you I've been in that weasel's brain for 60 seconds, and he was in mine. Brains are private places, muttering through unique and secret tapes—but the weasel and I both plugged into another tape simultaneously, for a sweet and shocking time. Can I help it if it was a blank?

This "plugging into another tape" reminds me of a conversation with a grad school friend. She once remarked, "You know, nature writing is just travel writing." And after chewing on it for about a decade, I have come to agree. Travel involves points of departure and ports of arrival. We toss things into a suitcase—toothbrush, passport, confidence—we kiss loved ones goodbye, we lock the house, and we hit the road. Yet writers who step barefoot through back doors into gardens or walk down their lanes to a creek can also be on profound journeys, no passports required, even if they can still smell morning coffee wafting through their own kitchen windows. Dillard may have been close to home when she encountered the weasel, but her inner journey was immense.

Consider *Pilgrim at Tinker Creek*. The first word in the title conjures a sacred journey. We might expect a travelogue about a long spiritual walk inspired by the famous pilgrimages such as the 500-mile El Camino de Santiago in Spain, the mountainous Kumano Kodo trail in Japan, or the Pilgrims' Way in England. But "at Tinker Creek" tells us Dillard doesn't leave Virginia. She and her readers travel while standing still (or, more likely, sitting, probably on a sycamore log over a creek): watching a monarch butterfly migration, playing king of the meadow with grasshoppers in a field, witnessing a giant water bug drain a frog's body and leave its crumpled skin to float downstream. These meditations are filled with exquisite metaphors that explore the eternal in the particular and are investigations into spiritual and soulful places.

The greatest travel and nature writing explores the islands, capes, and coves of our inner landscapes. As acclaimed travel writer Jan Morris puts it, "In a profounder sense the best travel writers are not really writing about travel at all. They are recording the effects of places or movements upon their own particular temperaments—recording the *experience* rather than the event, as they might make literary use of a love affair, an enigma or a tragedy." Whether nature writers sit on a streambank in Virginia or make a grueling ascent of Mount Everest, the best are also travel writers whose words have the power to create seismic shifts and continental drifts within us. This is the double helix of travel and nature writing: the artful way movement and stillness are woven with the visible and invisible to create meditations on our place in the world. Entering Dillard's world is like locking eyes with a wild animal.

In 1975, Dillard moved to an island in Puget Sound to live alone and explore profound questions about the will of God, time, death, and reality. Her 1977 book, *Holy the Firm*, ripples with questions about life's beauty and cruelty. In this search for holy fire, she writes about a friend's daughter who was burned in an airplane accident, about baptism on a beach, and about a moth who immolates in a candle flame.

One night a moth flew into the candle, was caught, burnt dry, and held. I must have been staring at the candle, or maybe I looked up when a shadow crossed my page; at any rate, I saw it all. A golden female moth, a biggish one with a two-inch wingspan, flapped into the fire, dropped her abdomen into the wet wax, stuck, flamed, frazzled, and fried in a second. Her moving wings ignited like tissue paper, enlarging the circle of light in the clearing and creating out of the darkness the sudden blue sleeves of my sweater, the green leaves of jewelweed by my side, the ragged red trunk of a pine. At once the light contracted again and the moth's wings vanished in a fine, foul smoke. At the same time her six legs clawed, curled, blackened, and ceased, disappearing utterly. And her head jerked in spasms, making a spattering noise; her antennae crisped and burned away, and her heaving mouth parts crackled like pistol fire. When it was all over, her head was, so far as I could determine, gone, gone the long way of her wings and legs. Had she been new, or old? Had she mated and laid her eggs, had she done her work? All that was left was the glowing horn shell of her abdomen and thorax—a fraying, partially collapsed gold tube jammed upright in the candle's round pool.

———

And then this moth-essence, this spectacular skeleton, began to act as a wick. She kept burning. The wax rose in the moth's body from her soaking abdomen to her thorax to the jagged hole where her head should be, and widened into flame, a saffron-yellow flame that robed her to the ground like any immolating monk. That candle had two wicks, two flames of identical height, side by side. The moth's head was fire. She burned for two hours, until I blew her out.

After death, the moth burns brighter. "The Death of the Moth" is one of Dillard's most personal short essays and explores a being's purpose after death. Aimed at emerging writers, it asks them to confront the question of sacrificing one's life in the name of writing and leaving art as a legacy. Yet the question of purpose after death is profound to consider on any level—artist or non-artist, human or nonhuman. Central to much of nature writing is the question of how best to live in the world. Dillard's work is a flame that draws us close with questions of how to live not just in the world but beyond it. Her writing reminds us we can stay close to home yet traverse widely and deeply, if we focus on how we perceive the unseen as well as the seen.

WORKS BY ANNIE DILLARD

POETRY

Tickets for a Prayer Wheel (1974)

Mornings Like This (1995)

NONFICTION

Pilgrim at Tinker Creek (1974)

Holy the Firm (1977)

Living by Fiction (1982)

Encounters with Chinese Writers (1984)

An American Childhood (1987)

The Writing Life (1989)

For the Time Being (1999)

ESSAY COLLECTIONS

Teaching a Stone to Talk (1982)

The Abundance: Narrative Essays Old and New (2016)

NOVELS

The Living (1992)

The Maytrees (2007)

GRETEL EHRLICH

Space has a spiritual equivalent
and can heal what is divided and
burdensome within us.

THE SOLACE OF OPEN SPACES

T WAS THE SUMMER of 1976. While Gretel Ehrlich was working as a producer on a film about sheepherders in the arid Big Horn Mountains of Wyoming, her lover was dying of cancer across the country in New York City. He was not yet thirty when he died. For two years afterward, Ehrlich was lost in grief.

When the rancher from the film project invited her back to Wyoming, Ehrlich left New York and became a sheepherder herself. What she called "a long arbitrary detour" became "the actual path." Life's impermanence taught her "loss was a kind of fullness," a theme that permeates much of her writing. She threw herself into hard ranch work—delivering lambs and calves, punching cattle, learning to ride—as a way of emptying herself in the open country and literally working through her loss. She ended up staying in Wyoming—a place she described as "tumbled and twisted, ribboned with faded, deathbed colors, thrust up and pulled down as if the place had been startled out of a deep sleep and thrown into pure light"—and marrying a young pack-trip outfitter. From 1979 to 1984, they bred cattle on an old homestead ranch on the west slope of the Big Horn Basin. As Ehrlich healed and found happiness again, she began writing long, descriptive letters to a friend in Hawaii about living in this part of the American West.

The Solace of Open Spaces emerged from this correspondence. Spare and elegant, the book is a collection of meditative essays on the people and landscapes of Wyoming. It earned Ehrlich comparisons with Thoreau and Walt Whitman, and established her as an essential voice in contemporary Western American literature. Readers are transported to the "musky-mint perfume of sagebrush," where evening entertainment could be watching the night sky. Essays like "About Men," "The Smooth Skull of Winter," "Obituary," "On Water," and "To Live in Two Worlds" are portraits of the people, animals, landscape, solitude, and space of her home. Her diamond-sharp prose contains both grace and muscularity, as she captures the self-reliance and vigor required for hard, physical work in these desolate badlands. The people attracted to hardscrab-ble lives—drunks, cowboys, ranchers, hermits, rascals, hoarders, misfits, sheepherders—are captured in realistic portraits, rather than romantic myths about how place shapes character.

When I'm in New York but feeling lonely for Wyoming I look for the Marlboro ads in the subway. What I'm aching to see is horse-flesh, the glint of a spur, a line of distant mountains, brimming creeks, and a reminder of the ranchers and cowboys I've ridden with for the last eight years. But the men I see in those posters with their stern, humorless looks remind me of no one I know here. In our hellbent earnestness to romanticize the cowboy we've ironically disesteemed his true character. If he's "strong and silent" it's because there's probably no one to talk to. If he "rides away into the sunset" it's because he's been on horseback since four in the morning moving cattle and he's trying, fifteen hours later, to get home to his family. If he's "a rugged individualist" he's also part of a team: ranch work is teamwork, and even the glorified open-range cowboys of the 1880s rode up and down the Chisholm Trail in the company of twenty or thirty other riders. Instead of the macho, trigger-happy man our culture has perversely wanted him to be, the cowboy is more apt to be conviv-ial, quirky, and softhearted. To be "tough" on a ranch has nothing to do with conquests and displays of power. More often than not, circumstances—like the colt he's riding or an unexpected bliz-zard—are overpowering him. It's not toughness but "toughing it out" that counts. In other words, this macho, cultural artifact the cowboy has become is simply a man who possesses resilience, patience, and an instinct for survival. "Cowboys are just like a pile of rocks—everything happens to them. They get climbed on, kicked, rained and snowed on, scuffed up by wind. Their job is 'just to take it,'" one old-timer told me.

A cowboy is someone who loves his work. Since the hours are long—ten to fifteen hours a day—and the pay is $30 he has to. What's required of him is an odd mixture of physical vigor and maternalism. His part of the beef-raising industry is to birth and nurture calves and take care of their mothers. For the most part his work is done on horseback and in a lifetime he sees and comes to know more animals than people. The ironic myth surrounding him is built on American notions of heroism: the index of a man's value as measured in physical courage. Such ideas have perverted manliness into a self-absorbed race for cheap thrills. In a rancher's world, courage has less to do with facing danger than with acting spontaneously—usually on behalf of an animal or another rider. If a cow is stuck in a boghole he throws a loop around her neck, takes his dally (a half hitch around the saddle horn), and pulls her out with horsepower. If a calf is born sick, he may take her home, warm her in front of the kitchen fire, and massage her legs until dawn. One friend, whose favorite horse was trying to swim a lake with hobbles on, dove under water to cut her legs loose with a knife, then swam her to shore, his arm around her neck lifeguard-style, and saved her from drowning. Because these incidents are usually linked to someone or something outside himself, the westerner's courage is selfless, a form of compassion.

Today, Western American writing is an established genre, but when Ehrlich began her career, the only major contemporary Western prose was Ivan Doig's 1978 *This House of Sky*. Like water flowing in a dry creek bed, other books about life in the West followed after Ehrlich's influential work. Some critics find *The Solace of Open Spaces* dated, as it doesn't address how the farming practices of cowboys and sheepherders displaced wildlife like bison and pronghorn antelope. That may be true, but the book is Ehrlich's lived experience—her focus was on her own healing. We may wish she had created greater resonance in this grief memoir by including losses felt by displaced indigenous people in the West, especially in her adopted Wyoming. But who are we to say how others work through sorrow? In later peregrinations and writing, she tackles grief on a large scale by writing extensively about the impact of climate change on native people.

On the strength and promise of *The Solace of Open Spaces* and her second book, *Heart Mountain* (1988), a novel about Japanese Americans in Wyoming's WWII internment camps, Ehrlich won a Guggenheim Fellowship, giving her opportunities to explore far beyond the American West—to the Arctic, to Japan, to Greenland, and to Hawaii—but before she could explore new terrain, something hit her.

Before electricity carved its blue path toward me, before the negative charge shot down from cloud to ground, before "streamers" jumped the positive charge back up from ground to cloud, before air expanded and contracted producing loud pressure pulses I could not hear because I was already dead, I had been walking.

When I started out on foot that August afternoon, the thunderstorm was blowing in fast. On the face of the mountain, a mile ahead, hard westerly gusts and sudden updrafts collided, pulling black clouds apart. Yet the storm looked harmless. When a distant thunderclap scared the dogs, I called them to my side and rubbed their ears: "Don't worry, you're okay as long as you're with me."

I woke in a pool of blood, lying on my stomach some distance from where I should have been, flung at an odd angle to one side of the dirt path. The whole sky had grown dark. Was it evening, and if so, which one? How many minutes or hours had elapsed since I lost consciousness, and where were the dogs? I tried to call out to them but my voice didn't work. The muscles in my throat were paralyzed and I couldn't swallow. Were the dogs dead? Everything was terribly wrong: I had trouble seeing, talking, breathing, and I couldn't move my legs or right arm. Nothing remained in my memory—no sounds, flashes, smells, no warnings of any kind. Had I been shot in the back? Had I suffered a stroke or heart attack? These thoughts were dark pools in the sand.

The sky was black. Was this a storm in the middle of the day or was it night with a storm traveling through? When thunder exploded over me, I knew I had been hit by lightning.

Ehrlich chronicles her recovery from this lightning strike in *A Match to the Heart* (1994). Few people have the mixed-fortune opportunity to write two healing memoirs. Ehrlich recalled, "When I got hit, my agent called the hospital and said, 'You have to stop using your life for material!'" The book is a mix of personal meditations and science writing, interviews with other survivors of lightning strikes, and an observation of open-heart surgery in an unsentimental and painstaking exploration of her body's own electrical circuitry and natural history. Her long and difficult recovery required stillness and rest, but once healthy, Ehrlich's focus as a nature writer shifted to places where she could explore the impermanence that runs through our lives—from the effects of climate change on melting landscapes in *This Cold Heaven: Seven Seasons in Greenland* (2001), *The Future of Ice: A Journey into Cold* (2004), and *In the Empire of Ice: Encounters in a Changing Landscape* (2010) to a tsunami's destruction in *Facing the Wave: A Journey in the Wake of the Tsunami* (2014).

Her timely trio of books on landscapes losing their icy winters, their glaciers, and their way of life illustrates Ehrlich's strength and versatility as a writer. At the same time, her work retains her signature mix of memoir, travelogue, science reportings, and poetic descriptions of place. The first, *This Cold Heaven*, chronicles seven seasons with Inuit subsistence hunters in Greenland. The second, *The Future of Ice*, records her six-month journey following winter from Tierra del Fuego to the top of the Svalbard archipelago in Norway all the way back to her cabin in Wyoming. Finally, she takes a year-long circumpolar trek in *In the Empire of Ice* and reports on how the tundra that has protected Inuit people for millennia is destabilized through pollution and greenhouse gas emissions.

Ehrlich has also published three collections of essays, a novel, a memoir, a biography, three books of poetry, ethnology/travel books, and a children's book, among others. Her work appears in *Harper's*, *New York Times Magazine*, *Time*, *National Geographic*, *Aperture*, *Architectural Digest*, *Orion*, *Outside*, and many other periodicals. Her first celebrated book, about the healing power of empty space, had its origins in a personal journey. Over thirty-five years, her writing has expanded far beyond herself and regional Western writing. She is one of the first nature writers to explore the impact of climate change on indigenous peoples in the Arctic. Like Gene Stratton-Porter and Mary Austin, Ehrlich is both poet and maverick. A practicing Buddhist for more than fifty years, she demonstrates through her writing how empathy and understanding of life's transience—from the death of a lover to the demise of ecosystems and old ways of life—can say far more about a rugged individualist than the myth of the Marlboro Man.

Losses, Ehrlich reminds us, can lead to awakenings.

MORE WESTERNS

JEANNE WILLIAMS

Born on the High Plains beside the tracks of the Santa Fe Trail, Williams has written sixty-nine novels, many evoking the dust storms and tumbleweeds of the Southwest. She set her first novel, *Tame the Wild Stallion* (1957), in Mexico and wrote it in the Lower Rio Grande Valley. Through her many strong female protagonists, readers learn how the settlement of the West was not solely a male enterprise. Her work includes *Home Mountain* (1990), *The Longest Road* (1993), and *The Unplowed Sky* (1994).

PAM HOUSTON

"I've always had this thing for cowboys, maybe because I was born in New Jersey," says the narrator in the title story of *Cowboys Are My Weakness* (1992). "But a real cowboy is hard to find these days, even in the West." Nearly three decades after her bestselling debut, Pam Houston returned to her Western roots with *Deep Creek: Finding Hope in the High Country* (2019), a reflection on the lessons her 120-acre ranch has taught her. "If *Cowboys Are My Weakness* was Pam Houston's call to millions of women—blasting us with self-recognition of how we give away our own power," wrote critic Amy Reardon, "then her new book is the response to that call."

TERRY TEMPEST WILLIAMS

By 1994, nine women in Terry Tempest Williams's family had undergone mastectomies. Seven died of cancer. In *Refuge: An Unnatural History of Family and Place* (1991), Williams weaves memoir and natural history to explore both her mother's cancer, caused by atomic fallout from bomb testing in Utah deserts, and the flooding of a beloved bird refuge. Her books and poetry collections cover everything from ecology and conservation to women's health.

LESLIE
MARMON SILKO

What she said:
The only cure
I know
is a good ceremony,
that's what she said.

CEREMONY

STORYTELLING is a form of mapping: it connects the self to the self, people to people, and people to places over time. Stories live on long after we do. For indigenous people, oral storytelling roots them in landscapes over millennia—not just a couple casual generations—and for these people, stories are more than yarns told over a fire. They are profound narratives of identity. Trauma—to an individual, to a people—can dislocate personal coordinates and unravel the narratives that help us navigate the world. It can lead to depression, grief, post-traumatic stress, addictions, and ostracization. Without unifying stories, we can become disconnected from ourselves, our loved ones, our history, and our surroundings.

Composure of the self and of a culture through storytelling is at the heart of Leslie Marmon Silko's *Ceremony* (1977), a twentieth-century masterpiece that distinguished her as the world's first female Native American novelist. It tells the story of Tayo, a shell-shocked veteran trying to regain his peace of mind and place in the world after returning home from the Second World War. When first published, it especially resonated with Vietnam veterans who had lost a cohesive sense of self and citzenship. As our understanding of mental health and post-traumatic stress disorder has grown, so has *Ceremony*'s relevance—in particular, its depiction of how old ways of knowing our physical world can be healing and therapeutic.

Tayo, of mixed Laguna Pueblo and white ancestry, has returned home to his reservation in New Mexico, having lost his will to live after enduring the Bataan Death March and a Japanese prisoner-of-war camp. He is alienated from his tribe, his family, and himself and filled with guilt and despair. Alcohol is an escape from self-loathing and from memories of fighting a white man's war. In a deliberately fractured narrative that alternates between prose and poetry, myth and memories, past and present, *Ceremony* tells the events of Tayo's broken life and how he slowly reconnects to plants, animals, and his Laguna Pueblo people through ancient rituals to become whole again.

It's a novel about the restorative power of stories and the vital role the natural world plays in the healing process.

"I am of mixed-breed ancestry, but what I know is Laguna," Silko has said of her storytelling focus. Mexican, Anglo-American, and Laguna Pueblo, she infuses all her work—novels, poems, films, short stories, and essays—with legends, myths, and ancient rituals. Raised in the sparse beauty of a New Mexican plateau and a recipient of a debut MacArthur Fellowship in 1981, Silko has been at the vanguard of the Native American Renaissance—a period of significant literary expansion by Native American writers since the 1960s, generally agreed to have been sparked by N. Scott Momaday's 1969 Pulitzer Prize–winning *House Made of Dawn*, a novel about the plight of a young Native American man torn between two cultures (but owing a great deal to earlier writers like Sarah Winnemucca, whose 1883 *Life Among the Piutes* is the first-known autobiography by a Native American woman). Before this time, outsiders often presumed to interpret unwritten Native American folktales and legends through film, books, and television. As indigenous Americans narrate their own lives, spiritualities, and diverse cultures, a rich and invigorated body of Native American literature, one that grounds and heals, has emerged.

Ceremony originated when Silko moved with her then-husband, John Silko, from New Mexico to Alaska in 1974. She left the sandstone and cottonwoods of home, where the annual rainfall was 13 inches, for the unknown Ketchikan, where it rained 160 inches a year and felt gray and claustrophobic. Separated from everything familiar, Silko struggled with feelings of deep dislocation along with migraines and nausea. "For me, writing is a way to transcend place and time," she has said about the way describing plants and places she loved and missed in *Ceremony* helped her recover her sense of self. "If you are sick in Navajo country, people say, 'You need a ceremony.' I often tell students that I wrote that book to save my life in a sense."

Building on the experiences of cousins who had returned from war damaged, the character of Tayo emerged. Her description of a mind lost and in distress is both haunting and beautiful.

> For a long time he had been white smoke. He did not realize that until he left the hospital, because white smoke had no consciousness of itself. It faded into the white world of their bed sheets and walls; it was sucked away by the words of doctors who tried to talk to the invisible scattered smoke. He had seen outlines of gray steel tables, outlines of the food they pushed into his mouth, which was only an outline too, like all the outlines he saw. They saw his outline but they did not realize it was hollow inside. He walked down floors that smelled of old wax and disinfectant, watching the outlines of his feet; as he walked, the days and seasons disappeared into a twilight at the corner of his eyes, a twilight he could catch only with a sudden motion, jerking his head to one side for a glimpse of green leaves pressed against the bars on the window. He inhabited a gray winter fog on a distant elk mountain where hunters are lost indefinitely and their own bones mark the boundaries.

Tayo's PTSD has prevented him from connecting with ancient stories, but with the ceremonial guidance of his tribe's medicine man, he finds a way of mapping himself back to *himself*, his people, and his Laguna Pueblo home. Events still occur to challenge him on the reservation, but little by little, Tayo recognizes he is part of a larger story. This reflects the more modern, less Freudian, approaches to trauma explored by literary scholar Michelle Balaev in *The Nature of Trauma in American Novels* (2012). She writes that, despite Western psychoanalytic talking cures, "retelling the traumatic past to another is less important than reconnecting to the land with its human, natural, and mythic histories that help the person reestablish a relationship to the social community of his home." The seasonal rhythms of mountains, oceans, skies, and deserts help take us out of our depression, anxiety, and alienation. In her essay "Landscape, History, and the Pueblo Imagination," Silko explains that "for Laguna Pueblo peoples, an intimate relationship between human and nonhuman is a necessary process of identity formation."

As Tayo steps with greater empathy through the world, capable now of focusing on the welfare of even small creatures, the white smoke of his former, traumatized self begins to fade. He is no longer disembodied nor dislocated. He understands how destructive forces in the world rewrote his narrative. He inhabits his own body again, reminded through stories and rituals of his identity and place in the wider community. In a telling hitchhiking scene, his new self emerges.

> He told the truck driver he didn't need to ride any farther. The sun was behind him and a warm dry wind from the southwest was blowing enough to cool the sweat on his forehead, and to dry out the wet cloth under the arms of his shirt. He walked down the ditch beside the highway, below the shoulder of the highway. He didn't want any more rides. He wanted to walk until he recognized himself again. Grasshoppers buzzed out of the weeds ahead of him; they were fading to a dry yellow color, from their bright green color of spring. Their wings flashed reflections of sun when they jumped. He looked down at the weeds and grass. He stepped carefully, pushing the toe of his boot into the weeds first to make sure the grasshoppers were gone before he set his foot down into the crackling leathery stalks of dead sunflowers.

Ceremony is timeless. Its invitation to appreciate ancient holistic healing is ever more relevant. Yet Silko's sharing of sacred, valuable, and little-known Laguna stories with the outside world has not been without controversy. Professor and Pueblo poet Paula Gunn Allen criticized the book for revealing secret tribal knowledge not intended for nonnatives. Allen cautioned that we must resist the idea of "treating Native spiritual life as a curious artifact" and realize that "Native people are people, and that their ways are not a spectacle but simply and significantly, a way of life." We can honor the non-Western approach to integrating the self with the natural world and should not misconstrue it as in-vogue, shallow environmental spirituality. It is a way of being.

Euroamerican culture seems to be catching up. There is growing awareness and appreciation of native knowledge as illustrated in the rise of terms such as ecotherapy, horticultural therapy, forest bathing, and biocentric living. I strongly resist categorizing the ceremonies created by Betonie the medicine man as "interventions," but they have the similar effect of relocating a person to a place. Tayo's newly heightened awareness of forces greater than himself—plants, animals, seasons, heritage—decreased his depression, isolation, and anxiety. In Silko's vivid descriptions, we see Tayo's emotions return. Read broadly, *Ceremony* reminds us that Tayo's story is a microcosm of the trauma of genocide—from Native Americans and African slaves to today's immigrants.

Ceremony is Silko's most recognized work on storytelling as a way of mapping a person and a people to a particular place. She carried the legacy of this forward in her second book, *Storyteller* (1981), a compilation of old photographs, tribal tales, poetry, and songs evoking recent and distant Native American life, in which she again contrasts Native and white cultures in spare and beautiful prose.

Where *Ceremony* evokes empathy, Silko's geographical novel *Almanac of the Dead* (1991) conjures horror. In this revision of European colonial history in America, map-knowledge is critiqued against plant-based knowledge, characters reject the legitimacy of appropriated land, and tribalism represents the egalitarian and ecocentric way to heal damage perpetrated by colonialism and racist white men obsessed with border walls. It is the imagining of a revolutionary future, decentered politics, and more ethical environmental and social practices.

WORKS BY LESLIE MARMON SILKO

NOVELS

Ceremony (1977)

Almanac of the Dead (1991)

Gardens in the Dunes (1999)

POETRY AND SHORT STORY COLLECTIONS

Laguna Women: Poems (1974)

Western Stories (1980)

Storyteller (1981)

Rain (1996)

Love Poem and Slim Canyon (1996)

Oceanstory (2011)

OTHER BOOKS

Sacred Water: Narratives and Pictures (1993)

The Turquoise Ledge: A Memoir (2010)

DIANE ACKERMAN

These days, startling though the thought is, we control our own legacy. We're not passive, we're not helpless. We're earth-movers. We can become Earth-restorers and Earth-guardians. We still have time and talent, and we have a great many choices. . . . Our mistakes are legion, but our imagination is immeasurable.

THE HUMAN AGE: THE WORLD SHAPED BY US

A GRADUATE SCHOOL friend once saw Diane Ackerman's *A Natural History of the Senses* in my bookbag and quipped, "Ackerman's work is *so* lush." I looked at him for a very long second and said, "That's precisely why I like her." An aficionado of Hemingway's short, tight prose, he rolled his eyes. I continued, "Her prose is less like a sleek bunch of tulips than an overflowing bouquet of peonies . . ." He began walking away. "And less a dry martini than a voluptuous red wine with a ripe plum start and a long velvety finish and—" I heard his laugh echo down our office hallway.

Ackerman is nature writing's Aphrodite: a historian and poet whose eloquent and iridescent words render complex subjects understandable and approachable. For those who want to box authors into a single discipline—science writer! romantic poet!— Ackerman's interdisciplinary approach as a poetic science storyteller can be flummoxing. A famous literary critic once drew her aside with avuncular concern and asked, "What's a nice girl like you doing writing about amino acids?" In the introduction to *The Moon by Whale Light: And Other Adventures Among Bats, Penguins, Crocodilians, and Whales* (1991), she described what it means to be a nature writer:

> My prose now seems to locate me among a small tribe often referred to as nature writers. How curious that label is, suggesting as it does that nature is somehow separate from our doings, that nature does not contain us, that it's possible to step *outside* nature, not merely as one of its more promising denizens but objectively, as a sort of extraterrestrial voyeur. Still, the label is a dignified one, and implies a pastoral ethic that we share, a devotion to the keenly observed detail, and a sense of sacredness. There is a way of beholding nature that is itself a form of prayer.

Ackerman's writing has long been a constellation of art and science. While completing her PhD at Cornell University in the 1970s, a poet and a scientist sat on her doctoral committee. Who was the poet? I don't know. But the scientist? Carl Sagan, renowned astronomer and Pulitzer Prize–winning author of the 1980 *Cosmos*, a book that explained complex astronomical ideas in a relatable, conversational style, and one of the bestselling science books of all time. She was Sagan's favorite poet, and he advised her on the technical aspects of her writing, including her first collection of poetry, *The Planets: A Cosmic Pastoral* (1976). "I just felt that the universe wasn't knowable from only one perspective," Ackerman has said about crossing boundaries between disciplines. "I wanted to be able to go exploring: follow my curiosity in both worlds."

Ackerman has written more than two dozen highly acclaimed works of poetry and nonfiction, including *New York Times* bestsellers *The Zookeeper's Wife* (2007) and *The Human Age: The World Shaped by Us* (2014) as well as the Pulitzer Prize finalist, *One Hundred Names for Love* (2011). Whether flying planes, working on a ranch, or exploring the natural history of love, she writes, she has said, for her own astonishment.

A Natural History of the Senses (1990), one of her bestselling books, is a ramble through the five senses with ravishing imagery and luscious descriptions. If I could pair this book with a perfume, it would be the complex composition of Chanel No. 5: an abundant bouquet of rose and jasmine, ylang-ylang and lily of the valley, patchouli and vanilla. Ackerman transports us from our air-conditioned, fluorescent-lit, digitally stimulated lives, back to our mammalian origins and the cave where our senses evolved. Composed of bite-sized essays, the book explores a range of sensual subjects, from why we ache for love and passion to how our eyes are placed to see as predators do. In her exploration of smell, she takes readers on a foray to a perfume laboratory in New York City to meet the people with such an acute sense of smell she describes them as "sensuous ghostwriters, inventors of rapture, creating the gold-plated aromas that influence and persuade us without us knowing." We also meet "an ancient Egyptian socialite attending a party [who] would wear a cone of unguent on top of her head; it would melt slowly, covering her face and shoulders with a trickle of perfumed syrup."

The following passage, from the layered essay "The Force of an Image: Ring Cycle," invites us to reimagine human vision, especially when our eyes settle upon rings.

Oh! the idea of rings in the hands of a poet.

In our mind's eye, that abstract seat of imagining, we picture the face of a lover, savor a kiss. When we think about him in passing, we have various thoughts; but when we actually picture him, as if he were a hologram, we feel a flush of emotion. There is much more to seeing than mere seeing. The visual image is a kind of tripwire for the emotions. One photo can remind us of an entire political regime, a war, a heroic moment, a tragedy. One gesture can symbolize the wide angles of parental love, the uncertainty and disorder of romantic love, the fun-house mirrors of adolescence, the quick transfusion of hope, the feeling of low-level wind shear in the heart we call loss. Look at a grassy hillside, and you can remember immediately what freshly cut grass smells like, how it feels when it's damp, the stains it leaves on your jeans, the sound you can make blowing over a grass blade held just so between your thumbs, and other assorted memories associated with grass: picnicking with the family; playing dodge ball in an orchard in the Midwest; herding cattle from the dusty New Mexico desert up to the high fields of lush green to graze; hiking through the Adirondacks; making love in a grassy field at the top of a hill, on a hot, breezy summer day, when the sun, shining through the clouds, lights one part of the hillside at a time, as if it were a room in which the lamp had been turned on. When we see an object, the whole peninsula of our senses wakes up to appraise the new sight. All the brain's shopkeepers consider it from their point of view, all the civil servants, all the accountants, all the students, all the farmers, all the mechanics. Together they all see the same sight—a grassy hillside—and each does a slightly different take on it, all of which adds up to what we see. Our other senses can trigger memories and emotions too, but the eyes are especially good at symbolic, aphoristic, many-faceted perceiving. Knowing this, governments are forever erecting monuments. Generally they don't look like much, but people stand in front of them and rush with emotion anyway. The eye regards most of life as monumental. And some shapes affect us much more than others.

For example, I've been following the space program closely for the past twenty years, and learning with robust delight about the solar system, thanks mainly to the Voyager spacecraft, which have been seen sending back home movies of Earth's closest relatives. What a lovely shock it's been to discover that half the planets have rings: not just Saturn, but Jupiter, Uranus, Neptune, and maybe even Pluto. And all the rings are different. Jupiter's dark, narrow rings contrast with Saturn's bright broad ribbons. Uranus's obsidian rings have baguette moons in tow. The solar system has quietly been running rings around all of us. How magical and how poignant. Few symbols have ever meant as much to us, regardless of our religion, politics, age, or gender, as rings. We give rings to symbolize infinite love and the close harmony of two souls. Rings remind us of the simple cells that were the oldest version of life, and the symphony of cells we now are. We reach for the rings on merry-go-rounds. Rings halo what is sacred. We draw rings around things to emphasize them. Sports often take place in the magic ring of the playing field. A sensory kaleidoscope unfolds in the circus ring. Rings symbolize the infinite: We are only ever beginning to end. Rings signal a pledge made, a vow taken. Rings suggest eternity, agelessness, and perfection. We chart time on the face of a clock, as points along a ring. On playgrounds, children shoot marbles into a chalked circle; they are prime movers, acting out planetary mechanics. We bring the world into focus with the globes of our eyes, worlds within worlds. We treasure the well-rounded soul we think we see in a loved one. We believe that, just as a strong circle can be made out of two weaker arcs, we can complete ourselves by linking our life to someone else's. We who crave the no-loose-ends, deathless symmetry of a ring praise the wonders of the universe as best we can, traveling along the ring of birth and death. The Apollo astronauts returned to earth changed by seeing the home planet floating in space. What they saw was a kind of visual aphorism, and it's one we all need to learn by heart.

Didn't I *tell* you?

As Ackerman bridges the gap between the subjective and the objective, the poet and the scientist, she is clearly enjoying her craft while also inviting us to be more aware of being alive. While scientists strive for detachment in their writing—the scientific method is based on the weight of evidence and is free of dogma—poets and essayists can indulge in language and, through the prism of personal experience, connect with readers in a way science writing cannot.

This versatility reflects Ackerman's panoply of interests over decades of writing. In *The Moon by Whale Light*, she describes how venturing into the natural world heightens her poetic awareness. "My mind will become a cyclone of intense alertness, in which details present themselves slowly, thoroughly, one at a time. I don't know how to describe what happens to me when I'm out in 'nature' and 'working'—it's a kind of rapture—but it's happened enough that I know to expect it."

From the stars to the sea, her exaltation of feelings and language contrasts her science writing with, say, Rachel Carson, who wrote evocatively but not sensually about the natural world. In *A Natural History of Love* (1994), Ackerman examines our evolutionary imperatives and the chemical reactions surrounding love and desire through a kaleidoscope of science and sensuality (although we should acknowledge the downside of this book's dated heteronormative slant). *The Rarest of the Rare* (1995) chronicles Ackerman's interactions with endangered species and imperiled habitats—golden lion tamarins, monk seals, the Amazon, Florida scrublands, the short-tailed albatross, and the migration of monarch butterflies—while explaining the agency of humans in the extinction process. *Deep Play* (1999) is an exploration of how immersion—a runner's high, making art, spiritual concentration—is an important part of our human existence. "The more an animal needs to learn in order to stay alive, the more it needs to play," she writes. "Without play, humans and many other animals would perish."

In *The Human Age*, which received both the 2015 PEN New England Henry David Thoreau Prize and National Outdoor Book Award, she confronts the impact of our species as the dominant force changing the planet. This sweeping narrative reviews recent history to show how our geoengineering—saturating the air with carbon dioxide, the oceans with fertilizer, and more—has resulted in climate change, a subject the best nature writers are now addressing. Weaving characteristic personal insights, scientific research, and interviews with meteorologists, bioethicists, immunologists, geneticists, geologists, and a cyborg anthropologist, she conveys all their fears about how humans are manipulating the planet—but concludes on a note of optimism:

> We understand ourselves on many more spine-tingling levels: how we're changing the planet, other creatures, and each other. This is not just the Human Age. It's also the age when we began to see, for the first time, the planet's interlaced, jitterbugging ecosystems—on the land, in the air, in the oceans, in society—and unmasked our own ecosystems. We've met many of our makers, the mad molecules.
>
> Thanks to revelations in neuroscience, genetics, and biology, we're bringing the life and times of *Homo sapiens sapiens* into a

much clearer focus. As the "Me" generation gives way to the "We" generation, we're growing more aware of the ties that bind us—even if we're less relaxed in face-to-face encounters.

We humans have so much in common that we can't seem to speak of comfortably: a genetic code, a niche on a small planet in a vast galaxy in an infinite universe; the underrated luxury of being at the top of our food chain; a familiar range of passions and fears; a mysterious, ill-defined evolution from creatures whose thoughts were like a vapor, and before that bits of chemical and chance so small they pass right through the mind's sieve without its being able to fully grasp them. We have in common, despite our extraordinary powers of invention, subtlety, and know-how, an ability to bore ourselves that is so horrifying we devote much of our short lives to activities designed mainly to make us seem more interesting to ourselves. We have in common a world our senses know voluptuously, from one splayed moment to the next, the wind touching one's chapped lips, a just-forgotten chore, the small unremarkable acts of mercy and heroism parents and lovers perform each day, the collective sort of creatures we are, whose qualities embarrass us when we stumble upon the moon, or Thomas Edison spending the last of his days in Florida trying to make rubber from goldenrod. We have in common a fidgeting, blooming, ever-startling universe, whose complex laws we all obey, whether we're born in Tierra del Fuego or Svalbard.

With her wide-ranging, deep-delving body of work, Ackerman is a treasure in this genre and beyond. Her research, language, imagery, and insights linger with us like a memorable fragrance, while challenging us to accept the urgency of today's environmental moment. As she has explained, this is the first time in our history on the planet that we have become aware of human impact and our ability to influence plants and animals on every continent and in every ocean. Her work asks us to hold a mirror to ourselves as one species, putting into perspective who we are and what kind of *animals* we want to be.

WORKS BY DIANE ACKERMAN

POETRY

The Planets:
A Cosmic Pastoral (1976)

Wife of Light (1978)

Lady Faustus (1983)

Reverse Thunder: A Dramatic Poem (1988)

Jaguar of Sweet Laughter: New and Selected Poems (1991)

I Praise My Destroyer (1998)

Origami Bridges (2002)

CHILDREN'S BOOKS

Bats: Shadows in the Night (1985)

Monk Seal Hideaway (1995)

Animal Sense, illustrated by Peter Sis (2003)

NONFICTION

Twilight of the Tenderfoot (1980)

On Extended Wings (1985)

A Natural History of the Senses (1990)

The Moon by Whale Light: And Other Adventures Among Bats,
Penguins, Crocodilians, and Whales (1991)

A Natural History of Love (1994)

The Rarest of the Rare (1995)

A Slender Thread (1997)

Deep Play (1999)

Cultivating Delight (2001)

An Alchemy of Mind: The Marvel and Mystery
of the Brain (2004)

The Zookeeper's Wife: A War Story (2007)

Dawn Light: Dancing with Cranes and Other Ways
to Start the Day (2009)

One Hundred Names for Love: A Stroke, a Marriage, and the
Language of Healing (2011)

The Human Age: The World Shaped by Us (2014)

ROBIN WALL KIMMERER

Listening in wild places, we are audiences in conversations not our own.

BRAIDING SWEETGRASS

A FEW YEARS AGO, I heard a memorable TED Talk that opened with the speaker describing how she had accomplished many goals in life but wished for one thing more. "I have a confession to make," she said, and paused for the audience to consider what regrets or secrets she would reveal. "I wish that I could photosynthesize. To make food out of light and water. To make medicines and give them away for free. To do the work of the world and for the world while standing silently in the sun. But I can't. I am not an autotroph, a producer, but a heterotroph. I am an animal. I am destined by my biology to be a consumer. I must take from the world in order to live. But if I could photosynthesize, I would be a berry."

A botanist and writer, Robin Wall Kimmerer then described her chosen berry, known in her indigenous culture as "heart berry," the leader of summer fruit, the first to ripen. In the language she was born into: "strawberry." And in the scientific language she was trained in: *Fragaria virginiana*. This intersection of science and ancient ways of knowing defines Kimmerer's work.

A few years after that TED Talk, I am following Kimmerer as she walks, a canvas knapsack slung over one shoulder, beaded earrings cascading through her salt-and-pepper curls, down a dirt path along the Exeter River in New Hampshire. I'm one of twenty teachers of nature and environmental writing. It's our summer holiday, but we've traveled from distant points—the Tetons, the Rockies, the Olympic Peninsula, Southern California, my small island in the Atlantic—for an immersive week at the Environmental Literature Institute at Phillips Exeter Academy. My new friends are all thoughtful and outdoorsy, and we look forward to how our field guide, Kimmerer, might introduce us to an older way of listening to and reading flowers, shrubs, and trees—and the opportunity to share this with our students.

A professor of environmental and forest biology at the State University of New York, Kimmerer is also a member of the Citizen

Potawatomi Nation. She writes essays for nature and culture journals such as *Orion* and award-winning books like *Gathering Moss: A Natural and Cultural History of Mosses* (2003), which won the prestigious John Burroughs Medal for nature writing, and *Braiding Sweetgrass: Indigenous Wisdom, Scientific Knowledge, and the Teaching of Plants* (2013), winner of the Sigurd F. Olson Nature Writing Award.

Swatting mosquitos from our bare legs and mindful of ticks, we follow Kimmerer along a dry, shaded path into the woods, attentive and open to her botanical stories. She stops at a white pine—a tall, straight tree ideal for ship masts—and strokes its serrated bark. Woodland trilliums dot the underbrush—their three white petals are symbolic, I think, of the way Kimmerer weaves the three elements of science, spirit, and story into her writing. At the pine, she describes in a soft voice how these trees and their canopies of feathered needles were important to peace, to indigenous governance, and to American democracy. Growing in clusters, they created sacred and healing spaces. I'm reminded of an important chapter in *Braiding Sweetgrass*, "Learning the Grammar of Animacy," in which she writes about her experience reading the botanical world this way.

I come here to listen, to nestle in the curve of the roots in a soft hollow of pine needles, to lean my bones against the column of white pine, to turn off the voice in my head until I can hear the voices outside it: the *shhh* of wind in needles, water trickling over rock, nuthatch tapping, chipmunks digging, beechnut falling, mosquito in my ear, and something more—something that is not me, for which we have no language, the wordless being of others in which we are never alone. After the drumbeat of my mother's heart, *this* was my first language.

I could spend a whole day listening. And a whole night. And in the morning, without my hearing it, there might be a mushroom that was not there the night before, cream white, pushed up from the pine needle duff, out of darkness to light, still glistening with the fluid of its passage. *Puhpowee.*

Listening in wild places, we are audience to conversations in a language not our own. I think now that it was a longing to comprehend this language I hear in the woods that led me to science, to learn over the years to speak fluent botany. A tongue that should not, by the way, be mistaken for the language of plants. I did learn another language in science, though, one of careful observation, an intimate vocabulary that names each little part. To name and describe you must first see, and science polishes the gift of seeing. I honor the strength of the language that has become a second tongue to me. But beneath the richness of its vocabulary and its descriptive power, something is missing, the same something that swells around you and in you when you listen to the world. Science can be a language of distance which reduces a being to its working parts; it is a language of objects. The language scientists speak, however precise, is based on a profound error in grammar, an omission, a grave loss in translation from the native languages of these shores.

My first taste of the missing language was the word *Puhpowee* on my tongue. I stumbled upon it in a book by the Anishinaabe ethnobotanist Keewaydinoquay, in a treatise on the traditional uses of fungi by our people. *Puhpowee*, she explained, translates as "the force which causes mushrooms to push up from the earth overnight." As a biologist, I was stunned that such a word existed. In all its technical vocabulary, Western science has no such term, no words to hold this mystery. You'd think that biologists would have words for life. But in scientific language our terminology is used to define the boundaries of our knowing. What lies beyond our grasp remains unnamed.

In the three syllables of this new word I could see an entire process of close observation in the damp morning woods, the formulation of a theory for which English has no equivalent. The makers of this word understood a world of being, full of unseen energies that animate everything. I've cherished it for many years, as a talisman, and longed for the people who gave a name to the life force of mushrooms. The language that holds *Puhpowee* is one that I wanted to speak. So when I learned that the word for rising, for emergence, belonged to the language of my ancestors, it became a signpost for me.

Had history been different, I would likely speak Bodewad-mimwin, or Potawatomi, an Anishinaabe language. But, like many of the three hundred and fifty indigenous languages of the Americas, Potawatomi is threatened, and I speak the language you read. The powers of assimilation did their work as my chance of hearing that language, and yours too, was washed from the mouths of Indian children in government boarding schools where speaking your native tongue was forbidden. Children like my grandfather, who was taken from his family when he was just a little boy of nine years old. This history scattered not only our words but also our people. Today I live far from our reservation, so even if I could speak the language, I would have no one to talk to. But a few summers ago, at our yearly tribal gathering, a language class was held and I slipped into the tent to listen.

Braiding Sweetgrass begins with an invitation to the reader, "Hold out your hands and let me lay upon them a sheaf of freshly picked sweetgrass, loose and flowing, like newly washed hair." It's a metaphor for the book's five unfolding sections: "Planting Sweetgrass," "Tending Sweetgrass," "Braiding Sweetgrass," "Picking Sweetgrass," and "Burning Sweetgrass." In each of these sections, Kimmerer shares stories of encounters with plants as a mother, scientist, botanist, tribal citizen, and teacher. Gratitude stories, cautionary tales. The consolation water lilies bring when her daughter Linden has left home for college. The deep symbiosis of The Three

Sisters: corn, beans, and pumpkins. The ceremony of laying salmon bones in streams to return nutrients to the world. And the way ceremonies help people transcend the realm of the individual to become part of a larger community.

As Kimmerer leads us along the shaded river path, she is adept at keeping her hands on each strand of narrative—the science, the spirit, and the story—to help develop a relationship of reciprocity with the natural world. Though less than a mile, our walk feels epic, as if I'm baby-stepping a thousand miles in unmapped territory. Do I really know plants? I can identify them but Kimmerer's deep knowing and ancient stories reverberate in me, showing me I know very little really. That morning I may have finished reading *Braiding Sweetgrass*, but I'll remain a novice in this language for quite some time.

Robin Wall Kimmerer

MORE INDIGENOUS WRITERS

LOUISE ERDRICH

As she walked back to her Ojibwe reservation in North Dakota one freezing night, June Kashpaw, a prostitute returning from her last call, died in a snowdrift. June's death opens *Love Medicine* (1984), Louise Erdrich's acclaimed debut novel, and prompts friends and three generations of her family to reflect upon their own lives and relationships with her. Their overlapping voices add a rich fluidity to this despairing narrative. A member of the Turtle Mountain Band of Chippewa Indians (of Ojibwe peoples) in Minnesota, Erdrich is an award-winning literary mainstay. Her wide body of work includes four nonfiction books, three poetry collections, several children's books, and many novels.

JOY HARJO

The first Native American to serve as US Poet Laureate, Joy Harjo has been writing for more than four decades. "To her, poems are 'carriers of dreams, knowledge and wisdom,'" wrote Carla Hayden, the Librarian of Congress, in June 2019. "And through them, she tells an American story of tradition and loss, reckoning and myth-making." A member of the Muscogee (Creek) Nation in Oklahoma, Harjo integrates prayer-chants and animal imagery into her work, as well as feminist and social justice poetic traditions. She is deeply concerned with oneness, remembrance, transcendence, and politics. Harjo has won numerous awards including an American Book Award for *In Mad Love and War* (1990) and the 2013 PEN Center USA Literary Award in creative nonfiction for her memoir, *Crazy Brave* (2012). She is also a musician and saxophonist and won a Native American Music Award for Best Female Artist of the Year in 2009.

PAULA GUNN ALLEN

The Sacred Hoop: Recovering the Feminine in American Indian Traditions (1986) is a pioneering collection of critical and literary essays. Credited with founding the field of Native American literary studies, Allen (1939–2008) asserted that Native American cultures were female-centered and therefore Native American literature was inherently feminist. Her mixed heritage, Lebanese on her father's side and Laguna Pueblo-Métis-Scot on her mother's, shaped her critical and creative visions. She reclaimed indigenous female mythologies and power from displacement and erasure by male-gendered, Euro-Christian creators—writing poetry, novels, and widely anthologized critical essays. Her book *Pocahontas: Medicine Woman, Spy, Entrepreneur, Diplomat* (2003) drew on overlooked sources to create striking new insights about an icon.

LAURET SAVOY

Trace

NOUN. A way or path.

    A course of action.

        Footprint or track.

            Vestige of a former presence.

            An impression.

                Minute amount.

                    A *life mark*.

VERB. To make one's way.

    To pace or step.

        To travel through.

        To discern.

            To mark or draw.

                To follow tracks or footprints.

                To pursue, to discover.

TRACE: MEMORY, HISTORY, RACE,
AND THE AMERICAN LANDSCAPE

KNOW SOMEDAY soon I'll take a walk with Lauret Savoy. I'd like it to be a long walk to hear all she has to say. It could be crunching along a trail near her home in the leafy hills of western Massachusetts. It could be the streets in Los Angeles or Washington, DC, where she lived as a child. It could be a plantation in South Carolina. It could be the US–Mexico border. Wherever it is, I know what I'll do: listen.

Until that time, we settle for a phone conversation. I quickly discover her gentle way of speaking in poetry. She tells me, "By the age of five, I believed I was a child born of sun-lit Earth and deep blue sky. When I looked at my skin, I saw the color of dry land in Southern California and the Southwest. And when I looked at my veins, it seemed that sky flowed in them. I believed I was made of sky and of land. That was what anchored the child-me."

You can understand why I want more opportunity to listen.

She tells me, "By 1968, my family had moved from California to Washington, DC, and we arrived in time to experience the riots. That was when I, as a small child, learned about racism. I was spat upon and I was hated. I needed to learn *who* I was then. That initial learning began in a struggle to answer or come to terms with questions that started to haunt me about origins: about who *I* was and who *we* were and what the American *land* was.

"That led me to try to trace not just my familial past but our nation's history: how the past and present have marked me and marked American society and marked the land. That led me to ask how geology and history and memory are related. The past that I come from and where we all come from is not so unlike the fragmented pieces of Earth history. But in the human past, the gaps are left by generations of silences, by losses of language and voice, and by displacement that involved movement on the land by choice as well as by force; it also involved forced servitude. When you think about history, gaps come from complex dimensions of lives flattened over time under the weight of ignorance and stereotype. What remains are dismembered narratives about who we are to each other and to this land. And what I needed to do was engage, interrogate, encounter, and understand the nature of the silences and the nature of what is known as well as unknown.

"I have been drawn to studying fragments—rocks, sand, the dust of lives—and trying to understand how they can be fitted together. For me, geology offers an elemental sense of place. The history of human experience on this continent owes so much to the history of the land itself, to the land's physical materials, texture, and structure. Yet the language and ideas of geology also offer metaphors for considering the deposition and erosion of human memory, the fragmentation and displacement of human experience. *Geo* and *logo* or 'understanding Earth' in the broadest sense."

The David B. Truman Professor of Environmental Studies and Geology at Mount Holyoke College, Savoy has a doctorate in geology, which helps her see patterns and fragments, gaps and traces in her winding search for her own and a larger history in the American landscape. Few of us have the combination of advanced scientific training and heritage (African American, European American, and Native American) to frame an inquiry about the intersection of land and identity as fascinatingly as Savoy does in *Trace: Memory, History, Race, and the American Landscape* (2015), a book that blends memoir, history, and the environment to uncover hidden legacies. She frames earth processes so differently from any other nature writer, male or female, that she can create seismic shifts in a reader's perspective on race, gender, and nature.

As I listen to Savoy braid sediment and sentiment, I think about the humbling disciplines of earth sciences. Glaciology, soil sciences, meteorology, oceanography, geomorphology, ecology, geology— each offers ways to comprehend spatial and temporal scales far greater than our blink-of-an-eye existence. If we pause our daily momentum to gaze at our own geographies, we can view yesteryears and wonder at what has been lost. The visible landscapes of our own bodies—that external terrain like high cheekbones, long tapered fingers, or the color of our eyes—may prompt us to think about the people who share those traits. My three children all have beautifully full lips. In family pictures, we can easily trace them to their father, then to his mother, his maternal grandmother, then to his maternal great-grandfather. After that, no visible records exist of this beautiful feature. Physical history drops away after a century or so for many of us, and with that memories.

Savoy writes about the invisible yesteryears her nation carries and she carries within herself, a history wrapped in the silence of the land. "If each of our lives is an instant, like a camera shutter opening then closing," she asks, "what can we make of our place in the world, of the latent image, for that instant?" In *Trace*, she tries to hold that shutter open a little longer, in pursuit of answers to questions of who she is and who Americans are, by taking road trips across America to trace history: visiting the headwaters of the Mississippi River in Minnesota, massacre sites in the American Southwest, the US–Mexico Border, the US Capital, and unmarked graves on a South Carolina plantation where "resident workers," as a teaching guide calls them, rather than the enslaved, are buried.

Savoy writes in *Trace*:

> In the dead of winter I like to walk on water, held above liquid depths of the nearby lake by a vast frozen plain.
>
> This ice demands respect. I look . . . again. Listen again . . . attentive to any *k-r-a-a-ck* or yielding to my weight. When the surface is more solid than a hardwood dance floor, and much thicker, I venture far. Even then I hear the *ga-loop*. A distant *plo-o-rp*. A muffled *gal-oosh*. Water undulating beneath ice and me.
>
> Sunlight appears to emanate from above and below on cloudless February days, raying through the crystalline lattice underfoot. With my eyes but inches from the surface, any sense of depth, of

refracted distance, yields to a sense of motion arrested. Air bubbles halt mid-ascent. White oak leaves descend as if on invisible steps, suspended for a season above the lake bottom.

The recent past lies beneath me in these marcescent leaves, plucked and blown here by January's heavy winds. Inches away, they are out of reach. I kneel within the next stratum.

Thoughts of time's passage always come to mind on such walks, thoughts of how memory of any form becomes inscribed in the land. The hills surrounding this lake and my home are worn remains of long-vanished mountains. Glacial debris from the last ice age produces a rock-crop in my garden each spring. Stone walls that two centuries ago bordered fields and pastures now thread the dark heart of forests.

Loren Eiseley wrote in *The Immense Journey* that human beings are denied the dimension of time, so rooted are we in our particular now. We cannot in person step backward or forward from our circumscribed pinpoints. I cannot touch a leaf encased in ice—nor can I feel the calloused hands that stacked these walls. Yet we make our lives among relics and ruins of former times, former worlds. Each of us is, too, a landscape inscribed by memory and loss.

I've long felt estranged from time and place, uncertain of where home lies. My skin, my eyes, my hair recall the blood of three continents as paths of ancestors—free and enslaved Africans, colonists from Europe, and peoples indigenous to this land—converge in me. But I've known little of them or their paths to my present. Though I've tracked long-bygone moments on this continent from rocks and fossils—those remnants of deep time—the traces of a more intimate, lineal past have seemed hidden or lost.

Yet to live in this country is to be marked by its still unfolding history. *Life marks* seen and unseen. From my circumscribed pinpoint, I must try to trace what has marked me. The way traverses many forms of memory and silence, of a people as well as a single person. And because our lives *take place* among the shadows of unnumbered years, the journey crosses America and time.

Despite the distance from England to Massachusetts, a muffled but distinct rapid drilling sound comes over the phone as Savoy and I speak. A hairy woodpecker has interrupted our conversation. In its search for prey, the bird, with speckled black-and-white wings and a red cap, is leaving its own traces in Savoy's wood-clad home. "Just a moment," she says and steps outside in the winter afternoon to shoo the bird off. An ocean away, it makes me smile to hear her hoot and holler. "I live on a long dirt road and have a lot of wildlife," she says before continuing her story.

"As a child, I questioned who I was and what I was after first experiencing racism. I didn't know. Part of that not knowing was having school lessons filled with stereotypes and biases. History was a story told of what happened. And those stories were told by people with the power of accepted voice. The story I was told diminished the place of people of color, people of mixed heritage, and women. I really consist of fragmented pieces that have been in part silenced—pieces in a heritage of blood, culture, custom, and circumstances that were not visible to me. What was visible was an incomplete self, a partial self. What I am and what I am doing requires coming to understand the wholeness that was there but not accessible to me for many reasons, from racism and different forms of othering to school lessons, media images, and familial silences."

Trace seems to be reaching back through fragmented history, in one chapter to a father Savoy did not know well, who died when she was a teenager. In her first year at Princeton, she discovered he had written a novel, *Alien Land*, published in 1949, more than a decade before her own birth. It was dedicated "to the child which my wife and I may someday have—and to the children of each American— in the fervent hope that at least one shall be brought to see more clearly the enduring need for simple humanity." Savoy has stated that much of her writing is an attempt to engage in a dialogue with the father she was unable to communicate with in life.

She and poet Alison Hawthorne Deming edited *The Colors of Nature* (2002, expanded and revised in 2011), a collection of pieces by thirty-two diverse writers, which explores the intersections of cultural identity and ecological awareness. This valuable and overdue book attends to omissions in the nature writing canon. Included are Jamaica Kincaid, Robin Wall Kimmerer, Nikky Finney, Ofelia Zepeda, bell hooks, Kimiko Hahn, Jeanne Wakatsuki Houston, and others. Savoy also co-edited *Bedrock: Writers on the Wonders of Geology* (2006) and co-authored *Living with the Changing California Coast* (2006). In helping spread the power of voice, Savoy is also showing us how to listen.

MORE EARTH SCIENCE

ALISON HAWTHORNE DEMING

Deming is an interdisciplinary cross-thinker, a poet who writes about science. From the minuscule to the stellar, she explores science, the physical world, and poetry through exquisite observations and memorable juxtapositions. Among her many volumes of poetry and nonfiction essays, there's no one best place to begin exploring her work, though the essay "Science and Poetry: A View from the Divide" is a good one. Her most recent work, *Stairway to Heaven* (2016), is a collection of poems reflecting on the loss of her mother and brother.

ANN ZWINGER

Zwinger (1925–2014) was one of nature writing's most prolific storytellers, known for the detail in her seventeen books about the canyons, rivers, trees, and deserts of the American West. She was a finalist for the 1973 National Book Award in science with co-author Beatrice Willard for *Land Above the Trees: A Guide to American Alpine Tundra*. In 1976, she received the John Burroughs Medal for distinguished contribution in natural history for *Run, River, Run: A Naturalist's Journey Down One of the Great Rivers of the West*.

M JACKSON

M Jackson is an American geographer, glaciologist, and National Geographic Society Explorer. In *While Glaciers Slept: Being Human in a Time of Climate Change* (2015) she combines science and personal narrative to explore parallels between the destruction of the planet as a result of climate change and a family facing the loss of parents. *The Secret Lives of Glaciers* (2019) folds together science, history, and personal stories from the Icelandic communities whose glaciers are slowly disappearing.

REBECCA SOLNIT

The stars we are given. The constellations we make. That is to say, stars exist in the cosmos, but constellations are the imaginary lines we draw between them, the readings we give the sky, the stories we tell.

STORMING THE GATES OF PARADISE:
LANDSCAPES FOR POLITICS

A COUPLE YEARS AGO, I was wandering through the French Quarter in New Orleans. It was early November and the shapely Mississippi River glistened under blue skies and feathery clouds. I walked without a map or plan through parks filled with banana trees and birds of paradise, past colorful Creole townhouses with double galleries of ornate ironwork and hanging ferns, past bistros serving alligator pie and Andouille sausage gumbo. Sugar filled the air, from the scent of deep-fried beignets to the sounds of sweet-fingered saxophones. On Chartres Street, a string band's French folk songs swirled up between buildings like a draft of birds. I walked along Royal Street, Bourbon Street, Dauphine Street, with stinging images of Hurricane Katrina in my mind, until I met the crescent of the Mississippi and followed its curve on raised banks. I wasn't physically lost. It's difficult to go astray in an ordered grid of streets abutting such an unmistakable river. But in other ways, I was adrift, frustrated by my inability to get beyond the city's painted surface to better understand its complex mélange of French, Spanish, African, British, and Native American histories.

Just as humidity and bewilderment peaked, I stepped through the doors of Faulkner House Books on Pirate's Alley. I needed to reconfigure my dizzied mental map of New Orleans beyond the visible markers of food, music, and architecture just outside the door. I brushed my hands along titles, until one literally stood out from the others—*Unfathomable City: A New Orleans Atlas* (2013) by Rebecca Solnit and native New Orleanian Rebecca Snedeker. I ran my hands over its tall tan cover, its shape reminding me of old driving atlases my grandparents used to stash in their car. I turned pages of essays accompanied by twenty-two curious, finely illustrated maps of New Orleans with subjects like "The Line-Up: Live Oak Corridors and Carnival Parade Routes," "Hot and Steamy: Selling Seafood, Selling Sex," and "Snakes and Ladders: What Rose Up, What Fell Down During Hurricane Katrina." From its classical typography to faded illustrations, the book's old-world cartological allure was an invitation to navigate New Orleans below and beyond visible markers. I opened to page one.

> "Fathom" is an Old English word that meant outstretched arms and an embrace by those arms. It came to mean a measurement of about 6 feet, the width a man's arm could reach, as well as the embrace of an idea. To fathom is to understand. Sailors kept the word in circulation as a measurement of depth, and it survives into the present day mostly as a negative, as unfathomable, the water so deep its depths cannot be plumbed, the phenomenon that cannot be fully grasped.
>
> New Orleans is all kinds of unfathomable, a city of amorphous boundaries, where land is forever turning into water, water devours land, and a thousand degrees of marshy, muddy, oozing in-between exists; where lines that elsewhere seem firmly drawn are blurry; where whatever you say requires more elaboration; where most rules are full of exceptions the way most land here is full of water.

Like New Orleans, Rebecca Solnit herself defies easy definition. The geography of her work seems equally immeasurable. Of course, I bought the book.

The second in a trilogy of inventive atlases including *Infinite City: A San Francisco Atlas* (2010) and *Nonstop Metropolis: A New York City Atlas* (2016), *Unfathomable City* illustrates Solnit's interest in the ways maps shape how we read and interact with the world. They reflect her desire to revive classic, beautifully illustrated paper maps we can write on, fold in our back pockets, and take control of at a time when many people navigate and perceive the world exclusively through digital devices. "Maps are ubiquitous in one sense and completely missing in another," she has explained, describing the medium as "a happy collision of visual data, language, and cartography all kind of working together." Since I knew I'd be wearing an overcoat and scarf the next day in England, I savored the warm early winter in New Orleans and walked to an open-air café. I bought a bag of beignets and a cup of coffee and found a spot near a jazz band, where I turned pages and peeled back the layers of this Great Southern Babylon.

Solnit is a writer, historian, and activist who links ideas and places like string to thumbtacks. Since the mid-1980s, she has written about an astonishing array of subjects—the environment, politics, landscapes, social justice, feminism, and art—inviting readers to think deeply and broadly about nature and culture. A longtime San Franciscan, she has written more than twenty books and countless penetrating cultural critiques in the *Guardian*, the *New Yorker, Literary Hub, TomDispatch*, and the *London Review of Books*—not to mention, she was the first woman in the history of *Harper's* magazine to write the bimonthly Easy Chair column. She has received a Guggenheim Fellowship, the Lannan Literary Award for nonfiction, and the Kirkus Prize, and was a finalist for the PEN/Diamonstein-Spielvogel Award for the Art of the Essay.

Through the prism of place—deserts, gardens, mines, wilderness—Solnit has explored the hidden histories of Yosemite National Park and the Nevada Test Site (*Savage Dreams: A Journey into the Hidden Wars of the American West,* 1994), the global impact of nonviolent activism over five decades (*Hope in the Dark: Untold Histories, Wild Possibilities,* 2004), the human nature of altruism during catastrophes (*A Paradise Built in Hell: The Extraordinary Communities that Arise in Disaster,* 2009), the boundaries of storytelling and the creation of our own narratives (*The Faraway Nearby,* 2013), and many more.

A Berkeley-educated journalist, Solnit dissolves the boundaries of traditional reportage by blending memoir, pellucid prose, and a strong sense of place to create radiant personal essays. Her voice is approachable and the journey sometimes meandering—as we read, we feel we are with her on a walk. When I was lucky enough to meet her after a reading, I was delighted to learn this luminosity is not limited to the page but shines the same in person: her unflinching blue eyes seem to see dimensions others overlook or refuse to examine.

Solnit is a leading voice in revising the feminist roadmap. Her first book for children, *Cinderella Liberator* (2019), illustrated by Arthur Rackham, is a progressive and modern retelling of the classic fairytale. Her essay "Men Explain Things to Me," which gifted us the term "mansplaining," is highly referenced and cited. This scathing and comic essay was drawn from her own encounter with the host of a dinner party. Upon hearing she was a writer, he asked her to describe her latest work. When she began to tell him about *River of Shadows: Eadweard Muybridge and the Technological Wild West* (2003), her book about "the annihilation of time and space and the industrialization of everyday life," the man bulldozed the conversation to summarize a book review he'd read about the very same subject—and he continued to hold forth, oblivious that there was someone more expert than him present, and despite Solnit's friend repeatedly telling him that, actually, Solnit was the author of the very book he was referencing. Mansplaining—the gendered and patronizing dynamic when men assume women don't know things, or the attitude that women are, as Solnit describes, "empty vessels to be filled with [men's] wisdom"—was dubbed Word of the Year by the *New York Times* in 2010.

This essay also led to Solnit's 2014 book, *Men Explain Things to Me,* a collection of seven essays about marriage equality, Virginia Woolf's embrace of doubt and ambiguity, the continuing ways women around the world are silenced, and much more. Her 2017 follow-up, *The Mother of All Questions,* is a collection of twelve feminist essays published during the #MeToo tidal wave—it covers ground familiar from *Men Explain Things to Me,* including the ways in which Rachel Carson was silenced. You get the feeling many women in its pages were treated to mansplaining.

Frankly, I want Solnit to explain things to me. After I moved to England, two of her books—*Wanderlust: A History of Walking* (2000) and *A Field Guide to Getting Lost* (2005)—became unexpected book-ends to my strange new expat life, helping me connect dots between past, present, and the unknown future. In both books, Solnit reflects how mystery and ambiguity, wandering and feeling lost, are inherent in life. I've learned that it's one thing to romantically sketch out a life abroad on a napkin in a café, but quite another to live out that transatlantic plan, especially when you hold one-way tickets to Europe and watch as the known life—farm, friends, family, job, city, community, culture, country (have I missed anything?)—becomes the past and the faraway nearby, as you climb through clouds and tears into the sky then land with a thump in a country where crosswalks are "zebra crossings," Englishmen wear yellow socks with dark suits, and the word "aluminium" is simply impossible to pronounce. Solnit's prose—personal, poetic, and wise—brought me perspective and comfort as I walked into an unknown time and space, both figuratively and literally.

In *Wanderlust*, Solnit asks profound questions about something basic: what does it mean to walk in the world? In a city? As a woman? On a pilgrimage, in a protest march, as a philosopher, or up a mountain? I read the book five years into my new expat life, when walking at the slow pace of my young children was a singular way of getting to know the new country underfoot. It deepened my understanding of walking in all settings—urban, rural, wild—from a historic perspective. It made me far more aware of the way societies have limited a woman's movement. Solnit also examines the literature of walking and profiles important perambulators in history, including William Wordsworth and Jean-Jacques Rousseau. *Wanderlust* is a fascinating exploration of the interplay between our bodies, our minds, and the world around us, but like so much of Solnit's writing, it's about far more—it's a field guide into the unknown, as we put one foot in front of the other to move forward.

On my tenth anniversary of expat life, I found *A Field Guide to Getting Lost* to be a meaningful glance backward. A slim volume of nine peregrinations around loss and getting lost, it's an exquisite mosaic of aesthetic criticism, autobiography, and cultural history that covers everything from hermit crabs and country music to Yves Klein's 1960 photograph *Leap into the Void.*

The world is blue at its edges and in its depths. This blue is the light that got lost. Light at the blue end of the spectrum does not travel the whole distance from the sun to us. It disperses among the molecules of the air, it scatters in water. Water is colorless, shallow water appears to be the color of whatever lies underneath it, but deep water is full of this scattered light, the purer the water the deeper the blue. The sky is blue for the same reason, but the blue at the horizon, the blue of land that seems to be dissolving into the sky, is a deeper, dreamier, melancholy blue, the blue at the farthest reaches of the places where you see for miles, the blue of distance. This light that does not touch us, does not travel the whole distance, the light that gets lost, gives us the beauty of the world, so much of which is in the color blue.

For many years, I have been moved by the blue at the far edge of what can be seen, that color of horizons, of remote mountain ranges, of anything far away. The color of that distance is the color of an emotion, the color of solitude and of desire, the color of there seen from here, the color of where you are not. And the color of where you can never go. For the blue is not in the place those miles away at the horizon, but in the atmospheric distance between you and the mountains. "Longing," says the poet Robert Hass, "because desire is full of endless distances." Blue is the color of longing for the distances you never arrive in, for the blue world. One soft humid early spring morning driving a winding road across Mount Tamalpais, the 2,500-foot mountain just north of the Golden Gate Bridge, a bend reveals a sudden vision of San

Francisco in shades of blue, a city in a dream, and I was filled with a tremendous yearning to live in that place of blue hills and blue buildings, though I do live there, I had just left there after breakfast, and the brown coffee and yellow eggs and green traffic lights filled me with no such desire, and besides I was looking forward to going hiking on the mountain's west slope.

We treat desire as a problem to be solved, address what desire is for and focus on that something and how to acquire it rather than on the nature and the sensation of desire, though often it is the distance between us and the object of desire that fills the space in between with the blue of longing. I wonder sometimes whether with a slight adjustment of perspective it could be cherished as a sensation on its own terms, since it is as inherent to the human condition as blue is to distance? If you can look across the distance without wanting to close it up, if you can own your longing in the same way that you own the beauty of that blue that can never be possessed? For something of this longing will, like the blue of distance, only be relocated, not assuaged, by acquisition and arrival, just as the mountains cease to be blue when you arrive among them and the blue instead tints the next beyond. Somewhere in this is the mystery of why tragedies are more beautiful than comedies and why we take a huge pleasure in the sadness of certain songs and stories. Something is always far away.

It makes sense that the mind-blowing maps in her atlas trilogy are absent in this field guide. When Solnit writes about the natural world, and anything else for that matter, it's always about more than what our physical eyes take in. *A Field Guide to Getting Lost* is about navigating inner landscapes of mystery, letting go of the finite, and embracing the unknown. When the familiar falls away, and fewer markers guide us, we begin to see possibilities in the once unfathomable.

WORKS BY REBECCA SOLNIT

*Secret Exhibition: Six California Artists
of the Cold War Era* (1991)

*Savage Dreams: A Journey into the Hidden Wars
of the American West* (1994)

A Book of Migrations: Some Passages in Ireland (1998)

Wanderlust: A History of Walking (2000)

*As Eve Said to the Serpent: On Landscape,
Gender, and Art* (2001)

*Hollow City: The Siege of San Francisco and
the Crisis of American Urbanism* (2002)

*River of Shadows: Eadweard Muybridge and
the Technological Wild West* (2003)

Hope in the Dark: Untold Histories, Wild Possibilities (2004)

A Field Guide to Getting Lost (2005)

Storming the Gates of Paradise: Landscapes for Politics (2007)

*A Paradise Built in Hell: The Extraordinary Communities
that Arise in Disaster* (2009)

A California Bestiary (2010)

Infinite City: A San Francisco Atlas (2010)

Ruins (2011)

The Faraway Nearby (2013)

Unfathomable City: A New Orleans Atlas (2013)

Men Explain Things to Me (2014)

The Encyclopedia of Trouble and Spaciousness (2014)

Nonstop Metropolis: A New York City Atlas (2016)

The Mother of All Questions (2017)

Call Them by Their True Names (2018)

*Drowned River: The Death and Rebirth of Glen Canyon
on the Colorado* (2018)

Cinderella Liberator (2019)

KATHLEEN JAMIE

Perhaps, aeons ago, this very Earth
– planet of tundra, mountains, oceans, glens,
formed thus inside her mother, then was born.

THIS WEIRD ESTATE

I N VICTORIAN LONDON, a mudlark was a destitute person, often a child, who scavenged through mud on the tidal River Thames for anything of value to sell—iron, coal, copper, rope, brick, bone, wood. It took me years of walking the Thames to realize that the people on the foreshore—heads down, Wellies on, poking rocks and slogging through mud—weren't oddballs but modern mudlarks. The Thames is a watery archaeological site, with black anaerobic mud that preserves whatever falls in, and its vigorous tide is constantly churning up artifacts, stories, and secrets—Roman pottery, medieval children's toys, messages in bottles, animal and human skeletons, the broken hearts and shattered dreams of lost (or tossed) wedding rings. These days, I have joined the mudlark ranks (having first obtained a permit), and my forays fill my studio with Staffordshire slipware, clay pipes, a seventeenth-century jetton, Roman pottery, and more.

In Cambridge University Library, upon delivery of the mountain of material I had requested while researching this book, I have a different kind of mudlark moment. Sifting through the pile, I come upon a singular object: a signed, limited edition poetry collection entitled *This Weird Estate* (2007), by Scottish writer Kathleen Jamie. Unsure what to make of it, I set the book flat on an oak table and run my hand over its raised felt cover, the color of pink flesh. Inside, I find six short poems, each accompanied by images of engravings and illustrated plates of human anatomy—all engrossing, detailed, and haunting—credited to Irish physician Richard Quain (1816–1898) and the Scottish physician John Lizars (1787–1860), both of whom were anatomists, surgeons, and medical authors.

Though it appears a thin, insubstantial thing, I'm able to recognize it, like the James II coin I plucked from between wet rocks on the Thames, as a gem. Within its distinctive covers, *This Weird Estate* explores our wild anatomies, from human ova to the planet Earth. In one image, a black-and-white X-ray of an infant, the girl appears to be in a sleeping or languid state—on her back, one knee raised, the other fallen to the side—but upon closer examination, I see her tiny bones are not yet fused; she must, I realize, shaken, have been still-born. The X-ray reveals an intricate landscape inside her that looks alive—arteries branch off her abdominal aortas like silhouettes of winter trees along a river. Tiny blood vessels in her brain resemble the twisted, lichen-covered dwarf oaks in Devon's Wistman's Wood. The poem beside this haunting image reads:

> At the end of my winter
> I walked in the wood,
> and she, in her kindness
> gave what she could
> of beard lichen, lungwort
> blueberry sprigs,
> tendrils of cold moss,
> broken birch twigs
> I bore home gladly
> these gifts of the wild;
> I arrange and arrange them,
> but they're not my lost child.

This Weird Estate is an illuminating glimpse into the intricate anatomical wilderness we all carry within. For this child, an unknown pathology has extinguished her beautiful ecosystem—why is unclear. The powerful interaction between the picture and the poem creates a cavalcade of unexpected feelings. Any woman who has carried a child, lost a child, or deeply longed to be with child, well knows the many meanings of "winter"—that grief after miscarriage, sorrow after an abortion, mourning after a child is stillborn, postpartum depression, the heartache of infertility.

Jamie's nuanced yet sinewy poems of maternal loss and grief highlight the deep connection between two bodies connected by an umbilical cord. The first poem in *This Weird Estate* is accompanied by an image of a cross-section of a brain, its veins and capillaries mapping out intricate circulation routes. It's written in a Scottish dialect, with words that conjure wildwoods, briars, and thorns. Another anatomical drawing is a tumor, or a tumorous womb after a hysterectomy. The narrator of the accompanying poem, entitled "Janet," talks directly to this unusual mass, reimagining it as a living thing she brought into the world: "Now you're born / among the beautiful / justified creatures of Earth." There is no skimming the surface with Kathleen Jamie's writing. Like walking the Thames at low tide, her poems force you to stop, bend down to examine that eye-catching thing you see, and contemplate other worlds washed ashore at your feet.

A professor of poetry at the University of Stirling, Jamie became interested in probing the past and exploring beyond what the eye can see when she was a teenager participating in an archaeological dig in the Scottish Highlands. Years later, after her mother's death, she began to also examine the human landscape as seen through a microscope and with X-ray. Her numerous books of poetry include *The Tree House* (2004), winner of the Forward Prize for best collection and a Scottish Arts Council Book of the Year Award; the Costa Book Award–winning *The Overhaul* (2012); and *The Bonniest Companie* (2015); all of which are set in Scotland and examine how its landscapes shape the humans who live there.

In her acclaimed essay collections *Findings* (2005) and *Sightlines* (2012), she is like a mudlark who scours remote Scottish island beaches and other remarkable settings for treasures in nature and language. "I have what Robert Louis Stevenson called 'a strong Scots accent of the mind' and my constellation of interests seem to include the natural world (widely defined), archaeology, medical humanities, and art," she writes on her website. "To produce work I've walked and sailed many miles, and benefitted from the company and expertise of visual artists, pathologists, curators, ornithologists, and from encounters with other species too, especially birds and whales."

In the *Findings* essay "Skyline," she writes about how she keeps binoculars on her desk, which she checks as often as others do their mobile phones, and observes peregrine falcons. "He lifted first one yellow talon then the other, like one who has chewing gum on his shoe." Unpretentious and profound, her prose is grounded in strong poetic insights. In "The Braan Salmon," she muses on the scent trail that draws the fish back to the spawning grounds, writing, "They say the day is coming—it may already be here—when there will be no wild creatures. That is, when no species on the planet will be able to further itself without reference or negotiation with us. When our intervention or restraint will be a factor in their continued existence. Every creature: salmon, sand martins, seals, flies. What does this matter?"

Jamie continues to train her gaze on wild places in *Sightlines*, winner of the 2014 John Burroughs Medal and recipient of the Orion Book Award. She travels to Shetland for gannets, to Bergen for whale skeletons, and to Rona for petrels. In Spain, subterranean prehistoric caves covered in Neolithic paintings spark this observation: "There was a time—until very recently in the scheme of things—when there were no wild animals, because every animal was wild; and humans were few." She sees patterns in bones, stones, and the earth. Her relationships with landscapes and living things permeate her writing. In "Aurora," *Sightlines*'s opening essay, she takes a cruise along Greenland's fjords to experience the red and green streamers of northern lights.

Kathleen Jamie

> Now it's after midnight, and dark. We have been to bed, lain in
> the dark in our cabins, but are up again, jackets and jerseys thrown
> over our pyjamas, boots, hats and gloves, and are again standing
> on the ship's foredeck, eight or ten of us, in twos or alone. Some
> lean on the rail, some stand in the middle of the deck. There is
> no electric light; the crew must have switched them off, so there
> is ship's equipment to negotiate in the darkness, winches and

a mast. Although there is no wind now, it's deeply cold and we move with care, because the metal deck underfoot is glazed with ice. If we speak at all, it's in whispers.

The land is featureless now, and the water black, but the heavens are vivacious. We are standing with heads tilted back, marvelling.

Luminous green, teal green, the aurora borealis glows almost directly overhead. It intensifies against the starry night like breath on a mirror, and it moves. Across the whole sky from east to west, the green lights shift and alter. Now it's an emerald veil, now with a surge it remakes itself into a swizzle which reaches toward some far-away place in the east. We're like an audience—some gaze directly, others have again raised long-lensed cameras—standing in the deep cold, looking up, keeping silence, but it's not a show, it's more like watching fluidity of mind; an intellectualism, after the passivity of icebergs. Not the performance of a finished work but a redrafting and recalculating. In fact, because the aurora's green is exactly the same glowing green as the ship's radar screen, as the readout which gives the latitude and longitude, the aurora looks less like a natural phenomenon, more like a feat of technology.

Some people say you can hear the northern lights, that they whoosh or whistle. Silence, icebergs, musk oxen, and now the aurora borealis—the phenomena of the Arctic. This is why we've come here. This is why we are out on the freezing deck at midnight. The lights alter again. Low voices, the rapid clickering of cameras.

Polly comes up beside me and pokes me as best she can through all the layers of clothes. With head tilted back she whispers, 'They are changing without moving', which is true, and I fall to wondering if there are other ways of changing without moving. Growing older perhaps, as we are. Reforming one's attitudes, maybe.

Bright teal green. Once upon a time, whaling ships had come to these latitudes, with orders to return heavy with oil and baleen.

> Now the aurora alters into long trailing verticals, and it makes me think of baleen. Sifting. Sifting what? Stars, souls, particles. You could fancy the northern night were a great whale whose jaws our ship were entering.

In *Surfacing* (2019), her latest collection of essays, Jamie considers human history and her own past. Important touchstones have shifted in her life: her children have left home; her father has died. Against the backdrop of a changing natural world—from Alaskan tundra thawing around a Yup'ik village to sand dunes in Scotland preserving the stone homes of Neolithic farmers—she explores the nature of time and what it means to live rooted in place. Changing without moving.

As for looking forward, Jamie's writing muse comes and goes. "There are times of intense writing, and times of silence. I've been publishing now for above thirty years, and still feel that it's all provisional." The muse and mudlarking must be the same—both wash ideas and artifacts ashore in unknown and unpredictable ways. Says Jamie of her journey, "I never can tell what will happen next."

MORE ON TIME, MEMORY, AND PLACE

KATHLEEN DEAN MOORE

Forests and rivers, deserts and islands were sources of healing for Kathleen Dean Moore after several loved ones died in a short time period. This resulted in her book, *Wild Comfort: The Solace of Nature* (2010). A retired professor, environmental philosopher, and writer, she is also the author, or co-editor, of more than a dozen books, and best known for her creative nonfiction essay collections including *Riverwalking: Reflections on Moving Water* (1995), *Holdfast: At Home in the Natural World* (1999), and *The Pine Island Paradox: Making Connections in a Disconnected World* (2004). Her environmental activism has also led to *Great Tide Rising: Towards Clarity and Moral Courage in a Time of Planetary Change* (2016), which followed her anthology *Moral Ground: Ethical Action for a Planet in Peril* (2010).

KATHLEEN NORRIS

While reading *Dakota: A Spiritual Geography* (1993) by poet and essayist Kathleen Norris, you might feel prairie winds blowing through the pages. In 1974, Norris and her husband moved from New York City to her grandparents' farm in isolated Lemmon, South Dakota, where she discovered a community of Benedictine monks. The resulting book is a spiritual meditation with a strong sense of place, in which Norris is concerned with slowing down, seeing more in less, and refining ideas about harsh and unforgiving places like the Great Plains. "Nature, in Dakota, can indeed be an experience of the Holy," she wrote. Her other books include *The Middle of the World* (1981), *The Cloister Walk* (1996), and *Journey: New and Selected Poems 1969–1999*.

Ray grew up in a poor, white, fundamentalist Christian family in a southern rural Georgia junkyard. "My homeland is about as ugly as a place gets," she wrote in *Ecology of a Cracker Childhood* (1999). She mourns the apocalyptic deforestation of the longleaf pine ecosystem, which once grew from Virginia to Florida to Texas. Author of six books, Ray focuses on rural life, agriculture, human rights, and environmental sustainability. "Southerners in general have a deep relationship with the land, history, and place," Ray has said of the region. "Which makes nature very important to the Southern psyche. Because of the terrain, our emphasis is more botanic than geologic, more rural than urban, and more deeply rooted in story."

CAROLYN FINNEY

What would it be like if John Muir walked into a meeting of the National Park Service Advisory Board and saw me there as a member?

IN CONVERSATION, JANUARY 2019

STORIES ABOUT our diverse human relationships with the natural world are more widely published now than when I was first learning about nature writing as an undergraduate, or later, when I taught courses such as American Literature of Nature and Place and Environmental Issues. In those days, I taught from the mighty tome, *The Norton Anthology of Nature Writing*. In it were excerpts of larger works mostly written by white men, clearly conveying the idea that writing about nature and the environment was the domain of a certain gender, class, and race. Which isn't to say that stories and poems by women and people of color didn't exist. A Norton editor, John Elder, tells me that with each revised edition of the anthologies, they have taken pains to include more of these narratives (the latest edition has close to 160 pieces of writing, nearly 50 by women—an improvement).

What percentage of visitors to America's national parks do you think are black? According to a survey commissioned by the National Park Service, it's 7 percent. If black people comprise nearly 14 percent of the US population, why don't more venture into America's public lands to see the bison and geysers of Yellowstone, the soaring pinnacles and spires in Utah's Arches, or the cliff dwellings of Pueblo people in Mesa Verde?

These are questions Carolyn Finney, a writer, performer, and cultural geographer, explores in her 2014 book, *Black Faces, White Spaces: Reimagining the Relationship of African Americans to the Great Outdoors*. A mix of memoir, scholarship, and history, the book traces the environmental legacy of slavery, racial violence, and Jim Crow segregation, while celebrating contributions black Americans have made to the environment. More scholarly than personal, Finney analyzes three main ideas: perception, representation, and access. Who has concern for the outdoors? Who recreates in American forests and parks? Who constructs stories and media stereotypes that perpetuate the "wilderness is whiteness" idea that keeps brown, black, and other nondominant groups "on the outside looking in"?

No matter your background, Finney's writing will illuminate issues of race and space to shift your understanding of how we access nature and are represented differently by media.

Finney opens *Black Faces, White Spaces* with a startling anecdote from one of her public speaking events, which invites readers to reflect upon their own assumptions and biases.

> I was especially fond of speaking about John Francis, a man who had spent twenty-two years walking across the United States to raise environmental awareness. On this particular day, I paused after saying "twenty-two years," waiting for the audience to murmur and look simultaneously surprised and impressed. Then, as I usually did, I added the punch line: "And for seventeen of those years, he did it without talking." A collective gasp ran through the audience: How is that possible? How did he communicate? Why did he do it? I loved this part—talking to people about how John earned his PhD during this period (without talking), became a representative for the United Nations and was one of the original architects of our oil spill policy that was instituted after the Exxon Valdez disaster infiltrated our seas and our environmental conversations.
>
> Pleased with myself, I ended this story by sharing how Hollywood was preparing to make a movie about his life. Won't it be amazing, even revolutionary, to see a mainstream movie about a black man walking across America to raise environmental awareness? As I continued talking amid laughs and nods of agreement, a young white woman timidly raised her hand. "Yes?" I smiled. "Well—uh—I'm not sure how to say this, but I have to tell you that as you were telling the story about John Francis, I just assumed he was white."

Did you also assume John Francis was white?

Finney's childhood is the driving force behind the scholarly analysis in *Black Faces, White Spaces*. She grew up on a twelve-acre estate of beech, oak, and fruit trees outside New York City, where, for fifty years, her parents worked as gardeners, chauffeurs, and housekeepers for a wealthy Jewish family. Her family were always permanent residents there, not property owners, and the only "colored" people in a wealthy and predominantly white area. While Finney grew to love her home, she learned some people there felt it "unnatural" for her family to occupy space in that privileged sphere.

Black Faces, White Spaces analyzes troubling issues relating to space and race, including systemic contradictions in American environmentalism and the lack of African American representation in a largely white environmental narrative. Finney explains that the dominance of white Eurocentric narratives in history and in nature writing provides "the context from which environmental organizations and African Americans draw their cues about how to think about the environment and themselves." She argues that most American stories of the great outdoors exclude brown and black people or don't account for the ways they may interact differently in outdoor spaces—say, fishing off a pier in Miami rather than wanting to drive to a national park. She explores the ways nature and the environment are racialized in America in the context of Hurricane Katrina's aftermath, and, when discussing the Wilderness Act of 1964, she examines how, though the act supposedly focused on conserving wilderness areas for "public purposes of recreation, scenic viewing, scientific understanding, education . . . and historical preservation," that access was limited for black people by their different historical experiences. And she shares stories from her travels.

For the past few years, I have been privileged to speak with black, white, and brown Americans across the country about race, racism, the media, and all matters deemed "environmental." In particular,

African Americans have shared with me their childhood stories from the woods and the 'hood, the North and the South, and from the 1930s to the 1980s. Whether working on a farm or hanging out on a stoop, their experiences of nature were usually welcomed by them, sometimes challenged by others, and were always bumping up against social, economic, and historical processes that served to remind them that their map of the world, while fluid, demanded a particularly fine-tuned compass that allowed them to navigate a landscape that was not always hospitable.

What I discovered/uncovered/recovered is the many ways in which—be it physical, artistic, or spiritual—black people have laid it all down in order to feed their children, plant their dreams, and share their experience and history with the environment. People like MaVynee Betsch who, in her middle years, gave away all her wealth to environmental causes and fought hard until her death in 2005 to conserve and protect both the natural resources of her home place, American Beach on Amelia Island in Florida, and the African American history that she believed was an intricate part of that landscape. Or Eddy Harris, who at the age of thirty during the 1980s, canoed the length of the Mississippi River to understand both the material and spiritual meaning of the river in American life and to explore what it meant to be a black man in contemporary society. Or Shelton Johnson, a black park ranger in Yosemite National Park who revived the story of Buffalo soldiers and their role in protecting the park by incorporating the story into the larger park narrative through interpretation, film, and the written word. Or people like my parents who simply wanted to feed their families and provide new opportunities and a better life for their children.

From Wynton Marsalis to Toni Morrison to Will Allen to Majora Carter to a man named Pearl, African Americans toiled, sang songs, wrote stories, and transformed the landscape with hard work, big dreams, and a belief that African Americans have and have always had an intimate, ever-changing and significant relationship with the natural environment.

Black Faces, White Spaces deepens our understanding of why environmental justice—defined by the Environmental Protection Agency as "the fair treatment and meaningful involvement of all people regardless of race, color, national origin, or income with respect to the development, implementation, and enforcement of environmental laws, regulations, and policies"—is vital to fair societies everywhere. Finney's book is vital in shaping our understanding of how and why people of color are adversely affected by lack of access to wild and natural places.

As the nature-writing genre becomes more inclusive, it not only creates space for more diverse authors but also for a wider range of styles—from lyrical, personal meditations to scholarly academic work. Finney's next book will be more narrative, expanding on the personal side of *Black Faces, White Spaces* to delve into her family's relationship with land, race, and belonging. "I want to explore how my parents and I created our map of the world, informed by who we imagine ourselves to be and what we imagine to be possible," she tells me in an animated and passionate conversation. "The book will have a number of layers. It will be personal—my own adoption, my search for my biological parents, and my experience growing up on that estate. It will explore my years of backpacking abroad in the late eighties and nineties and living in Nepal. It will also explore what I call 'Bringing Black to America'—the narrative of slavery and how it informs blackness today—and 'Dream Time,' what I call radical presence in shaping a transformative future."

As a former professional actor and independent scholar, Finney also plans to broaden her stage presence by developing a one-woman performance piece entitled *The N Word: Nature, Revisited*. Based on race and public lands, it will be a conversation between herself and John Muir. Her inspiration is Anna Deavere Smith's *Twilight: Los*

Angeles, 1992, a play comprising a series of monologues taken from interviews with real people impacted by the riots in Los Angeles that year. "I have been influenced by John Muir as much as anybody," she says, her voice circumspect. "But I also have mixed feelings about him. He was brilliantly committed to all things about nature, but in his book *A Thousand-Mile Walk to the Gulf* (1916), in his own words, he says a lot of racist things about black people along the way." She pauses when she says this to me. "How do we hold that?"

How *do* we?

MORE ENVIRONMENTAL JUSTICE

DIANNE D. GLAVE

Forced labor in cotton fields, bodies hanging from trees, crossing the ocean on a slave ship—images of the African American experience in the natural world are melded with violence and injustice. Each chapter of *Rooted in the Earth: Reclaiming the African American Environmental Heritage* (2010) opens with a fictional account of a black protagonist surviving hardship and disconnection. With scenes that range from farming in Africa to Michelle Obama planting a vegetable garden at the White House, Glave, a pastor and historian, overturns stereotypes and reclaims black environmental history while addressing environmental justice.

VANDANA SHIVA

Shiva's father was a forest conservationist, her mother a farmer who loved the natural world in India. Shiva became an environmental activist, scholar, and food advocate interested in biodiversity and indigenous knowledge. She has written more than twenty books, including *Staying Alive: Women, Ecology, and Development* (1988), which revised how people perceived women in the third world. Her other notable books include *Stolen Harvest: The Hijacking of the Global Food Supply* (2000) and *Soil Not Oil: Environmental Justice in an Age of Climate Crisis* (2007).

NAOMI KLEIN

Klein was a student at the University of Toronto in 1989 when a man declaring war on feminism murdered fourteen female engineering students at École Polytechnique. She described the event as the wakeup call that spurred her to action. Now the Gloria Steinem Chair in Media, Culture, and Feminist Studies at Rutgers University, Klein is an award-winning Canadian author, filmmaker, and climate activist often cited as an influential thinker. She is known for her political analysis and criticism of capitalism and corporate globalization. *This Changes Everything: Capitalism vs. the Climate* (2014) was an instant *New York Times* bestseller, and her subsequent work has built on that platform, with books that include *No Is Not Enough: Resisting Trump's Shock Politics and Winning the World We Need* (2017), *The Battle for Paradise: Puerto Rico Takes on the Disaster Capitalists* (2018) and *On Fire: The (Burning) Case for a Green New Deal* (2019).

HELEN
MACDONALD

Vast flocks of fieldfares netted the sky, turning it
to something strangely like a sixteenth-century
sleeve sewn with pearls.

H IS FOR HAWK

T'S AN INDIAN SUMMER in Cambridge, England—a liminal October moment before autumn fully arrives and summer lets go. Students and professors hurry across tree-lined commons, past ivy-covered colleges bathed in low warm light.

I'm sitting in a mahogany boat on the dreamy River Cam. The punter stands at the back with a long pole and gently nudges us away from modern life. We glide into the ancient world behind the backs of England's oldest colleges—past Henry VIII's Trinity College, past the ornate stained-glass chapel of King's College Chapel, and under the Bridge of Sighs. Trees drop their first leaves like red and gold embers into the water, a hint of autumn, while cormorants sun themselves and an elegant heron spears a fish on the banks of the Wren Library.

In my handbag, I carry *H Is for Hawk* (2014) by Helen Macdonald. Though set here in Cambridge, the book is actually about a parallel landscape, and the way it can hide, even alongside college gardens and civilized scholarship. Exquisitely described by Macdonald, this landscape is an invisible wilderness, one people carry inside themselves, and living with it can feel like navigating a labyrinth or spiraling downward in darkness. The wilderness is depression—a low recess that can be episodic or long-term, brought on by grief, trauma, or unexplained imbalances of chemicals in our minds.

Macdonald is a British writer, poet, illustrator, historian, and former research fellow in the Department of History and Philosophy of Science at Jesus College here at Cambridge University. Upon the unexpected death of her father, she became depressed and withdrew from the world to process, cope, and recover. An experienced falconer, long fascinated by the high-strung, temperamental, murderous birds of prey called goshawks, she adopted one and named her Mabel.

Training Mabel eventually led to her recovery.

H Is for Hawk is a masterpiece of literary nonfiction that braids memoir, literary biography, and falconer's diary into a beautiful example of new nature writing. The book became an international bestseller and an instant classic, showered with accolades, from the 2014 Costa Book of the Year award to the Samuel Johnson Prize for Nonfiction. Macdonald endeavors to answer the fundamental question of how best to live in the world by exploring the mental architecture of grief and loss, the role wild animals play in our imaginations, the power of memory, relationships between fathers and daughters, and how gender and sex shape access to nature. The title, *H Is for Hawk*, comes from a child's alphabet game and the process of learning to read, which for Helen refers to making sense of the world again after it was rendered incomprehensible.

There's something about birds—their mellifluous songs, painted plumage, graceful flight—that elicits some of our best nature writing. *H Is for Hawk* naturally draws comparisons with J. A. Baker's 1967 work of genius, *The Peregrine*. Like Baker, Macdonald tries to enter "the light-drenched prism of the hawk's mind," to inhabit the kind of mental remove inherent in wild animals. She trains her goshawk, Mabel, and the goshawk trains her as well—to soar above human troubles for a while. She writes, "The hawk was a fire that burned my hurts away. There could be no regret or mourning in her. No past or future. She lived in the present only, and that was my refuge." In processing her father's death, Macdonald shunned family and friends, becoming solitary and inward. Hawking provided a distraction from herself, a way of being self-possessed outside human emotions.

The book is a genre-buster, weaving parallel narratives in language that dares to be dark, full of expletives, and funny. You don't often see these traits in nature writing, which is a shame because too much reverential, heard-in-church-on-Sunday language can lead to a bored reader. Like all good poetry, every word in *H Is for Hawk* is worthy of reading aloud, but an especially crystalline passage is Macdonald's description of Mabel.

> The feathers down her front are the colour of sunned newsprint, of tea-stained paper, and each is marked darkly towards its tip with a leaf-bladed spearhead, so from her throat to her feet she is patterned with a shower of falling raindrops. Her wings are the colour of stained oak, their covert feathers edged in palest teak, barred flight-feathers folded quietly beneath. And there's a strange grey tint to her that is felt, rather than seen, a kind of silvery light like a rainy sky reflected from the surface of a river. She looks new. Looks as if the world cannot touch her. As if everything that exists and is observed rolls off like drops of water from her oiled and close-packed feathers. And the more I sit with her, the more I marvel at how reptilian she is. The lucency of her pale, round eyes. The waxy yellow skin about her Bakelite-black beak. The way she snakes her small head from side to side to focus on distant objects. Half the time she seems as alien as a snake, a thing hammered of metal and scales and glass. But then I see ineffably birdlike things about her, familiar qualities that turn her into something loveable and close. She scratches her fluffy chin with one awkward, taloned foot; sneezes when bits of errant down get up her nose. And when I look again she seems neither bird nor reptile, but a creature shaped by a million years of evolution for a life she's not yet lived. Those long, barred tailfeathers and short, broad wings are perfectly shaped for sharp turns and brutal acceleration through a world of woodland obstacles; the patterns on her plumage will hide her in perfect, camouflaging drifts of light and shade.

The act of releasing the hawk off her leather glove brings Helen closer to her father, Alisdair, who spent his professional life looking through a camera lens as a press photographer and his younger days searching the skies as a boy obsessed with plane-spotting. "I must have inherited being a watcher from Dad," she writes. As Mabel soars into the fields around Cambridge, and Macdonald cranes her neck skyward to watch her fly, she mirrors her father's way of looking at the world. As I, myself, float on the Cam, past green fields and gardens, I'm reminded of ways Mabel begins to unexpectedly rewild Macdonald. In a scene that takes place in Jesus Green, not far from my boat, Mabel's effect on Macdonald's senses is striking.

> Keys in pocket, hawk on fist, and off we go. Leaving the house that evening is frightening. Somewhere in my mind ropes uncoil and fall. It feels like an unmooring, as if I were an airship ascending on its maiden flight into darkness. Stepping over the low railings into the park I head for the thick black avenue of limes and the lamplit leaves beneath. Everything seems hot and clean and dangerous and my senses are screwed to their utmost, as if someone had told me the park was full of hungry lions. Night air moves in the spaces between trees. Moths make dusty circles about the lamps. I look down and see each pale blade of grass casts two separate shadows from the two nearest lamps, and so do I, and in the distance comes the collapsing echo of a moving train and somewhere closer a dog barks twice and there's broken glass by the path and next to it a feather from the breast of a woodpigeon judging by its size and curl. It lies upon the grass as if held just above it, gleaming softly in the darkness.
>
> "Bloody hell, Mabel," I whisper. "Who spiked my tea with acid?"

As well as cracking good scenes, what enhances the structure of *H Is for Hawk* are the parallel narratives, including an examination of falconry's culture of masculinity. Macdonald deepens her own story by describing how, in English culture, living space became gendered over time: hunting fields masculine, indoor rooms feminine. She recalls being introduced to the historically aristocratic sport of falconry at age twelve—her parents tolerated her obsession with birds of prey and allowed her to tag along with Eton-accented male falconers despite her working-class Irish background. Then Macdonald flips the script—after hunting forays, she brings Mabel into her home to sit on a perch (in contrast to her male mentors, who housed their hawks separately). Together they watch bad television and play catch with wadded balls of paper. Bringing a murderous goshawk into a domestic sphere undercuts dominant ideas about falconry's inherent masculinity.

In another fascinating gender comparison, Macdonald weaves in the sad tale of English author T. H. White, whose 1951 book, *The Goshawk*, tells a very different story about the psychological role of animals in our lives. Best known for his Arthurian novels, collected in *The Once and Future King* (1958), White's lifelong interest in natural history led him to adopt a goshawk and to train it in traditional rather than modern methods. A gay man, forced like other homosexuals at the time to keep his desires suppressed, White turned to hawking as an escape from loneliness and lingering childhood abuse issues. The practice allowed him to maintain the fiction of playing it straight. His experience of hawking serves as a counterpoint to Macdonald's own. She writes:

> I found there were myriad definitions of this thing called tragedy that had wormed its way through the history of literature; and the simplest of all was this: that it is the story of a figure who, through some moral flaw or personal failing, falls through force of circumstance to his doom.
>
> It was the Tragedy paper that led me to read Freud, because he was still fashionable back then, and because psychoanalysts had their shot at explaining tragedy too. After reading him I began to see all sorts of psychological transferences in my falconry books. I saw those nineteenth-century falconers were projecting onto their hawks all the male qualities they thought threatened by modern

life: wildness, power, virility, independence and strength. By identifying with their hawks as they trained them, they could *introject*, or repossess, those qualities. At the same time, they could exercise their power by "civilising" a wild and primitive creature. Masculinity and conquest: two imperial myths for the price of one. The Victorian falconer assumed the power and strength of the hawk. The hawk assumed the manners of the man.

For White, too, falconry involved strange projections, but of very different qualities. His young German goshawk was a living expression of all the dark, discreditable desires within himself he'd tried to repress for years: it was a thing fey, fairy, feral, ferocious and cruel. He had tried for so long to be a gentleman. Tried to fit in, to adhere to all the rules of civilised society, to be normal, to be like everyone else. But his years at Stowe and his analysis and the fear of war had brought him to breaking point. He had refused humanity in favour of hawks, but he could not escape himself. Once again White was engaged in a battle to civilise the perversity and unruliness within himself. Only now he had put those things in the hawk, and he was trying to civilise them there. He found himself in a strange, locked battle with a bird that was all the things he longed for, but had always fought against. It was a terrible paradox. A proper tragedy. No wonder living with Gos brought him nearly to madness.

He is lost. The barn is a dungeon. He is swimmingly, drunkenly tired. A chill summer wind blows through the walls. White owls hunt outside: powdery, reed-thin shrieks under a low orange moon. He is an executioner, he thinks, and he should be wearing a mask. A black one that conceals his face. He has been measuring time in the bates of the hawk, in the hundreds of times he's lifted the screaming captive back onto his glove. The barn is the Bastille. The hawk is a prisoner. The falconer is a man in riding breeches and a checked coat. He stands in a Rembrandt interior. A pile of sticks and empty jars on the brick floor;

cobwebs on the walls. A broken grate. A barrel of Flowers beer. A pool of light from the oil-lamp, and the hawk. The hawk, the hawk, the hawk. It is on his fist, all the sepia arrowheads on its pale breast dishevelled and frayed from his hands. The man is swaying backwards and forwards like a man on a ship, as if the ground beneath him pitched and rolled like the sea. He is trying to stay awake. He is trying to keep the hawk awake. The hawk is trying to close its eyes and sleep but the swaying pulls it back. I am free, the man is telling himself. *Free.*

H Is for Hawk is Macdonald's best-known work, but it's not her only book inspired by birds. Her undergraduate collection of poetry, *Shaler's Fish* (2001), teems with birdsong, flint eggs, down, wet feathers, and dark plumes. She trained hawks in the Middle East, and her doctoral dissertation at Cambridge focused on the "history of natural history and how we relate to the natural world." Her research in the Archives of Falconry at the World Center for Birds of Prey in Boise, Idaho, bewitched her with medieval manuscripts, sealskin parkas, and other cultural fragments. The remarkable ideas she couldn't fit into her dissertation became *Falcon*, her 2006 book about "the cultural history of falconry and birds of prey across thousands of years, with musings on anatomy, physiology, hunting strategies, flight mechanics, and conservation philosophy and practice."

Today her essays appear in the *New York Times Magazine*. Her work continues to build on a theme in *H Is for Hawk*: investigating how humans see the natural world and the way that affects what we value. In 2019, she edited *Vesper Flights*, a collection of best-loved pieces on a range of subjects, including the nature of nostalgia, science fiction, and an account of a refugee's flight to the United Kingdom. As ever, birds wing through these stories—cranes in Hungary, swans on the River Thames, golden orioles in Suffolk's poplar forests—perfect metaphors to talk about time, memory, love, loss, and how we make sense of the world.

Back on the River Cam, my guide and I reach the wooden Mathematical Bridge, gently turn around, and float back to the dock at Magdalen. Musing on *H Is for Hawk* has left me feeling as if I've journeyed through a wild and hidden place. The punter extends his hand, and I step, changed, back into modern life.

MORE BIRD LIFE

MABEL OSGOOD WRIGHT

Wilderness vanishing under rapid American growth was a deep concern of Mabel Osgood Wright (1859–1934), especially birds and their diminishing habitats. Her first book, *The Friendship of Nature: A New England Chronicle of Birds and Flowers* (1894), was a collection of essays. *Birdcraft: A Field Book of Two Hundred Song, Game, and Water Birds* (1895) is the prototype for modern birding field guides. Wright wrote more than a dozen books on birds and gardens, including *Flowers and Ferns in Their Haunts* (1901), *The Garden of a Commuter's Wife, Recorded by the Gardener* (1902), and *The Making of Birdcraft Sanctuary* (1922). She was the first president of the Connecticut Audubon Society.

LYANDA LYNN HAUPT

Birds make numerous luminous flights into the books of Seattleite Lyanda Lynn Haupt. *Mozart's Starling* (2017) is the story of the composer and his pet bird, a tale that has captivated linguists, ornithologists, music historians, and Mozart aficionados. Her other books include *The Urban Bestiary: Encountering the Everyday Wild* (2013), a finalist for the Orion Book Award; *Crow Planet: Essential Wisdom from the Urban Wilderness* (2009), winner of a Sigurd F. Olson Nature Writing Award; *Pilgrim on the Great Bird Continent: The Importance of Everything and Other Lessons from Darwin's Lost Notebooks* (2006); and *Rare Encounters with Ordinary Birds: Notes from a Northwest Year* (2001), winner of a Washington State Book Award.

POLLY ATKIN

Herons, jackdaws, owls, and bees—along with deer, foxes, rabbits—appear throughout *Basic Nest Architecture* (2017), an evocative poetry collection by Cumbrian writer Polly Atkin. The book is themed around three ideas—"place as nest, the mind as nest, and the body as nest"—and explores what it means to inhabit a place, to desire communion with the non-human world, and to live with chronic illness. "It's too easy, almost, when you're struggling to move across the ground on badly designed legs, to look at birds and think of them as freer, better, more at home in their element," she said. "Wrapped around that is a question about the way humans use birds to help them think, and the symbolism and mythology of birds." Her stellar "Why Is It Always a Poem Is a Walk?" in the *New Welsh Reader* provides an important critique of access and disabilities in ecopoetry, nature writing, and environmental movements. By asking who has access to nature, and who writes about it, Atkin challenges the notion that the majority of mainstream nature writing is authored by abled, hyper-fit men.

SACI LLOYD

My plan for the rest of my life is to set myself on
fire with enthusiasm so people will come for miles to
watch me burn. I. Will. Roar. For. Nature.

PERSONAL CORRESPONDENCE, DECEMBER 2018

BRITISH AUTHOR Saci Lloyd and I walk through Epping Forest, an ancient royal hunting ground near her home in north London. She is wearing red trousers, a full-length coat, and a fur hat that looks like a cat curled in the sun on her head. "One day I was here and looked down," she recalls, holding a bag of bread, "and I see the black wing of a crow in the grass." Possibly a hundred crows surround us now. "There were crows all around me like this—and I heard loud *caw caw caws*— and so I moved a respectful distance away, and just watched. And I realized then that they were mourning and having a crow funeral. I watched one crow after another fly down and lament over that wing for half an hour."

We toss the entourage of birds scraps of bread then set out on a meadow path toward a woodland. Sunlight splinters autumn clouds. "The crows are being sentinels now. But—ha ha! Look over there!" she says as a blue-winged corvid darts from oak to oak. "That is a jay's blue flash of magic. They are associated with Mercury, the messenger, because they go between two worlds. That's what crows are, too. Messengers between two worlds."

We amble across a low ditch lined in beech trees which looks like the pale of a former deer park. I look both ways as if crossing a street. It feels like I'm stepping out of urban London into the past. An older man bounds toward us with a white bag at his side. There's a *fantastico* flurry of greetings and exclamations in Italian. It's Gerardo! He's Saci's Italian friend! And he has mushrooms!

Strolling with Lloyd feels like being an extra in a Fellini film—yet she is a futurist, an acclaimed writer of "cli-fi." This robust fiction subgenre has sprung from the ticking clock of climate change and explores the consequences of a warming planet. As real-life disasters grow more dire, and readers seek a glimpse into possible futures, cli-fi is growing in acclaim, output, and popularity. Lloyd's books include *The Carbon Diaries 2015* (2009), *The Carbon Diaries 2017* (2009), *Momentum* (2011), *Quantum Drop* (2013), and *It's the End of the World As We Know It* (2015)—all are grounded in themes of reduced natural resources and the pressures that come with it.

The Carbon Diaries have gained a cult following in America and Britain and have been translated into more than fifteen languages. These gritty eco-thrillers take an immediate, accessible route to exploring the ways a warming planet changes the world—through the personal journals of feisty Laura Brown. She's a sixteen-year-old living in Britain, one of the first countries to create mandatory carbon rationing to reduce its consumption by 60 percent. Laura is juggling the usual teenage stuff—passing classes, playing in a band, trying to get the attention of a fit boy named Ravi—while trying to manage life with a carbon debit card. Her diary entries are sweary and sassy. They are misspelled and myopic. And they document a typical self-absorbed teenager in an atypical world collapsing under droughts, riots, diseases, and floods.

Fri, Jan 2nd

11 p.m. In bed now. *Jeeesus*, Kieran's got himself in a real state over rationing.

'I'm all washed up. Finished,' he kept moaning. 'It's the hunter-gatherer, macho, sink-unblocker's world now. What'll become of a little skinny hairdresser guy like me?'

Kieran goes to the gym about six times a week, so I told him he had gorgeous pecs, which usually sorts him out.

'Yeah, yeah, but what's the use when there'll be no clubs, no weekenders in Ibiza, no chilled Laurent-Perrier, no Versace? A male hairdresser can't be taken seriously without a lifestyle!'

'Like you do any of that stuff anyway,' I snorted. 'You're always moaning about those scene queens.'

'I know, I know—but they're taking my right to choose away!'

I checked he wasn't being ironic, but his mouth was all drawn down like a little boy.

When I got home, my parents were asleep in front of the TV screen, every single light in the house was blazing and Kim was in the bath with the stereo and her bedroom HD on. I don't know what's gonna happen to this family once rationing really kicks in.

Lloyd's books are vivid and action-packed with a strong sense of place, but the thing that distinguishes her stories from most climate change dystopia? "It's probably that I include a lot of jokes," she says as we walk. Lloyd is effervescent and mirthful in person and on paper, and my face hurts from laughing at her dry one-liners. "If anything," she says in a serious moment, "I have in mind the urban kids I teach graphics and design to. Nature for them is something on the television or in Africa, as opposed to something right outside a window. They have no upbringing in nature and so the humor is the bridge to get them there to care."

Because only a handful of nature writers have written with satire and jest—among them Edward Abbey, Bill Bryson, Suzanne Roberts, David Quammen, Robert Michael Pyle, and Ellen Meloy—there's the impression that, in these serious times, humor only subverts the cause. With biodiversity loss and climate change, naturally the stakes are high—who wants to be the one cracking jokes at a funeral? But Lloyd shows that writing about the most serious issues facing our times doesn't need to feel like going to Sunday school. We can still laugh while fighting the good fight. Lloyd illustrates this in the way Laura's year progresses. Her diary entries reflect how these new carbon reduction policies are affecting her friends, family, and nation. Reading *The Carbon Diaries* or *Momentum* makes me wonder what kind of future awaits our children and grandchildren, the generation who now leads climate rallies with young activists like Greta Thunberg. Despite the chaos her characters experience firsthand, Lloyd has written narratives that are warm and relatable. And they pop with graphics—report cards, carbon points, band concert posters, and drawings—that help readers understand this version of "normal" teenage life in the new abnormal of climate change.

Weds, July 29th

10 p.m. After more than 24 hours of solid talk they've passed the emergency law. Big sections of the country are going to be cut off. We are first on the list. Thames Water's cutting all London houses, borough by borough. There'll be a standpipe for every 20 homes. The weird thing is when they announced it I didn't feel anything. That's starting to happen loads. Even with Ravi. I know I really like him, but I can't always seem to connect.

Dad stood in the garden with Shiva, looking at the dried-up beds.

'All that work for nothing. I can barely keep it all going with our shower water. Once they switch us off, I don't know what's going to happen.' He shook his head. 'I'm going to join the march on Thames Water's headquarters in Reading tomorrow. We've got to force them to do *something*, at least start building a bloody desalination plant. Y'know, for making clean water out of the sea.'

Shiva frowned. 'How does it work?'

'Not sure—something to do with osmosis and the Thames.'

'But Nicholas, the Thames is a freshwater river. Where's the salt?'

'Well, a lot of it's tidal, so I guess they do it closer to the sea.'

'But . . . '

'What?'

'It sounds like a big process. Isn't it going to burn a lot of fuel?'

'Yeah well, I guess that's the choice now—pollute or burn.' Dad stamped his foot. 'There's got to be another way to get water in this town.'

For readers who have grown tired of fantasy novels about the orphan with a lightning bolt scar waving magic wands, Lloyd's kind of worldbuilding feeds a real, churning, and expanding ecological consciousness. And while the name "cli-fi" may be new, the genre is not. It stretches at least back to Jules Verne's 1889 *The Purchase of the North Pole*, about removing the four seasons by changing the tilt of the Earth's axis, continues through *The Wind from Nowhere*, J. G. Ballard's 1961 novel about worldwide hurricanes that destroy civilization, and boasts plentiful contemporary examples, including *Oryx and Crake* (2003) by Margaret Atwood, *The Windup Girl* (2009) by Paolo Bacigalupi, and *Flight Behavior* (2012) by Barbara Kingsolver.

Writers of cli-fi and solarpunk—the optimistic literary movement that imagines thriving local communities in balance with the environment—question and critique how different worlds might be imagined. "There is no time anymore," Lloyd emphasizes as we walk through clusters of birch trees, "because we are now officially in a state of emergency. It is one thing to burn your own house down, but to burn down the houses of the other great lineages—these other wonderful forms of life with far greater and nobler lineages than us—is absolutely *unacceptable* to me. There are those who say, 'No, no, don't frighten people. That's not the way to reach them.'" She stops and reflects for a moment. "There are ways to get through an emergency but *lying* about what it is will not do it. It's very sad for me to see that not only is alliance-building difficult, it is an article of faith for those with right-wing views to see that climate change is a left-wing socialist hoax—it adds another layer of horror to the thing." Young people, she says, accept that climate change is an existential threat we have a limited window to fix before the point of no return.

"I don't know if we are going to make it as a species," Lloyd reflects. "I'm fifty-fifty on it, but I'm not going to sit on the side and let things go to oblivion. The earth is going to be fine, but it is not going to be with us." I hear real sadness and anger in her voice. "There is just going to be a great biodiversity loss."

In this cloud of sobering thoughts, we head through the woods single file. I hear the cawing of crows again, and it takes me back to my childhood in California, where they flew in languid streams across pink skies at dusk, and my grandmother, looking across cornfields, would say, "It's roosting time." I think of the young readers who love Lloyd's writing and how they are growing up in a different climate, literally, than Lloyd and I did. I remember two of my favorite books: *Where the Wild Things Are* (1963) by Maurice Sendak and *The Lorax* (1971) by Dr. Seuss.

Nearly fifty years after Seuss's fable about the danger posed by autocratic corporate greed, newspapers lead with worrying headlines about our impact on Earth: shrinking ice sheets, rising sea levels, retreating glaciers, longer droughts, bigger hurricanes, tornado wildfires, ocean plastic, and endangered species. Naturally children will always need books that nurture their hearts and imaginations, but young people growing up in the Anthropocene are asking, "Where *are* the wild things?" Sixty percent of mammals, birds, fish, and reptiles have been wiped out since *The Lorax* was published. Brave, imaginative, and scientifically literate writers like Lloyd are responding with powerful new storytelling.

We walk through a grove of oaks with canopies like enormous parasols. "*Shhh,*" Lloyd whispers, looking up. Blue tits, coal tits, and robins pirouette between the lacework of branches, plucking seeds and insects and emitting crystalline whistles and chirps. "If you listen," she says, "there are lots of conversations going on around us now. You can think about the voices of the birds and right now they are giving companion calls. Right now, they are saying, 'Hey! I'm okay. You okay?' 'I'm okay.' 'You okay?' This is considered baseline and it means all is peaceful here."

We listen to this tree music for a long time. After a while, we turn back toward the open meadows where Lloyd's bulldog Lola is tearing through grass. I can't shake the image of the crow funeral. I think for a moment how Lloyd and other intrepid female cli-fi writers—Edan

Lepucki, Claire Vaye Watkins, Nnedi Okorafor—are like these crows lamenting the black wing of nature lying in the grass, calling out as messengers between two worlds: "All is not well. All is not well . . . "

Over tea and Italian biscuits back at her house, Lloyd shows me a solar oven in her yard. She describes her next book, too—a science fiction fable. The lead character is a talking stick bug named Stacy Blumenthal, who is trapped in a biodome with a cast of other non-human characters. The biodome is heating, and their quest is to work together to find a solution. I laugh so hard at her description that tears run down my face.

She has offered to give me a ride to the nearby Tube station in her new hybrid van—a vehicle, she tells me, that will soon be wrapped in vinyl to resemble a spaceship. I imagine it will be a whimsical mash-up of *Galaxy Quest*, the science fiction action-comedy film, with a serious environmental message. "Yes!" she says. She plans to maneuver her spaceship through the streets of London for workshops on climate change and the impact of environmental inaction.

"It's going to be called *Earthship II: No More Passengers, Only Crew*. Of course, I would love to be played by Sigourney Weaver, but the sad truth is I'm Doctor Lazarus. I am just glad it's taking a while for the vinyl to come in because it's given me time to practice driving. Honestly, who wants to be slow reversing a spaceship in public?"

MORE CLI-FI

The Completionist (2018) by Siobhan Adcock

Disasters in the First World (2017) by Olivia Clare

Future Home of the Living God (2017) by Louise Erdrich

The Broken Earth Series (2015–17) by N. K. Jemisin

Flight Behavior (2012) by Barbara Kingsolver

California (2014) by Edan Lepucki

The Honey Farm (2018) by Harriet Alida Lye

Who Fears Death (2010) by Nnedi Okorafor

The Collapse of Western Civilization: A View from the Future (2014) by Naomi Oreskes and Erik M. Conway

South Pole Station (2017) by Ashley Shelby

Station Eleven (2014) by Emily St. John Mandel

Gold Fame Citrus (2015) by Claire Vaye Watkins

A Catalogue of Sunlight at the End of the World (2017) by A. C. Wise

ANDREA WULF

I am not a typical nature writer. In nature writing, you allow yourself to be in the writing. Maybe it's because I am German, and Germans like their academic non-fiction, but I just don't like using the word "I." In fact, "nature writer" doesn't even exist as a category in German. It doesn't translate.

IN CONVERSATION, JULY 2018

N THE SHIFTING LIGHT of the garden courtyard, Andrea Wulf and I are surrounded by purple *Verbena bonariensis* and old-fashioned violets. I take note of them and wonder if, like me, Andrea is thinking of the horticultural backstories and the driven nurserymen or swashbuckling plant hunters behind these flowers. She and I belong to a small club of people who think of gardens as cultural artifacts—she as a design historian, I as a garden historian—and long before we meet for this summer lunch in London, I have admired how she tells horticultural and natural history through narrative nonfiction.

Through vivid scene-making and extensive research, her five books read like adventure novels that immerse readers in the past. We travel to the tops of mountains for extraordinary moments of discovery and into quiet greenhouses where new plants are cultivated. Over coffee, the two of us discuss the way her primary source research, including original letters, manuscripts, books, and travel to original sites, creates unforgettable scenes. "I might have become a painter had I not become a writer," she explains, in a light, German-inflected accent. "When I am writing, I often close my eyes and walk through landscapes in my mind."

Experiencing different landscapes has long been part of her life. Born in India and raised in Germany, Wulf was a student of applied cultural studies at the Leuphana University of Lüneburg and design history at the Royal College of Art in London. After moving to England, she was drawn to narrative nonfiction and the range of techniques it borrows from fiction to make conventional nonfiction come alive—enhanced sense of place, dialogue, enriched language, flexible time structures, more detailed characterization, and first-person narration. On one end of this narrative spectrum lies memoir: authors fully immerse themselves as subjects in the story—think Gene Stratton-Porter's birding books and Vita Sackville-West's garden writing. On the other end is literary journalism: authors report on events—think Susan Fenimore Cooper's diary of Cooperstown and Rachel Carson's environmental investigations. Whether because she is a German historian or because nature writing isn't part of her cultural tradition, Wulf prefers literary reportage to first-person narrative.

Her first three books—*This Other Eden: Seven Great Gardens and 300 Years of English History* (2005), *The Brother Gardeners: Botany, Empire and the Birth of an Obsession* (2008), and *The Founding Gardeners: The Revolutionary Generation, Nature, and the Shaping of the American Nation* (2011)—emerged from her interest in the Enlightenment, that intellectual movement of the late seventeenth and early eighteenth centuries to which all the writers in this book are, to some degree, reacting. "The Enlightenment is the moment," Wulf said, "when we became the modern human that we are today. We moved away from the belief that the world was just a divine clockwork, to the elevation of reason as the faculty to make sense of it all, to focusing on the self as the veil through which we see the world."

In *The Brother Gardeners*, Wulf explores how England became a nation of gardeners through the achievements of a dedicated group of men with green thumbs, business acumen, and botanical wanderlust. Gardens are no different from architecture, literature, and music—they are mirrors of society. During the Enlightenment, dreary plots devoid of flowers half the year grew to be "gardens of the world" filled with exotic specimens collected by intrepid plant hunters. In the book's opening, it's the summer of 1716, and we are in the potting shed of Thomas Fairchild, leading English nurseryman of the day. We peer over his shoulder as he gently brushes a feather across sweet William then draws its tip across a carnation pink. He is creating the world's first man-made hybrid, *Dianthus caryophyllus* × *D. barbatus*, known today as "Fairchild's Mule." In another scene, we step aboard the ship *Endeavour* during the extraordinary South Pacific and Australian adventures of Swedish scientist Daniel Solander and English botanist Joseph Banks. We feel invested in the relationship between English merchant Peter Collinson and American botanist John Bartram as they worked together for decades as plant exporter and importer. *The Brother Gardeners* illuminates how much of our modern gardens are living legacies, pulsating with with extraordinary human stories.

Wulf's third garden history book, *The Founding Gardeners,* is an eloquent ecological and historical narrative that situates in time the botanical passions of the first four US presidents—Washington, Adams, Jefferson, and Madison. Their private gardens, farms, and forests reflected their unique vision for colonial self-sufficiency and an independent New World republic. Wulf constructs an inclusive narrative of all people working the land, one that addresses the institution of slavery in the creation of Southern estates and plantations—including a particular freezing winter day when Washington's enslaved workers created an arboretum for him by transplanting trees from a nearby woodland in the dead of winter. In the chapter "Tho' an old man, I am but a young gardener," Wulf captures how Jefferson longed for the refuge of his gardens at Monticello as he rode home after declining to run for a third presidential term.

A lone rider battled through a fierce snowstorm in the foothills of Virginia's Blue Ridge Mountains. The snow was so deep that the roads were almost impassable, and for the last seven hours an ice-cold wind had cut through the rider's heavy coat. It was mid-March 1809, but instead of the first green flush of spring the forests were hidden under a stark white blanket, while the layers of mountain ridges had all but disappeared in the hypnotizing dance of light flakes. The traveler was sixty-five-year-old Thomas Jefferson, who had left Washington four days earlier after James Madison's inauguration as the fourth president of the United States. Seventy miles into his journey home he had overtaken his estate manager, Edmund Bacon, who led two wagons' worth of Jefferson's belongings from the White House and one filled with shrubs from the capital's nurseries. Jefferson could have traveled the remaining fifty miles in his carriage but was anxious not to waste any more time—he had waited for this moment for so long, and a snowstorm was not going to stop him.

"Never did a prisoner, released from his chains, feel such relief as I shall on shaking off the shackles of power," claimed the third president of the United States, who had described his final years in office as "the most tedious of my life." Desperately lonely in the capital, even his daily rides in the countryside had started to bore him. Like George Washington before him, Jefferson longed to tend to his plantation and garden, and had made the decision to follow Washington's example and not run for a third term. Increasingly his letters to friends and family had mentioned this pining to return to "the enjoyments of rural life." "My views and attentions," he wrote to fellow gardener William Hamilton in Philadelphia, "are all turned homewards." He was so excited about his garden in particular, he said to Hamilton, that "the subject runs away with me whenever I get on it."

As a fan of narrative nonfiction, I ask Wulf about her writing process. She says such detailed scenes and character insights emerge from detailed book proposals, which provide "scaffolding" for the depth of storytelling. "I am not a kissed-by-the-muse kind of writer," she tells me. "I am a crafter. I go through dozens of drafts and hone until someone finally pulls the manuscript out of my hands. It is always two steps forward, one step back. I just feel that it is never done."

Chasing Venus: The Race to Measure the Heavens (2012) reflects Wulf's shift from earthly pleasures to heavenly pursuits. It's the story of how ambitious eighteenth-century scientists from Sweden, Britain, Russia, France, Germany, and the American colonies worked together to answer one of the most pressing questions of the 1700s: how far is the Earth from the sun? Scientists believed the transits of

Venus in 1761 and 1769—when our nearest planet moves across the face of the sun—held the answers. *Chasing Venus* shows how science is not an ivory tower activity but a discipline that takes place in a human and historical frame of personal journeys and great sacrifices.

The same can be said for the extraordinary life of Alexander von Humboldt, "the lost hero of science," whose daring vision of the Earth as one great living organism was as bold as the man himself. When we think of the most famous scientists, Darwin, Newton, and Einstein come to mind. Though during his life Humboldt's fame was second only to Napoleon's, until Wulf's *The Invention of Nature: Alexander von Humboldt's New World* (2015), few people today knew of Humboldt, the Prussian scientist, naturalist, and geologist whose vision of nature as interconnected has become commonplace. His philosophy so deeply influences the way we understand the natural world that the man behind the science has disappeared. Wulf's Humboldt book shot into the literary stratosphere. Reviewers everywhere tripped over themselves finding new adjectives to describe it. Best Book of the Year in 2015 for the *New York Times,* the *Atlantic,* and the *Economist.* Winner of the 2016 Costa Biography Award and the Royal Society Insight Investment Science Book Prize. Recipient of the Sigurd F. Olson Nature Writing Award and the James Wright Award for Nature Writing. A top ten bestseller in Germany for more than a year.

We learn in *The Invention of Nature* that more places and things on Earth are named after Humboldt than anyone else. Mountains, glaciers, forests. Rivers, colleges, plants. The Humboldt Current. The Humboldt squid. A giant sinkhole. And it's not limited to Earth— two asteroids bear his name, as well as a basin on the moon. "To him, everything is connected," Wulf explains to me. "Rachel Carson makes that connection with *Silent Spring* and you can only do that if you see nature as the web of life." Wulf drew on Humboldt's original letters, manuscripts, sketches, scraps of paper, and books to write as deeply about his science as his character. She slept in Venezuelan rainforests, walked around Walden Pond, and hiked in Yosemite National Park. She climbed Chimborazo in Ecuador to capture Humboldt's pivotal ascent in 1802, the moment he took everything he knew about the natural world and wove it into a cohesive vision that would change worldviews forever.

On 22 June they arrived at the foot of the volcano where they spent a fitful night in a small village. Early the next morning, Humboldt's team began the ascent together with a group of local porters. They crossed the grassy plains and slopes on mules until they reached an altitude of 13,500 feet. As the rocks became steeper, they left the animals behind and continued on foot. The weather was turning against them. It had snowed during the night and the air was cold. Unlike the previous days, the summit of Chimborazo was shrouded in fog. Once in a while, the fog lifted granting them a brief yet tantalizing glimpse of the peak. It would be a long day.

At 15,600 feet their porters refused to go on. Humboldt, Bonpland, Montúfar and José divided the instruments between them and continued on their own. The fog held Chimborazo's summit in its embrace. Soon they were crawling on all fours along a high ridge that narrowed to a dangerous two inches with steep cliffs falling away to their left and right—fittingly the Spanish called this ridge the *cuchilla*, or 'knife edge'. Humboldt looked determinedly ahead. It didn't help that the cold had numbed their hands and feet, nor that the foot that he had injured during a previous climb had become infected. Every step was leaden at this height. Nauseous and dizzy with altitude sickness, their eyes bloodshot and their gums bleeding, they suffered from a constant vertigo which, Humboldt later admitted, 'was very dangerous, given the situation we were in'. On Pichincha, Humboldt's altitude sickness had been so severe that he had fainted. Here on the *cuchilla*, it could be fatal.

Despite these difficulties, Humboldt still had the energy to set up his instruments every few hundred feet as they ascended. The icy wind had chilled the brass instruments and handling the delicate screws and levers with half-frozen hands was almost impossible. He plunged his thermometer into the ground, read the barometer and collected air samples to analyse its chemical components. He measured humidity and tested the boiling point of water at different altitudes. They also kicked boulders down the precipitous slopes to test how far they would roll.

After an hour of treacherous climbing, the ridge became a little less steep but now sharp rocks tore their shoes and their feet began to bleed. Then, suddenly, the fog lifted, revealing Chimborazo's white peak glinting in the sun, a little over 1,000 feet above them—but they also saw that their narrow ridge had ended. Instead, they were confronted by the mouth of a huge crevasse which opened in front of them. To get around it would have involved walking across a field of deep snow but by now it was 1 p.m. and the sun had melted the icy crust that covered the snow. When Montúfar gingerly tried to tread on it, he sank so deeply that he completely disappeared. There was no way to cross. As they paused, Humboldt took out the barometer again and measured their altitude at 19,413 feet. Though they wouldn't make it to the summit, it still felt like being on the top of the world. No one had ever come this high—not even the early balloonists in Europe.

Looking down Chimborazo's slopes and the mountain ranges in the distance, everything that Humboldt had seen in the previous years came together. His brother Wilhelm had long believed that Alexander's mind was made 'to connect ideas, to detect chains of things'. As he stood that day on Chimborazo, Humboldt absorbed what lay in front of him while his mind reached back to all the plants, rock formations and measurements that he had seen and taken on the slopes of the Alps, the Pyrenees and in Tenerife. Everything that he had ever observed fell into place.

Nature, Humboldt realized, was a web of life and a global force. He was, a colleague later said, the first to understand that everything was interwoven as with 'a thousand threads'. This new idea of nature was to change the way people understood the world.

Humboldt is haughty and generous, curious and cosmopolitan—a man whose personality hid personal insecurities, whose drive into nature repressed his sexual orientation, and whose lack of empathy with people blunted some relationships. "He was so curious about so many things," Wulf tells me. "He never stuck with any one idea." She discusses how Humboldt's ideas influenced other important scientists and how his observations of the Americas—slavery, environmental devastation, and colonialism—showed for the first time the severe impact Europeans had had on native populations. He was the first person to observe human-made climate change.

The summer afternoon sunlight is shifting as Andrea and I relax beside our empty coffee cups. In the murmur of modern London outside the restaurant, our conversation winds down. We look ahead to our own travel and writing projects. Andrea tells me she's finishing dialogue on a graphic novel, *The Adventures of Alexander von Humboldt* (2019). She explains that 2019 marks the 250th anniversary of Humboldt's birth. From South America to Germany, she will be speaking at celebrations around the world, reviving the important story of a great naturalist. Listening to her plans for the year, I get the feeling this might be one of the few times over the next eighteen months that she will be sitting still.

MORE TRAVEL AND NATURE WRITING

ISABELLA BIRD

Isabella Bird (1831–1904) dismissed stifling Victorian gender conventions to become a trailblazing British explorer, photographer, writer, and naturalist. It wasn't easy. From childhood, Bird suffered from numerous ailments, including a tumor removed from her back at nineteen. Her doctor's prescription? Open-air. Bird took this remedy to the next level and spent a long life taking sea voyages to lands few men, let alone women, ever visited. Her father gave her £100 in 1854 with permission to stay away from home for as long as funds lasted. Vivid letters home became her first book, *An Englishwoman in America* (1856). Though generally classified as travel writing—*Six Months Among the Palm Groves, Coral Reefs, and Volcanoes of the Sandwich Islands* (1875), *Unbeaten Tracks in Japan* (1881), *Journeys in Persia and Kurdistan* (1891), *Among the Tibetans* (1894)—Bird's books offer glimpses into the natural worlds she visited. Her most famous book was *A Lady's Life in the Rocky Mountains* (1879). Bird was a household name in the late nineteenth century and the first woman elected to the Royal Geographical Society.

ISAK DINESEN

Baroness Karen von Blixen-Finecke (1885–1962) could also be called Baroness Boss. She managed a coffee plantation in Africa. She had a love affair with English game hunter Denys Finch Hatton. She was enamored with the idea of vultures picking her remains clean when she died. She wrote her superlative and best-known work, *Out of Africa* (1937), a lyrical memoir about her life in the Ngong Hills in Kenya (then called British East Africa) from 1914 to 1931, under the pen name Isak Dinesen. The film adaptation won seven Academy Awards, but ever-Hollywood, the film focuses more on romance than the daily life Dinesen captured in her writing, including beautiful descriptions of African landscapes and dignified portraits of the people who worked on her land.

ELIZABETH DODD

"The contemporary nature writer lives not only in a different century," Dodd wrote to me, "but a different world from the one inhabited by Henry David Thoreau, Susan Fenimore Cooper, and other American forebears." Whether hiking to find ancient petroglyphs or canoeing rivers to access ancient trees, Dodd takes readers to places that invite us to consider time, place, art, legacies, and our relationships with other-than-human dimensions. She explains, "Today's nature writers can celebrate wonder or environmentalist effort on the local level, but any such writing exists within a context, whether explicitly named or not, of global threat." Her creative nonfiction books include *Horizon's Lens: My Time on the Turning World* (2012), *In the Mind's Eye: Essays Across the Animate World* (2008), and *Prospect: Journeys and Landscapes* (2003). Her poetry collections are *Archetypal Light* (2001) and *Like Memory, Caverns* (1992).

CAMILLE T. DUNGY

Outside long enough, I lose the contours of my body
and become part of something larger.

"A GOOD HIKE"

N THE TITLE POEM of Camille T. Dungy's *Trophic Cascade* (2018), the setting is Yellowstone, but the poem's rhythmic accretion of imagery puts me at the beach, watching the ocean pound the shore. Line by line, momentum builds in waves. From songbirds and birds-of-prey to new berries on brush, the reintroduction of wolves reconstructs an ecosystem like a river shapes the land, like pregnancy changes a body. A classic example of trophic cascade, the presence of the wolf, a top predator, has a ripple effect on the landscape, surprising even scientists. In the hands of a poet, this subject illuminates even greater truths.

TROPHIC CASCADE

After the reintroduction of gray wolves
to Yellowstone and, as anticipated, their culling
of deer, trees grew beyond the deer stunt
of the mid century. In their up reach
songbirds nested, who scattered
seed for underbrush, and in that cover
warrened snowshoe hare. Weasel and water shrew
returned, also vole, and came soon hawk
and falcon, bald eagle, kestrel, and with them
hawk shadow, falcon shadow. Eagle shade
and kestrel shade haunted newly-berried
runnels where mule deer no longer rummaged, cautious
as they were, now, of being surprised by wolves. Berries
brought bear, while undergrowth and willows, growing
now right down to the river, brought beavers,
who dam. Muskrats came to the dams, and tadpoles.
Came, too, the night song of the fathers
of tadpoles. With water striders, the dark
gray American dipper bobbed in fresh pools
of the river, and fish stayed, and the bear, who
fished, also culled deer fawns and to their kill scraps
came vulture and coyote, long gone in the region

until now, and their scat scattered seed, and more

trees, brush, and berries grew up along the river

that had run straight and so flooded but thus dammed,

compelled to meander, is less prone to overrun. Don't

you tell me this is not the same as my story. All this

life born from one hungry animal, this whole,

new landscape, the course of the river changed,

I know this. I reintroduced myself to myself, this time

a mother. After which, nothing was ever the same.

"Trophic Cascade" reaches its full potential when Dungy makes her personal revelation at the end. A master of poetic synthesis, she fuses fact, observation, and revelation to offer poetry's inevitable surprise: motherhood has rewilded her. Having a child has done to her inner landscape what wolves have done to Yellowstone. Making the experience of motherhood a central topic in this collection of nature writing sets Dungy apart from most of the nature-writing tradition. In her powerful parallel of the trophic cascade progression, Dungy becomes new to herself in a fierce and sweeping story of interconnection. It is a poem to be read again and again.

Throughout Dungy's fourth collection of poetry, motherhood and nature intersect. When I ask her about *Trophic Cascade*'s natural history, she tells me, "I am never not thinking about nature. Because I don't understand a way we can be honest about who we are without understanding that we *are* nature." In person at poetry readings, Dungy is as generous, attentive, and spirited as she is on paper. Her smile is warm and infectious, and her purple and pink shoe collection reflects her playful whimsy. "I was really caught by the story of the Yellowstone River and so I wrote into it, asking myself, '*Why does this matter to me?*' My daughter was three and a half at the time. Piece by piece, the poem came together. And it was as much of a revelation to me as it was to the reader." One of the last things Dungy did to the poem was to push it to the right margin, shifting from the normal way of seeing a poem and anchoring it to the page in a satisfying way. "It just felt right that way," she says.

While motherhood is a framework for seeing anew, Dungy also explores violence, joy, and environmental degradation. She writes about hiking in the Sierras while newly pregnant, the first time her baby sleeps through the night, and her daughter's first birthday—intimate moments set to the rhythms of the natural world. In "There are these moments of permission," she delicately describes how finding time for herself as a new mother is akin to the space between raindrops. Throughout the collection, her environmental imagination is cross-pollinated with gender, race, history, and the ways being an African-American woman brings an extra layer of complication to motherhood. She wonders in "Conspiracy," for example, if people think she is being "quaintly primitive" by carrying her baby on her back with a brightly patterned African cloth. She wonders if she might be mistaken for her own child's nanny. As a collection, *Trophic Cascade* draws a picture of how we protect our young and adapt to life's challenging conditions while also adjusting to losses and mourning our elders.

"I've actually gotten pushback for writing about motherhood," says Dungy, a professor of poetry at Colorado State University. This resistance comes even in light of her acclaimed body of work. She edited the highly influential *Black Nature: Four Centuries of African American Nature Poetry* (2009) and has written four volumes of poetry, including the sonnet collection *What to Eat, What to Drink, What to Leave for Poison* (2006), *Suck on the Marrow* (2010), and *Smith Blue* (2011). Her honors include an American Book Award and fellowships from the Guggenheim Foundation, the Sustainable Arts Foundation, and the National Endowment for the Arts in both prose and poetry. Her debut collection of personal essays, *Guidebook to Relative Strangers: Journeys into Race, Motherhood, and History* (2017), was nominated for the National Book Critics Circle Award in criticism. The book centers on the first three years of her daughter's life and chronicles Dungy's own journey balancing new motherhood with a demanding career of travel and teaching.

"People sometimes give a patronizing response. 'Oh, you're writing about nature?' and 'Oh, you're writing about motherhood?' as if they are sentimental topics. I have heard that dismissive tone a lot, implying that writing about nature and motherhood is a marginal cottage industry and not a serious literature topic." As she talks, I recall seeing a spate of recent articles concerning "mom books," from such publications as *Harper's*, *Slate*, the *Paris Review*, the *Los Angeles Review of Books*, and the *New York Times*, all of which declared, finally and in so many words, that motherhood is a rich life experience worth celebrating and exploring. Despite this welcome, if long-overdue pronouncement, these articles tend to be somewhat problematic themselves—penned by white authors reviewing the work of other white authors. Without poems, essays, and books from brown and black mothers, the "mom book" genre can feel like a monologue on a universal experience instead of a productive conversation.

Choosing to write about motherhood as a black woman can feel, Dungy tells me, like playing into something that has been turned against black mothers. "One of the interesting elements of writing as an African American author alongside the environmental movement is that, historically, we've been described as animals in derogatory, violent, and deeply damaging ways. And that dangerous and dominant attempt to animalize black people is something we are always pushing against. In this context, it's problematic for me to write from this motherhood perspective because I'm saying, 'Hey, I am a mammal.' That's transgressive. The way people have been made into animals against their will for the power of others is problematic." She pauses and says, "And yet, in writing, it is actually easier for me to think of myself as an animal. I have all these things in common with the greater-than-human world, and the alliances I have with plants and animals can be life-affirming and deeply beneficial."

Dungy's bold anthology *Black Nature* features nearly two hundred poems by black men and women, from eighteenth-century slave Phillis Wheatley to poet laureate Rita Dove. It challenges the notion that the tradition of nature writing is solely grounded in pastoral landscapes and Euro-American perspectives. Black writers, Dungy tells me, were writing even if they weren't being seen. The voices within the collection show nature as a source of hope with seeds of survival as well as the devastating legacy of slavery and people forced to work the land. As she writes in its introduction, the book's ten thematically organized sections "are a representative sampling of poems from each major movement in black American poetics as well as the newer poetry of contemporary poets still in the process of publishing their own collections." Some examples in the anthology show how writers have moved "beyond personal, cultural, and political struggles into spaces of deep appreciation, connection, healing, and peace," while other voices illustrate a distaste for wilderness. Take her own poem "Language" and contrast it with the tangible anger and injustice in "The Natural World" by G. E. Patterson, which is featured in *Black Nature*.

LANGUAGE *by Camille T. Dungy*

Silence is one part of speech, the war cry
of wind down a mountain pass another.
A stranger's voice echoing through lonely
valleys, a lover's voice rising so close
it's your own tongue: these are keys to cipher,
the way the high hawk's key unlocks the throat
of the sky and the coyote's yip knocks
it shut, the way the aspens' bells conform
to the breeze while the rapid's drum defines
resistance. Sage speaks with one voice, pinyon
with another. Rock, wind her hand, water
her brush, spells and then scatters her demands.
Some notes tear and pebble our paths. Some notes
gather: the bank we map our lives around.

THE NATURAL WORLD *by G. E. Patterson*

You got here trees all dappled with sunlight and shit
You got trees green with lots of leaves
You got fruit-bearing trees   made for climbing
   good for something.

I got trees too   My trees stainless steel poles
with no flags   My trees streetlights redyellowgreen
glass shattered on the ground

You got birds waking you up in the morning
Birds waking you up in the morning   TweetTweet
ChirpChirp That's how it is for y'all
                 mutherfuckers

I got birds too   My birds
loud as jackhammers   My birds
loud as police sirens   My birds
loud as gunfire   My birds
electric gas-powered

My birds   My birds killers

These kinds of contrasts, from Dungy's almost pastoral language to Patterson's young, urban African-American, male perspective, turn *Black Nature* into a mind-blowing, essential collection every aficionado of this genre should read. It is the definitive volume for appreciating the range and depth of human relationships with the natural world.

"My vision for *Black Nature* formed at the same moment the ecopoetics movement was flourishing," Dungy says. "Ecopoetics has distanced itself from the ways we have come to understand 'nature poetry' and the glorification of some beautiful space or the sense of 'I climbed the mountain and found myself.' It frequently talks about the degradation of the land and eco-justice questions, which are paired with other justice movements. Ecopoetics complicates our interconnection. It brings the Anthropocene into the ways we observe the non-human world. And therefore poetry that brings in economic and personal history while bringing the person into the nature—there is more space for that in ecopoetics. *Black Nature* landed at just the right time."

Dungy's beautiful, timely, and approachable writing awakens an inclusive sense of belonging in the world. What does she want people to get out of her poems? "Beauty and the heightened craft that comes from looking at everyday objects with respect," she tells me. "There is, for example, a difference between the crocheting we do for scarves versus for doilies. And I want people to look at that extra careful needlework that brings it from an everyday piece of needlework to heightened craft. I want people to enjoy my poems as everyday language but also to experience the extra care."

Camille T. Dungy

MORE POETRY

JANE CLARKE

"Writing is such a curious mixture of the conscious and unconscious," Irish poet Jane Clark told me, "that it's hard to fully explain either the compulsion or the process." Clarke is the author of *The River* (2015), *All the Way Home* (2019), and *When the Tree Falls* (2019)—collections of poems distilled to their essence, reticent and intimate, subtle and vivid. With a farming and psychotherapy background, Clarke feels life on the farm where she grew up gave her the imagery and language best attuned to her internal world. "I didn't choose to write 'nature poetry,' rather it chose me. There was no other way for me to express what I wanted and needed to express." Finely crafted images of natural life—drystone walls, Rhode Island Red chickens, the smell of burnt barley—are a backdrop in *The River* to convey the beauty and brutality of farming, the memories of parents, and the life of land and animals.

AIMEE NEZHUKUMATATHIL

"Poetry offers an attention to the world, to beauty, and to love," writes Nezhukumatathil. "I think that's a form of activism: inviting people in this hurting world to see animals and nature and human relationships differently, and to take refuge in beauty." Drawing upon her Filipina and Malayali Indian background, Nezhukumatathil has written numerous award-winning poetry collections, including *Oceanic* (2018), *Lucky Fish* (2011), *At the Drive-in Volcano* (2007), and *Miracle Fruit* (2003). Her poetry is playful and fun to read aloud. It tastes like ripe fruit on the tongue—and is filled with lush landscapes. With poet Ross Gay, she co-wrote the epistolary chapbook, *Lace and Pyrite: Letters from Two Gardens* (2014). She is also poetry editor at *Orion*, a leading magazine focused on nature, culture, and the environment.

JENNY JOHNSON

Jenny Johnson's debut poetry collection, *In Full Velvet* (2017), explores luxurious liminal moments of life through imagery of the natural world. An important contribution to contemporary lesbian literature, Johnson's work expands our understanding of community, diversity, identity, and the body in queer landscapes. In "Aria," as Aretha Franklin sings "You Make Me Feel Like a Natural Woman," Johnson wonders what is natural to transgender bodies. In "The Bus Ride," she captures desire and attraction: "When she turns from the window and sees me / she is as lovely as a thrush seeing for the first time all sides of the sky. / Let this be a ballet without intermission: the grace of this ride beside her / on the green vinyl, soft thunderclaps in the quarry. / Let me be her afternoon jay, hot silo, red shale crumbling–." For more on the natural world by lesbian authors, Johnson herself recommends *Strange as This Weather Has Been* (2007) by Ann Pancake, *Bestiary* (2016) by Donika Kelly, *Rocket Fantastic* (2017) by Gabrielle Calvocoressi, and *Last Psalm at Sea Level* (2014) by Meg Day.

ELENA
PASSARELLO

Of all the images that make our world, animal images are particularly buried inside us. We feel the pull of them before we know to name them, or how to even fully see them. It is as if they are always waiting, crude sketches of themselves, in the recesses of our bodies.

ANIMALS STRIKE CURIOUS POSES

T HERE IS A JOKE in Elena Passarello's 2017 virtuoso essay collection, *Animals Strike Curious Poses*, that involves nipples, pickles, peekaboo, and "Purple Rain." It's entirely drawn from the vocabulary of Koko, the western lowland gorilla who used more than one thousand words of sign language. There's the tale of Mike, the traveling headless chicken from Colorado, and the swirl of existential questions about his will to live eighteen months after he met the chopping block in 1945. There's the creative collaboration between Mozart and his starling, who in 1784 heard the maestro's Piano Concerto in G and sang it back, rearranged and improved, hesitant grace notes replaced by confident crotchets, a fermata added to the end of the first measure to add dramatic pause—all revisions Mozart retained. And there's the opening story of Yuka, the 40,000-year-old strawberry-blonde Pleistocene woolly mammoth discovered in 2010 by tusk hunters in the softening permafrost of the Siberian wilderness.

Animals Strike Curious Poses—a line borrowed from Prince's song "When Doves Cry"—examines our relationships to animals and the ways they reshape our relationship to the natural world. In each exquisite essay, some traditional, others genre-bending, a famous animal is profiled. Not knowing how Passarello will craft one essay to the next lends the reading experience an unexpected pliability, akin to attending the Edinburgh's Festival Fringe and not knowing what acts will appear on stage.

Each animal featured in this modern bestiary has been named by humans in some way. Each animal is a performer in some way, too— even the mummified mammoth, on display so long after her death. Passarello's interest in the performative nature of each animal is an extension of her ten years in regional theater and professional voice-overs prior to her second career as a writing professor at Oregon State University.

"I'm very drawn not just to human bodies in performance," Passarello tells me, about the connections between theater and writing, "but to other creatures forced to live before audiences." This theme is also seen in her wildly inventive debut essay collection, *Let Me Clear My Throat*, an exploration of vocal expression and how a few famous voices such as Marlon Brando's "Stella!" and the Wilhelm scream became cultural icons. Her own voice is distinctive, both as a writer and an actor. (Don't miss the performance that made Passarello the first woman to win the annual *Streetcar Named Desire* Stella Screaming Contest in New Orleans.) She explains, "My interest in (or receptiveness to) changing the form, voice, and mode of each essay that I write, rather than honing a signature style, probably comes from theater as well. As an actor, you change nearly everything about your presentation as you move from role to role. Over the course of a year's worth of jobs, your entire universe reboots several times over." As droll and witty in person as on paper, Passarello is a virtuoso essayist known for her highly researched pieces, which have earned her much praise, including the prestigious Whiting Award for Nonfiction, a grant intended to help emerging writers focus on writing full-time.

Animals Strike Curious Poses is the best book on animals I have read. It's also hilarious. I'm talking laugh-out-loud, alarm-other-patrons-in-the-cafe level humor. Passarello's writing is playful, and a tender poignancy underlies each story. Her work reflects a depth of empathy that may be related to her ability to inhabit different characters on stage, and her spirited style reminds me of what Ellen Meloy once wrote: "A great deal of nature writing sounds like a cross between a chloroform stupor and a high mass." Not in this menagerie. Most of Passarello's essays face outward, but in one of the few personal memoir pieces, she reflects upon her childhood memories of "Lancelot the Living Unicorn."

That same year as the Humphrey story and the zoo camp, my grandparents took me to the Ringling Brothers and Barnum

& Bailey Circus. This was their year of Lancelot—"the Living Unicorn," as he was billed on the 1985 souvenir program. I bought the program with three dollars of my own money and, after the circus, thumbed through it for weeks until the glossy pages fell to pieces. It said the Living Unicorn had just wandered into the big top one day the previous year, provenance unknown. Lancelot was ageless; there were no facts to weight him down other than the fact that, according to the program, he ate rose petals for dinner. In the full-color photographs, he usually stood next to a spangly, Miss-America-cute woman, his long white hair—not so much a mane as a suit of poodle curls—gleaming and very possibly permed.

The horn at the top of his head was prodigious: twice as thick as that of the title character in *The Last Unicorn*. It was also covered in opalescent pink paint, trunking up from Lancelot's forehead in a glittery shaft. In one photograph, he appeared with two children about my age. The blond boy in the photo smiled out toward the photographer, but the little girl next to Lancelot stared right at the unicorn with unabashed awe, like she'd forgotten all about the person taking her picture. Lancelot himself gazed into the middle distance, looking like a little, white Rick James. Who knows what he was thinking.

The program also featured a pullout poster that I taped to my closet door. It was a Lisa Frank–style portrait of Lancelot in a hot pink frame, above the caption "I Saw the Living Unicorn!" I'm not certain how many differences I noticed, back then, between the illustrated poster unicorn and the photographed one. But now, it's obvious that the drawn unicorn is horsier, with a straight-up mane, a fuller muzzle, and a longer, broader neck. The eyes are much less hircine, and they stare straight into the viewer.

At the circus, Lancelot didn't gallop in; he rode. His entrance was on a hydraulic float trimmed in Grecian curlicues, with a curved dais at the top of it, slathered in gold paint. On the dais was a waving handler, dressed sort of like Glinda the Good Witch, who stood beside Lancelot. The unicorn himself had a tiny gold pedestal atop the dais, on which he could only arrange his two front feet.

A follow spot stuck to the vehicle as it zoomed around the ring; Lancelot stood erect, but sort of jostled in the motion of the float. Schmaltzy orchestral music boomed from the Civic Center speakers. From my seat, Lancelot was little more than a white furry blob. But when his shellacked horn, firm and proud on his cranium, caught the spotlight, everyone around me inhaled. He was much smaller than a horse—maybe pony-sized—which, being small myself, I found exciting.

I now wonder why the circus didn't just strap a horn to an actual pony. They could have easily used showbiz magic to sell that trick from an arena-sized distance. But the circus was working a different angle with this critter that, even from yards away, was no horned horse. Perhaps they needed a horn that would look more legitimately rooted in photo close-ups. They knew I would obsess over that program, so they wanted a unicorn that would read biologically true at home, away from the smoke and spotlight. But I think it's more likely that they wanted to surprise us over anything else, even if that surprise involved a ridiculous specimen. It's brilliant circus logic: that this jarring, not-horse-body was so weird, it would make sense when you learned it subsisted on flower petals. In other words, the circus hoped the more unnatural Lancelot looked, the happier I'd be.

This philosophical concern for the ways we humans need and use—as well as misuse—animals runs through the collection. Was the intention to form a larger meditation? "Yes," Passarello tells me in conversation. "In order for all that to work, a collection's overall subject needs to be nimble, layered, and open to multiple approaches. Animals, with their consistent presence throughout human culture, had that kind of potential." She modeled this on the bestiaries of medieval Europe, which added the restriction that she couldn't have multiple essays on the same species. "Like a bestiary," she continues, "I made sure each essay was a mix of both biological fact and the 'facts' of a particular human's or group of humans' imagination. I tried to make a series of wild essays that built a portrait of humankind looking at animals for the past thirty-nine millennia."

"I'm as likely to write about the social practices of birdwatchers as I am the birds they seek," Passarello says of her fascination with the nature of human thought and obsession, be it a song, a speech, or a salamander. When I ask her about her next steps, she says, "I'm challenging myself in two ways. I want to try to make a book-length work, rather than a collection. I also would like to try to *do* some kind of task or attempt a trade that I have no business attempting, in hopes of writing a sort of George Plimpton–esque memoir of failure. The thing I do will probably involve performance."

Whatever her next project, I know it will be exquisite in construction, rich in research, and strong in voice. *Encore!*

MORE ANIMAL LIFE

BRENDA PETERSON

Peterson is a memoirist, novelist, and nature writer in the Puget Sound area who has authored twenty books, many reflecting her interest in the relationship between humans and animals, including *Living by Water: True Stories of Nature and Spirit* (1990), *Build Me an Ark: A Life with Animals* (2001), and *Wolf Nation: The Life, Death, and Return of Wild American Wolves* (2017). Her anthology *Intimate Nature: The Bond Between Women and Animals* (1998), co-edited by Linda Hogan and Deena Metzger, features original stories, essays, and poems by female nature writers and scientists.

MIRIAM DARLINGTON

Written with a delightful, self-deprecating sense of humor, *Otter Country* (2012) chronicles Darlington's search for and encounters with Britain's sleek and whiskered wild otter. In similar terrain, *Owl Sense* (2018) records Darlington's second wild-animal quest—this time to see all thirteen native owl species in Europe. Among other exciting journeys, readers travel with Darlington to Finland to find the eagle owl and to Serbia to sight the long-eared owl.

JENNIFER ACKERMAN

Author of seven books on science, nature, and human biology, Ackerman travels around the world to report, in highly entertaining ways, on cutting-edge research and shifts our understanding of what it really means to have a bird brain. *The Genius of Birds* (2016) was described by *Scientific American* as a "lyrical testimony to the wonders of avian intelligence."

AMY LIPTROT

I've swapped disco lights for celestial lights but
I'm still surrounded by dancers. I am orbited by
sixty-seven moons.

THE OUTRUN

A FTER YEARS OF HEDONISM and drowning in booze in London, Amy Liptrot washed ashore on her native Orkney Islands in Scotland. The journey back to the northern landscape and sheep farm where she was raised was intentional—a deliberate way to curate her inner life and recover her own self. She traded living on the edge in London for living on another edge, the far north of Scotland, an experience she captured in her raw and glistening debut memoir, *The Outrun*, winner of the Wainwright Prize for best nature, travel, and outdoor writing in Britain in 2016.

Liptrot's celebrated book is both a modern recovery story and classic nature writing—a celebration of a particular place and the search for how best to live in the world. In unflinching detail, she captures her lost and difficult years adrift in London—a blur of drunkenness, vomit, assaults, and sexual encounters, as well as lost jobs, lost boyfriends, and lost friends. Hitting rock bottom prompted her to change and enter rehab. The move back home helps her pinpoint the root cause of her addiction and shields her from the people and places that interrupt her sobriety.

The best nature writing shows close, repeated observations of patterns and rhythms in the natural world. Liptrot's first step toward healing is grounded in deep symbolism: rebuilding the drystone dykes that have crumbled on her family's farm. Hands on stones, the repetitious work slows her, roots her, and shifts her thinking from the days and months of her own life to decades and centuries beyond herself. By slowing down, she is able to observe her personal geography. She thinks of the original fence builders while meditating on permanence and works toward fencing off her past and moving into the future to, as she writes, "see if these forces will weave me down, like coping stones, and stop the jolting."

I'm repairing these dykes at the same time as I'm putting myself back together. I am building my defences, and each time I don't take a drink when I feel like it, I am strengthening new pathways in my brain. I have to break the walls down a bit more before I can start to build them up again. I have to work with the stones I've got and can't spend too long worrying if I'm making the perfect wall. I just have to get on with placing stones.

Stone by stone, day by day, season by season, Liptrot harnesses the therapeutic powers of the islands to do something extraordinary—construct a new inner landscape. Physically removed from her previous life, the fresh air and open sky of the Orkneys are palliatives and clarifiers that give her the space and simplicity to create a healthy mental map. While reading, I wondered if isolation in the far north would help or hinder her sobriety, but in gritty and graceful prose, Liptrot slowly recovers herself under the night sky, in the sea, and among wildlife. As a reader, I rooted for her to drink in the wisdom of the world where she now lived.

And she does. Exquisitely. She reflects upon tides, swims in the icy sea, tracks puffins and terns, and learns island folklore, rural traditions, and constellations. Stripping down to an elemental existence—cloud-spotting, bird-watching, lambing—she begins to see herself and her remote surroundings anew. "My center of gravity has moved north," she writes. Becoming a nighttime "corncrake wife," which involves counting rare corncrakes for the Royal Society for the Protection of Birds, also offers her a new kind of nightlife, one that invites mindful parallels between herself and the plight of the bird.

Since before I started the job, I've been reading *Moby-Dick*. I've been reading it for so long it feels like I've been on a three-year round-the-world whaling trip, carrying it back and forth every day, hefty in my shoulder bag, like a harpoon. I'm storm-crazed Captain Ahab, but instead of a whale I'm chasing an elusive bird. Although I've heard almost thirty males, I still haven't seen one. The corncrake is always just beyond me.

On tough nights, I start to ask myself questions. Why save this bird, a bird seldom seen, a relic from the crofting times, a bird unable to adapt to modern land use? What difference does it make? And then I learn that, in 1977, corncrake remains were excavated from the Pictish and Viking Age site in Buckquoy, in Orkney's West Mainland. It shocks me to discover that corncrakes had been here for thousands of years, yet in less than a century we have all but wiped them out. Their decline is undoubtedly down to human activity so it seems right that we should take responsibility to conserve the last few.

An isolated male, perhaps the only corncrake on his island, calls for three, four, five hours a night for months. One was heard calling on Flotta all summer, and I am delighted to learn that chicks were seen at the end of the season—he found a mate, after all.

I reach a total of thirty-two calling corncrakes heard in Orkney during the season, just one more than last year. Each male that calls from the same spot for more than a few days is assumed to be accompanied by a female. Although numbers still remain low, since RSPB's Corncrake Initiative has been running, there has been a slight upward trend in Orkney. Unlike the fabled drowning sailors, the corncrakes are struggling against death and somehow it is as if my fate becomes intertwined with that of the bird. I'm trying to cling to a normal life and stay sober. They are clinging to existence.

My friend told me about when her mother died, leaving behind a husband and three young children. The family went on holiday in America, and my friend described her dad as 'just driving'. You might feel that you can't go on, yet you do, just driving to give yourself something to do while things settle, shift and gain form, until the way that life is going to be makes itself clear. I'm driving on, one-kilometre grid square by one-kilometre grid square. Imperceptibly, the churning in my chest is subsiding. Like when I cycled at night in London, I find relief by being in motion. One night, I realise I'm feeling easier and more normal, even lucky to live and work here in Orkney.

This is a different kind of nightlife. The life I had in the city—parties and clubs—is no longer there for me but these never-nights, marking off grid references and following maps in the mist, they are my own. I've found no corncrakes tonight but dawn is coming. I've got a flask of coffee and I can hear seals.

There are wonderful moments. I make eye contact with a short-eared owl, plentiful this year and known locally as 'catty faces'. It's on a fence post next to where I park, and we both turn our heads and see each other. I gasp, the owl flies. One still-pink dawn, just before midsummer, I stop at the Ring of Brodgar on the way home. There's no one around, and I take all my clothes off and run around the Neolithic stone circle.

Then, just after three a.m., when I finish my survey one night towards the end of the seven weeks, I pull away slowly in the car and something unexpected happens: I see a corncrake. It's just a moment but it's in the road right in front of me, running into the grass verge. Its image—the pink beak and ginger wing—keeps darting through my mind: just a second that confirmed the existence I'd spent months searching for. My first and only corncrake. Usually dawn comes slowly but tonight I drive out of a cloud and suddenly it's a new day.

The Outrun is one of the latest shimmering reminders of nature's palliative powers for people across ages, cultures, and geographies. It follows the tradition of Ehrlich's *The Solace of Open Spaces*, Silko's *Ceremony*, and Oliver's poetry. Liptrot's immersion in the elements of Orkney shows how slow, repeated contact with the natural world can help us see our place in the family of things. Her book reflects recent research in psychology, epidemiology, urban design, medicine, and the restorative effects of open, undeveloped natural spaces—parks, forests, river corridors, beaches, fields—on health.

An often-quoted 1984 study showed that patients in hospital rooms with a view of trees had shorter hospitalizations, less need for pain medication, and fewer negative comments in nurse's notes compared to patients with views of brick walls. We are meant to be in nature—even a picture of a tree can have a restorative effect on our minds. Nature offers hope. Nature offers renewal. Close contact with nature can rewrite our inner geographies and save lives.

"A book ends," Liptrot has said in the years since *The Outrun* was published, "but life continues—I wrote a book about my mental wobbliness and my recovery, and those things don't end. You realize that things are ongoing and relentless, and just to keep writing it."

MORE RECOVERY NARRATIVES

SUE HUBBELL

At the age of fifty, Sue Hubbell (1935–2018) was divorced, in debt, and in charge of 300 beehives. She began writing to supplement her income and became the author of eight books including *A Country Year: Living the Questions* (1986) and *A Book of Bees: And How to Keep Them* (1988). A former librarian, she wrote personal essays about life transitions and the new gender roles farm work required. "My bees cover one thousand square miles of land that I do not own in their foraging flights," she wrote in *A Country Year*, "flying from flower to flower for which I pay no rent, stealing nectar but pollinating plants in return. It is an unruly, benign kind of agriculture, and making a living by it has such a wild, anarchistic, raffish appeal that it unsuits me for any other, except possibly robbing banks."

OLIVIA LAING

More than sixty years after Virginia Woolf drowned herself in the Ouse, Laing set out on a midsummer meander along the 42-mile length of that Sussex river. In *To the River: A Journey Beneath the Surface* (2011), she memorably reflects upon Woolf's life and her own relationships to history, memory, and place. The journey is meditative, melancholic, and metaphoric—as the river clarifies and redirects her thoughts from the personal to the universal.

JESSICA LEE

A Canadian of Welsh and Chinese ancestry, Lee is an emerging nature writer. Her debut, *Turning: A Swimming Memoir* (2017), blends memoir and nature writing as she attempts to swim fifty-two lakes in fifty-two weeks as a cure for heartbreak. The founder and editor of *Willowherb Review*, a literary magazine that aims to promote diversity in nature writing, she has a PhD in environmental history and aesthetics and lives in Berlin.

ELIZABETH RUSH

I suspect fewer people will resist the term "climate change" not just when the floodwaters arrive at their doorsteps but also when they get to tell their stories and sense that they have been heard. When the words they alight upon, excavate, and share become part of the vernacular we use to describe these uncanny and improbable days, *that* is when this phenomenon will become more than a catalyst for cataclysm.

RISING

T
HE VERY WEEK Elizabeth Rush's book *Rising: Dispatches from the New American Shore* (2018) arrived in the post, my brother's home in Northern California burned to the ground. Under orange, apocalyptic skies, Tony and his wife, Julia, grabbed important documents, ordered their teenagers into cars, and sped downhill through pine, madrone, and manzanita—by day's end, the forest would be a charred no-man's land. People died. Cars melted. Even the dirt burned. Homemade quilts, handwritten letters, and hope chests turned to ash and blew around Mount Shasta and beyond. A week later, the family returned to find only a hoe and a spade hanging unscathed in a metal garden shed.

Fire, burning. Water, rising. Feathers from the same bird.

That strange and unsettled week, as we witnessed firsthand these changes of the Anthropocene, I began to think of rising seas as slow diseases and wildfires as quick, brutal stabs. Different afflictions, equally fatal.

Two hundred years ago, Dorothy Wordsworth was chastised by relatives for taking long moonlight walks alone. Now look at where we walk and what we write about. In *Rising*, Elizabeth Rush strides along American coastlines on the other side of the Industrial Revolution to report on the most pressing issue of our day: climate change. Winner of the 2018 National Outdoor Book Award in natural history, *Rising* combines the best of lyrical nature writing and science journalism to turn an oft-politicized issue into an accessible human story. A professor of creative nonfiction at Brown University, Rush is part of a generation that simply accepts climate change as reality. She knows from experience how rising sea levels are transforming coastal communities throughout the world. Her work does something that other superb writing on climate change does not— it brings poetic feeling and a personal narrative to the subject. And her warm and informed presence is felt in the opening pages, where she encounters tupelos—dead due to saline inundation—and urges us to remember their names.

Whenever I can, I pull away from my computer screen and ride back out to Jacob's Point. There I wander in a landscape we do not yet have a name for, a marsh inundated by too much of the very thing that shaped it. I have read about the disappearance of tree frogs in Panama, the droughts scraping across Kenya, the heat waves killing thousands in Paris and Andhra Pradesh and Chicago and Dhaka and São Paulo. I have written about communities affected by sea level rise. But *my* life has seemed so removed, so buffered from those events.

At Jacob's Point I am finally glimpsing the hem of the specter's dressing gown. The tupelos, the dead tupelos that line the edge of this disappearing marshland, are my Delphi, my portal, my proof, the stone I pick up and drop in my pocket to remember. I see them and know that the erosion of species, of land, and, if we are not careful, of the very words we use to name the plants and animals that are disappearing is not a political lever or a fever dream. I see them and remember that those who live on the margins of our society are the most vulnerable, and that the story of species vanishing is repeating itself in nearly every borderland.

In a hundred years none of these trees will be here. No object thick with pitch to make the mind recollect. And if we do not call them by their names we will lose not only the trees themselves but also all trace of their having ever been. Looking at the bare tupelos at the farthest edge of Jacob's Point, I am reminded of something John Bear Mitchell said when my students asked him how the Penobscot people of Maine have responded to centuries of environmental change. "Our ceremonies and language still include the caribou, even though they don't live here anymore. . . . The change is in how we acknowledge them." His response surprised my students. He seemed to be saying: learn the names now, and you will at least be able to preserve what is being threatened in our collective memory, if not in the physical world. His faith in language clearly eclipsed their own.

And then there is the pleasure in it. I like my excursions best when I am alone. Waking early to ride to a slender little marsh that most overlook. The wild blackberries, ripe from summer heat, seemingly fruiting just for me. The black needlerush dried in logarithmic spirals, and patches of salt marsh cordgrass that look like jackstraws and blowdowns in an aging forest. Both bearing the delicate trace of the last outgoing tide.

Beyond the stand of tupelos, the marsh still hums with the low-grade sound of honeybees hunting in loosestrife. The ospreys cast their creosote shadows over cicadas and lamb's-quarters and bayberry. This tiny journey into the marsh feels like a grand field trip. Mud snails wrestle in the ebb tide, a great egret hunches at the far horizon scanning for mummichogs, and the sea balm rushes through the tree of heaven. I walk out only a fifth of a mile farther than most people go, and yet there is so much happening, so many unexpected gifts and self-made surprises.

Dropping down, I arrive at the water's edge. I pull on my bathing suit and dive into the bay, but not before stubbing my toe on a barnacle-covered rock submerged just beneath the surface. I care intensely about being here, about coming back alone and often, and I don't really understand why.

Sometimes the key arrives before the lock.

Sometimes the password arrives before the impasse.

Speak it and enter a world transformed by salt and blue.

Say: *tupelo.*

Rush weaves testimonials into her personal essays like willow branches in the hands of a basketmaker, to give those most impacted by rising seas the opportunity to speak for themselves. Walking coastlines in Louisiana, Rhode Island, Maine, Florida, California, and Oregon, she gathers stories from people living and working on the front lines. "In my mind," she has said, "writing and reporting about people—especially vulnerable ones—is an act of empathy." Rush made a deliberate decision to put at the heart of her book stories of everyday people whose lives and livelihoods are being fundamentally reshaped by climate change. "Every human being has the ability to tell a story and to make sense of the world around them with storytelling," she has said.

Anecdote has no place in formal scientific papers, but climate change becomes a more compelling subject when personal story-telling is allowed to illustrate how the abstract concept forcefully impacts real people. In *Rising*, science and data are given faces and narratives. "One of my goals," Rush said in a talk, "was to step out-side of the traditional climate change discourse—to not use jargon like 'parts per million' to make my point—but instead focus on the emotional impact of our changing world, to show what it's like to watch the land where you have made your life slowly disappear beneath higher tides and stronger storms."

In vital ways, *Rising* probes how environmental issues intersect with class and race. By integrating stories of vulnerable communities on the margins of the land and of society, Rush makes environmental justice central to the climate conversation and advocates for voices that often go ignored. She cautions that people who live in and on wetlands "are often, though not always, lower income or people of color—indigenous peoples, blacks, Hispanics, recent immigrants—and they are not getting multi-million-dollar infrastructure design solutions to help them adapt to climate change." Sea level rise is deepening social problems and class differences, and in many places these preexisting structural inequalities will determine which com-munities profit or lose, escape or suffer, as issues go unaddressed. In a polyphonic approach inspired by Svetlana Alexievich's *Voices from Chernobyl: The Oral History of a Nuclear Disaster* (1997), Rush includes firsthand accounts like that of Marilynn Wiggins of Pensacola, Florida, who lays bare the reality of environmental injus-tice based on race and place:

We're flooding worse now, but girl, the flooding has always been bad. And because we're a black neighborhood the city doesn't pay us no mind. Any house that sits on the ground, that's on slab, those people flood out all the time. We're surrounded by water. The Gulf of Mexico is right there and we've got the rainwater coming at us from the other side. A long time ago, I hear this was a wetland. Back when I was younger I used to drive school buses for a living and there were many mornings that I couldn't get to my bus because the floodwater was so high. I would walk out my front door and the water would hit me at my waist.

Plus on top of it all we had the old sewage treatment plant down here and the mosquito control plant. They were handing out poison. I mean they made high-powered chemicals right around the corner. There were toxins in the soil and underground at Corrine Jones Park, right here on Intendencia Street. So the people who owned the mosquito plant had to pay $250,000 to the park. Some of the nearby residents were complaining, saying, "How's it possible for the poisonous chemicals to travel from the old plant across the street to the park without our homes being affected?" But we haven't been able to get Ashton Hayward, the mayor of Pensacola, to come see what is actually going on out here. My neighbors next door complain that they have black dust coming out of their faucet. But we haven't heard from the people who test the water yet. It seems like I'm always waiting for someone to get back to me.

Back in 2014, the flooding was very serious. My house is six or seven feet higher than my neighbors', and even so the porch was ripped off. But next door, I tell you, the ones with the half-dead cypress out back, they were flooded *out*. The water went into all those cottages and halfway houses and those people lost everything they had. Many of them just left. The worst part is that when there's a great flood you can still smell the sewage—you would think that the plant was still up and running. But it's not. It closed after Hurricane Ivan.

Across Pensacola, in a lot of black and minority neighborhoods, they're placing retention ponds to try to control, at least a little, the water that's here. But you have to remember that these retention ponds are also a concern for a lot of residents. When they replace the parks where the kids used to play, it can be devastating. Of course the retention pond is needed but it was needed forty years ago. Where were they forty years ago? Can someone answer me that?

With this conversational and confessional dynamic, Rush invites us to interrogate our own understanding of how a warming planet, melting ice, and rising seas impact the lives of real people.

Rush is also giving the melting ice itself a voice. In 2019, she was the Antarctic artist and writer-in-residence for the National Science Foundation and joined scientists from the United States and Great Britain for a fifty-day scientific "cruise" to the Thwaites Glacier. The International Thwaites Collaboration aims to investigate the unstable glacier's current and past behavior to better understand when it might collapse and the effect it will have on future sea level rise. Rush tells me her next book will weave together what she's learned through this experience with meditations on motherhood.

In the meantime, she writes essays like "Atlas with Shifting Edges," in which she travels the West Coast on a book tour for *Rising* and must calculate "the carbon cost of running up the coast to promote [her] book on climate change." As fire season hits the region where my brother lives and the air she drives through grows thick with smoke, Rush listens to the stories of friends and strangers and admits, "The more floods and wildfires I hear about, the more hours I spend at the edge where water and land meet, the less inclined I am toward linearity, toward the idea that all of this loss will inevitably deliver us to some already determined future, where loss is all there is. . . . Together we watch the water's edge wobble. We wonder what to call the feeling of losing the places that shaped us, a word for the way our very lives drive them further and further into the past."

Whatever that word is, and however devastating, naming and knowing can help prevent these afflictions from becoming fatal.

Elizabeth Rush

ELIZABETH KOLBERT

Kolbert is an American environmental journalist best known for her Pulitzer Prize–winning books *The Sixth Extinction: An Unnatural History* (2014) and *Field Notes from a Catastrophe: Man, Nature, and Climate Change* (2006). Both books combine superb field reporting on and analysis of the effects of humans on the planet.

KATHARINE HAYHOE

A Canadian atmospheric scientist and professor of political science, Hayhoe has won numerous prizes for her scientific communications including the Stephen H. Schneider Award in 2018. She is well-known for her book *A Climate for Change: Global Warming Facts for Faith-Based Decisions* (2009) co-written with Andrew Farley. The book explains the science of global warming, the impact of humans on climate, and the role the Christian faith plays in the issue.

NAOMI ORESKES

Oreskes is an American historian of science at Harvard University. She has written six books, including *Merchants of Doubt: How a Handful of Scientists Obscured the Truth on Issues from Tobacco Smoke to Global Warming* (2010) and *The Collapse of Western Civilization: A View from the Future* (2014). Both are co-authored with Erik M. Conway. In the first, a work of nonfiction, she and Conway explain how a group of politically connected "experts" ran campaigns to discredit the sound research of actual climate scientists. The second is a book of science-based fiction, set in the year 2393. This is the year of the Great Collapse, a dramatization based on facts and scientific projections of what could happen to civilization with continued soaring temperatures, rising sea levels, widespread drought, and disintegration of the West Antarctic Ice Sheet.

AFTERWORD

A PECULIAR THING HAPPENED while writing this book. I felt time compress: the past, present, and future all in dialogue with each other. As my knowledge of these poets, ramblers, and mavericks deepened, and I read their thoughts and feelings about the natural world, the writing process became a time warp. I imagined them gathered in coffee shops, gardens, and meadows, all conversing—Mary Austin listening intently to Leslie Marmon Silko's stories of Southwest indigenous peoples, and Carolyn Merchant fascinated, as a historian, with how Dorothy Wordsworth perceived the world. I imagined Gene Stratton-Porter heartily laughing at Elena Passarello's humorous bird stories. And I wanted to listen in on Lauret Savoy talking science with an intent Susan Fenimore Cooper.

In the two centuries that separate the writings of our first and last writers, a new climate has emerged. The physical world is warmer and less wild. The cultural world is more inclusive and empowering. In this span of time, women have taken ownership of our own narratives by stepping in front of the anonymous moniker "By A Lady" to proudly use our names, dismissing male chaperones to take a walk on our own, thank you very much. Though this freedom unfortunately does not yet extend to women the world over, the tradition of predominantly American and British nature writing provides a special prism through which to measure not just women's progress in Western society but also momentous global changes in the natural world.

New voices are emerging. In the words of Ursula Le Guin, "We will be wanting the voices of writers who can see alternatives to how we live now and can see through our fear-stricken society and its obsessive technologies, to other ways of being. And even imagine some real grounds for hope." From instilling this hope to warning us of the consequences of our inactions, and from offering poetic and spiritual expression to offering alternative realities, nature writing is a genre like no other, one women have used and continue to use to share uniquely wise ways of being in this rare and beautiful world.

ACKNOWLEDGMENTS

GRATITUDE GOES TO MANY PEOPLE in far-flung places who helped shape this book. Thanks to the editors at *Outside* magazine who published my initial response to an outdated feature. In Cambridge, thanks to Robert Macfarlane for stirring early interest in that response. In the Lake District, thanks to James Rebanks for leading me to Dorothy Wordsworth, and to Poppy Garrett at Dove Cottage for research assistance. At Lancaster University, thanks to Simon Bainbridge for insights into early female mountaineering history. In New York, thanks to Jennifer Griffiths at Fenimore Art Museum, Hugh MacDougall with the James Fenimore Cooper Society, and Jessie Ravage for a summertime ramble and paddle around Cooperstown. In Idaho, thanks to Rochelle Johnson for insights into Susan Fenimore Cooper. In Indiana, thanks to Terri Gorney with Friends of the Limberlost and to Curt Burnette with the Limberlost State Historic Site for your generosity of time.

In California, thanks to Matthew Hengst of the Southern California Mountaineers Association. In Scotland, thanks to Steven McColl, for without your eye-catching cobalt suit, a path would never have opened on the Cairngorms and walking with James Littlejohn, to whom I owe great thanks as well. Thanks also to

Erlend Clouston for the personal stories of Nan Shepherd. In Suffolk, thanks to Charlotte Peacock for cheerleading my angle on Nan Shepherd. In Devon, warm thanks to Terrie Windling for wisdom and recommendations, and to caped crusader Heather Sheppard for persevering with permissions. In Wales, thanks to Paul Dodgson for discussions of creative nonfiction and initial feedback. In France, thanks to Bridget Holding for early reading.

In Oregon at Timber Press, thanks to Andrew Beckman for championing this project and giving me the freedom to follow my instincts. Special thanks to Jacoba Lawson for sensitive editing and keeping an eagle eye for infelicities. In Germany, warmest thanks to Gisela Goppel for such evocative author illustrations.

Thanks to my supportive family—with love to Rolf Aalto for appreciating the space I need to explore and write. Heartfelt appreciation especially to our mostly grown children, August, Tess, and Stellan Aalto, for sensitive feedback on these essays.

To Reginald Lewis, teacher, gardener and hunter, who passed away during the writing of this book, infinite gratitude from a daughter to her father—for the green eyes, green thumb, and good guidance that instilled a lifelong appreciation for seeing this rare and beautiful world.

To all the trailblazing writers in these pages, thank you for having the courage to put pen to paper, even in challenging times. Some of you have long felt like friends, even if you lived in a different century. Many of you are new friends, whose future essays and books I look forward to reading. It has been my honor and pleasure celebrating your lives, literature, and legacies.

SOURCES

Abbott, Rebecca L. "Mabel Osgood Wright, A Friend of Nature." *Sacred Heart University Review*: Vol. 18, issue 1, 1998.

Achenbach, Joel. "Why Carl Sagan Is Truly Irreplaceable." *Smithsonian Magazine*. March 2014.

Ackerman, Diane. *The Human Age*. New York: W. W. Norton and Company, 2014.

———. *The Moon by Whale Light*. New York: Random House, 1991.

———. *A Natural History of the Senses*. New York: Random House, 1990.

———. *On Extended Wings*. New York: Atheneum, 1985.

———. *Twilight of the Tenderfoot*. New York: William Morrow and Company, 1980.

———. *The Zookeeper's Wife*. New York: W. W. Norton and Company, 2007.

Acocella, Joan. "Happy Birthday, 'O Pioneers!'" *The New Yorker*. 30 December 2013.

Adcock, Siobhan. "The Vanguard of Climate Fiction." *Literary Hub*. 5 July 2018.

"After the Death of Nature: Carolyn Merchant and the Future of Human-Nature Relations, A Symposium." University of California, Berkeley. PDF. May 2018.

Allen, Paula Gunn. "Special Problems in Teaching Leslie Marmon Silko's 'Ceremony.'" *American Indian Quarterly*: Vol. 14, no. 4, 1990.

Altman, Rebecca. "American Beauties." *Topic Magazine*. August 2018.

——. "American petro-topia." *Aeon*. 11 March 2015.

——. "How the Benzene Tree Polluted the World." *The Atlantic*. 4 October 2017.

——. "The Legacy of Plastic." TEDx, San Francisco, 25 Oct 2017. Accessed 2 February 2019. www.youtube.com/watch?v=zAUWEHdrIBc.

——. "Time bombing the future." *Aeon*. 2 January 2019.

American Forests, "A History of Innovation." Accessed 28 July 2018. www.americanforests.org/about-us/history.

Anderson, Lorraine. *Sisters of the Earth*. New York: Vintage, 1991.

Annie Dillard, Official Website. Accessed 27 October 2018. www.annie-dillard.com.

Atkin, Polly. *Basic Nest Architecture*. Bridgend: Seren, 2017.

——. "Being Mutant." Official Website. Accessed 22 July 2019. pollyatkin.com/2015/08/23/being-mutant/.

——. Email correspondence with Kathryn Aalto. 15 July 2019.

——. "A Q&A with Polly Atkin for Wildlines @ The Leeds Library." *The State of the Arts*. 13 March 2018.

——. "Why Is It Always a Poem Is a Walk?" *New Welsh Reader*: Issue 120, May 2019.

"The Audacious Natural Word: A Review of Camille Dungy's 'Black Nature.'" *Obsidian*: Vol. 10, no. 2, 22 October 2009.

Austin, Mary. *California*. 1914. Project Gutenberg. Accessed 29 May 2019. www.gutenberg.org/ebooks/44764.

——. "Can Prayer Be Answered." *The New York Times*. 29 July 1934.

——. *Earth Horizon*. Boston: Houghton Mifflin Company, 1932.

——. *The Land of Little Rain*. Boston: Houghton Mifflin Company, 1903.

"Author Gretel Ehrlich on Dialogue." Idaho Public Television. Sun Valley Writers' Conference 2014. Accessed 11 December 2018. www.youtube.com/watch?v=MVeh9WsDza8.

Bainbridge, Simon. "Women in the Mountains 1787-1829." The Wordsworth Trust.

Baker, J. A. *The Peregrine: 50th Anniversary Edition*. New York: HarperCollins, 2017.

Balaev, Michelle. *The Nature of Trauma in American Novels*. Evanston: Northwestern University Press, 2012.

Bill Moyer's Journal. Transcript of 21 September 2007 episode. Accessed 19 September 2018. www.pbs.org/moyers/journal/09212007/transcript1.html.

Blunt, Alison. *Travel, Gender, and Imperialism*. New York: The Guildford Press, 1994.

Bogan, Louise. "Profiles—American Classic." *The New Yorker*. 8 August 1931.

Brady, Amy. "Recommended cli-fi." Email correspondence with Kathryn Aalto. 3 December 2018.

Branch, Michael P. "Are You Serious? A Modest Proposal for Environmental Humor." *The Oxford Handbook of Ecocriticism*. Oxford: Oxford University Press, 2014.

Brand, Russell. "#004 Feminism – Can It Change the World?" An Interview with Anne Phillips. *Under the Skin with Russell Brand*. 30 March 2017.

British Library Learning. "The campaign for women's suffrage: an introduction." 6 February 2018. Accessed 22 June 2018. www.bl.uk/votes-for-women/articles/the-campaign-for-womens-suffrage-an-introduction.

Bryant, Kenzie. "How Mary Oliver's 'The Summer Day' Became an American Sensation." *Vanity Fair*. 17 January 2019.

Buell, Lawrence. *The Environmental Imagination*. Cambridge: The Belknap Press of Harvard University Press, 1996.

Buni, Catherine. "Toward a Wider View of 'Nature Writing.'" *Los Angeles Review of Books*. 10 January 2016.

Cairngorms National Park. Accessed 15 February 2019. cairngorms.co.uk/discover-explore/landscapes-scenery/the-mountains.

Cape Cod Landscape History. Cape Cod National Seashore displays. Province Lands Visitor's Center. 22 September 2018.

Carrington, Damien. "Humanity has wiped out 60% of animal populations since 1970, report finds." *The Guardian*. 29 October 2018.

Carson, Rachel. *Silent Spring*. Boston: Houghton Mifflin Company, 1962.

———. "Silent Spring – I." *The New Yorker*. 16 June 1962.

———"What's the Reason Why: A Symposium by Best-Selling Authors." *New York Times Book Review*. 2 December 1962.

Carter, Tara Ann. "First and Second Wave Native American Literature." Yale National Initiative. Accessed 30 May 2018. teachers.yale.edu/curriculum/viewer/initiative_16.01.03_u.d.

Cather, Willa. *My Ántonia*. Boston: Haughton Mifflin Company, 1918.

———. *O Pioneers!*. Boston: Haughton Mifflin Company, 1913.

Caws, Mary-Ann. *Vita Sackville-West: Selected Writings*. New York: Palgrave, 2002.

Chaney, Anthony. "Anthony Chaney on Carolyn Merchant's 'The Death of Nature' (1980)." Society for U.S. Intellectual History. 27 March 2016.

Clayton, John. "The Old West's Female Champion: Caroline Lockhart and Wyoming's Cowboy Heritage." WyoHistory.org. 8 November 2014.

Clouston, Erlend. Interview with Kathryn Aalto. 31 August 2018.

Cocker, Mark. "Death of the naturalist: Why is the 'new nature writing' so tame?" *The New Statesman America*. 17 June 2015.

Cooper, Brittney. "The racial politics of time." TEDWomen 2016. Oct 2016. Accessed 1 March 2018. www.ted.com/talks/brittney_cooper_the_racial_politics_of_time.

Cooper, Susan Fenimore. *Rural Hours*. New York: G. P. Putnam, 1850.

Cronon, William. "The Trouble with Wilderness; Or, Getting Back to the Wrong Nature." *Uncommon Ground*. New York: W. W. Norton and Company, 1995.

Cushway, Philip. *Of Poetry and Protest*. New York: W. W. Norton and Company, 2016.

Darwin Correspondence Project. "Letter no. 3796." DCP-LET-3796. Accessed 8 May 2018. www.darwinproject.ac.uk/letter/?docId=letters/ DCP-LETT-3796.xml;query=3796;brand=default.

"Deep Play by Diane Ackerman." *Kirkus Review*. 1 May 1999.

Deming, Alison Hawthorne. "Mt. Lemmon, Steward Observatory, 1990." *Science and Other Poems*. Baton Rouge: Louisiana State University Press, 1994.

Dennison, Matthew. "Vita Sackville-West: her gardening legacy." *The Telegraph*. 22 June 2012.

DeSalvo, Louise and Mitchell A. Leaska. *The Letters of Vita Sackville-West and Virginia Woolf*. New York: Morrow, 1985.

"Diane Ackerman." American Academy of Arts and Sciences Celebration of Arts and Humanities. 7 June 2018. Accessed 20 January 2019. www. youtube.com/watch?v=Jx_i1A-hhLY

"Diane Ackerman." *Kirkus TV* Interview. Accessed 20 January 2019. www. kirkusreviews.com/tv/video/kirkus-tv-diane-ackerman/

Diaz, Natalie. "New Poetry by Indigenous Women." *Literary Hub*. 15 August 2018.

Dickinson, Emily. *Letters of Emily Dickinson*. Edited by Mabel Loomis Todd. "Letter to Mrs. J. C. Greenough, 1885." New York: Dover, 2004.

Dillard, Annie. *The Annie Dillard Reader*. New York: HarperCollins, 1994.

———. *Holy the Firm*. New York: Harper and Row, 1977.

———. *Mornings Like This*. New York: HarperCollins, 1995.

———. *Pilgrim at Tinker Creek*. New York: HarperCollins Perennial Classics, 1998.

———. *Teaching a Stone to Talk*. New York: Harper and Row, 1982.

———. *Tickets For a Prayer Wheel*. Middletown: Wesleyan University Press, 1974.

Dingfelder, Sadie. "What's next for Helen Macdonald, author of 'H Is for Hawk.'" *The Washington Post*. 17 March 2016.

Dodd, Elizabeth. Email correspondence with Kathryn Aalto. 11 June 2019.

Doward, Jamie. "Hawks, butterflies, coasts, and footpaths: How nature writing turned to literary gold." *The Guardian.* 22 March 2015.

Dungy, Camille. "Diversity and Inclusion in Conservation." Department of Human Dimensions of Natural Resources, Colorado State University. 5 Mar 2018. Accessed 17 May 2018. www.youtube.com/watch?v=jDzEXmWRr7Q.

———. "A Good Hike." *Terrain.org.* 29 June 2017.

———. Interview with Kathryn Aalto. 20 December 2018.

———. *Smith Blue.* Carbondale: Southern Illinois University Press, 2011.

———. *Suck on the Marrow.* Los Angeles: Red Hen Press, 2010.

———. *Trophic Cascade.* Middletown: Wesleyan University Press, 2017.

Ehrlich, Gretel. *Arctic Heart.* Santa Barbara: Capra Press, 1992.

———. *Cowboy Island.* Carpinteria: Santa Cruz Island Foundation, 2000.

———. *Drinking Dry Clouds.* Santa Barbara: Capra Press, 1991.

———. *Heart Mountain.* New York: Viking, 1988.

———. *A Match to the Heart.* New York: Pantheon Books, 1994.

———. *The Solace of Open Spaces.* New York: Viking, 1985.

Ehrlich, Paul R., David S. Dobkin, and Darryl Wheye. "DDT and Birds." Stanford Birds. Accessed 22 April 2018. web.stanford.edu/group/stanfordbirds/text/essays/DDT_and_Birds.html.

Elder, John. Email correspondence with Kathryn Aalto. 10 November 2016.

"Elizabeth Rush: Rising." Exeter TV98. Discussion hosted by Water Street Books. 20 July 2018. www.youtube.com/watch?v=RvCnepK472I.

Elkin, Lauren. "Why All the Books About Motherhood?" *The Paris Review.* 17 July 2018.

Ellis-Petersen, Hannah. "Helen Macdonald's 'extraordinary' memoir wins Samuel Johnson Prize." *The Guardian.* 4 November 2014.

Falconer, Rachel. *Kathleen Jamie.* Edinburgh: Edinburgh University Press, 2015.

Finney, Carolyn. *Black Faces, White Spaces.* Chapel Hill: University of North Carolina Press, 2014.

Franklin, Ruth. "What Mary Oliver's Critics Don't Understand." *The New Yorker.* 20 November 2017.

Freeman, Michael. "Snowdon descriptions of ascents by women." Early Tourists in Wales. Accessed 22 February 2019. sublimewales.wordpress.com.

Furman, Necah Stewart. "Western Author Caroline Lockhart and Her Perspectives on Wyoming." *Montana: The Magazine of Western History*: Vol. 36, no. 1, 1986.

Gadsby, Hannah. *Nanette*. Netflix. Accessed 10 July 2018.

Garbes, Angela. "Why Are We Only Talking About 'Mom Books' by White Women?" *New York, The Cut*. 1 November 2018.

Gaskell, Elizabeth. *Life of Charlotte Bronte*. New York: Penguin Classics, 1998.

"Gene Stratton-Porter: Voice of the Limberlost." Ball State University Libraries and Indiana University. Accessed 16 June 2018. www.youtube.com/watch?v=kvOWDOfxbLw.

Genzlinger, Neil. "Sue Hubbell, Who Wrote of Bees and Self-Reliance, Dies at 83." *The New York Times*. 18 October 2018.

Gerrard, Greg. *The Oxford Handbook of Ecocriticism*. Oxford: Oxford University Press, 2014.

Goodyear, Dana. "Zen Master: Gary Snyder and the art of life." *The New Yorker*. 13 October 2008.

Gormley, Terri. "Gene's Fort Wayne Book Signing." PDF.

Green, Lucy Bryan. "On Naming Women and Mountains." *The Nashville Review*. 1 August 2014.

Gregory, Alice. "How Rebecca Solnit Became the Voice of Resistance." *The New York Times Style Magazine*. 8 August 2017.

Gretel Ehrlich: 1987 Winner in Nonfiction. Whiting Award. Accessed 3 October 2018. www.whiting.org/awards/winners/gretel-ehrlich.

Grey, Mary. "Ecofeminism and Christian Theology." *The Furrow*: Vol. 51, no. 9, 2000.

Gurton-Wachter, Lily. "The Stranger Guest: The Literature of Pregnancy and New Motherhood." *Los Angeles Review of Books*. 29 July 2016.

Haberman, Clyde. "Rachel Carson, DDT, and the Fight Against Malaria." *The New York Times*. 22 January 2017.

"Helen Macdonald: H Is for Hawk." Chicago Humanities Festival. 11 May 2016. Accessed 12 October 2018. www.youtube.com/watch?v=ctXwRwj2xp8.

"Helen Macdonald Interview," Book View Now, 2016 AWP Conference and Book Fair. Accessed 11 October 2018. video.tpt.org/video/book-vie w-now-helen-macdonald-interview-2016-awp-conference-book-fair/.

Henderson, Caspar. "The Best Books on Pollution Recommended by Rebecca Altman." Five Books. Accessed 2 February 2018. fivebooks. com/best-books/pollution.

Hengst, Matthew. "Climbing Mount Mary Austin." Email correspondence. 12 September 2018.

Henson, Pamela M. "Reviewed Work: *The Nature Study Movement: The Forgotten Popularizer of America's Conservation Ethic* by Kevin C. Armitage." *History of Education Quarterly*: Vol. 51, no. 1, 2011.

"Historical Timeline of Provincetown, Massachusetts." Town of Provincetown. Accessed 2018. www.provincetown-ma.gov/DocumentCenter/Home/View/874.

Houston, Pam. *Cowboys Are My Weakness*. New York: W. W. Norton and Company, 2005.

"In Search of the Novel, Leslie Marmon Silko." *Annenberg Learner*. 26 August 2013.

Jamie, Kathleen. About. Kathleen Jamie website. Accessed 17 November 2018. www.kathleenjamie.com/about/.

———. *Among Muslims*. London: Sort Of Books, 2002.

———. *Findings*. London: Sort Of Books, 2005.

———. *Sightlines: A Conversation with the Natural World*. London: Sort Of Books, 2012.

———. *This Weird Estate*. Edinburgh: Scotland and Medicine, 2007.

Johnson, Rochelle. Email correspondence with Kathryn Aalto. 13 January 2019.

Jordan, Philip D. "Reviewed Work: *Indiana Authors and Their Books, 1816-1916: Biographical sketches of authors who published during the first century of Indiana statehood with lists of their books* by R. E. Banta." *The Mississippi Valley Historical Review*: Vol. 36, no. 3, 1949.

Joy Harjo. The Poetry Foundation. Accessed 20 February 2019. www.poetryfoundation.org/poets/joy-harjo

Jukes, Thomas H. "DDT, Human Health, and the Environment." *Boston College Environmental Affairs Law Review*: Vol. 1, issue 3, 1971.

Kaufman, H. G. "Preparations for Arbor and Bird Day." *The Journal of Education*: Vol. 67, no. 12, 1908.

Keats, John. "La Belle Dame sans Merci: A Ballad."

Kimmerer, Robin Wall. *Braiding Sweetgrass*. Minneapolis: Milkweed, 2015.

——. *Gathering Moss*. Corvallis: Oregon State University Press, 2003.

——. "Reclaiming the Honorable Harvest." TEDxSitka. 18 August 2012. Accessed 2 June 2018. www.youtube.com/watch?v=Lz1vgfZ3etE.

——. A Walk Along the Exeter River. Environmental Literature Institute at Exeter. Phillips Exeter Academy. 23–28 June 2017.

Klinkenborg, Verlyn. "Appreciations: Ellen Meloy." *The New York Times*. 4 Nov 2011.

Knole. National Trust. Accessed 5 April 2018. www.nationaltrust.org.uk/knole.

Kuman, Maxine. "Imitations of Mortality." *Women's Review of Books*. 7 April 1993.

Lawless, Debra. *Provincetown*. Charleston: The History Press, 2011.

Lear, Linda. *Rachel Carson*. New York: Henry Holt, 1997.

Lee, John M. "Silent Spring is Now a Noisy Summer; Pesticide Industry up in Arms." *The New York Times*. 22 July 1962.

Leslie Marmon Silko. The Poetry Foundation. Accessed 27 November 2018. www.poetryfoundation.org/poets/leslie-marmon-silko.

Lezard, Nicholas. "Review of *Lyrical Ballads by William Wordsworth and ST Coleridge*, edited by Fiona Stafford." *The Guardian*. 16 July 2013.

"Librarian of Congress Names Joy Harjo the Nation's 23rd Poet Laureate." Library of Congress. Accessed 20 June 2019. www.loc.gov/item/prn-19-066/librarian-of-congress-names-joy-harjo-the-nations-23rd-poet-laureate/2019-06-19/.

Lilley, Deborah. "New British Nature Writing." *Oxford Handbooks Online*. April 2017.

Limberlost. Indiana State Museum Historic Site. Accessed 21 July 2018. www.indianamuseum.org/limberlost-state-historic-site.

Liptrot, Amy. "The Corncrake Wife." 5 x 15 Stories. 16 September 2016. Accessed 12 December 2018. www.youtube.com/watch?v=A66HZNwxpK4.

———. *The Outrun*. Edinburgh: Canongate, 2016.

Lloyd, Saci. *The Carbon Diaries 2015*. London: Hodder Children's Books, 2008.

———. Interview with Kathryn Aalto. 20 November 2018.

———. *It's the End of the World as We Know It*. London: Hodder Children's Books, 2015.

———. *Momentum*. London: Hodder Children's Books, 2011.

"Loblolly Marsh Preserve." Indiana Department of Natural Resources. PDF.

Lopate, Phillip. *The Art of the Personal Essay*. New York: Doubleday, 1994.

Lopez, Barry. "A Way Out of Our Predicament." Sacred Land Film Project. 17 August 2018. Accessed 20 May 2018. www.youtube.com/watch?v=Diu_aaXUZzM.

Macdonald, Helen. Email correspondence with Kathryn Aalto. 15 June 2017.

———. *Falcon*. London: Reaktion, 2006.

———. "H Is for Hawk." 5 x 15 Stories. 11 June 2015. Accessed 10 Oct 2018. www.youtube.com/watch?v=rpM6HvjfmeQ.

———. *H Is for Hawk*. London: Jonathan Cape, 2014.

———. "Helen Macdonald on structuring a book." Writers in Conversation. 28 June 2017. Accessed 10 October 2018. www.youtube.com/watch?v=tOrZrVDjrcs.

———. *Shaler's Fish*. Buckfastleigh: Etruscan, 2001.

Macfarlane, Robert. "An Impish Spirit." *The Guardian*. 30 March 2005.

———. Quoted in Eleanor Bell's "Into the Centre of Things: Poetic Travel Narratives in the Work of Kathleen Jamie and Nan Shepherd." *Kathleen Jamie: Essays and Poems on Her Work*. Edinburgh: Edinburgh University Press, 2015.

———. "Why We Need Nature Writing." *The New Statesman*. 2 September 2015.

———. *The Wild Places*. New York: Penguin, 2007.

Malcolm, Janet. "Capitalist Pastorale." *New York Review of Books*. 15 January 2015.

Harriette Martineau. Martineau Society. Accessed 18 August 2018. martineausociety.co.uk/the-martineaus/harriet-martineau/.

"Mary Oliver: Listening to the World." *On Being with Krista Tippett*. 5 February 2015.

McKie, Robin. "Rachel Carson and the Legacy of Silent Spring." *The Guardian*. 26 May 2012.

McLaughlin, Dorothy. "Silent Spring Revisited." PBS, *Frontline: Fooling With Nature*.

McNew, Janet. "Mary Oliver and the Tradition of Romantic Nature Poetry." *Contemporary Literature*: Vol. 30, no. 1, 1989.

Merchant, Carolyn. *American Environmental History*. New York: Columbia University Press, 2007.

———. *The Death of Nature*. San Francisco: Harper and Row, 1980.

———. "The Death of Nature: A Retrospective." *Organization and Environment*: Vol. 11, no. 2, June 1998.

———. *Ecological Revolutions*. Chapel Hill: University of North Carolina Press, 2010.

———. "Environmentalism: From the Control of Nature to Partnership with Carolyn Merchant." UC Berkeley Graduate Lecture Series. UCTV. 26 July 2010. Accessed 30 May 2018. www.uctv.tv/shows/Environmentalism-From-the-Control-of-Nature-to-Partnership-with-Carolyn-Merchant-19243.

———. Merchant Symposium. Cooperative New School for Urban Studies and Environmental Justice. 4 May 2018. Accessed 1 December 2018. www.youtube.com/watch?v=23AXo_5YwKo.

———. Profile. Department of Environmental Science, Policy, and Management. University of California, Berkeley. Accessed 1 December 2018. ourenvironment.berkeley.edu/people/carolyn-merchant.

———. *Reinventing Eden*. New York: Routledge, 2003.

Milspaw, Yvonne J. "The Sacred Hoop: Recovering the Feminine in American Indian Traditions by Paula Gunn Allen." *The Journal of American Folklore*: Vol. 103, no. 408, 1990.

Morris, Gregory L. *Gretel Ehrlich*. Western Writers Series. Boise: Boise State University, 2001.

Milne, Lorus and Margery. "There's Poison All Around Us Now." *New York Times Book Review*. 23 September 1962.

Morris, Jan. "The Allure of Travel Writing." *Smithsonian Magazine*. Sept 2009.

Mount Mary Austin. U.S. Board on Geographic Names. United States Geological Survey. Accessed 4 July 2018. geonames.usgs.gov/apex/f?p=gnispq:3:0::NO::P3_FID:1659072.

Muir, John. *Our National Parks*. Boston: Haughton Mifflin Company, 1901.

Maloney, Wendi. "Native American Heritage Month: Celebrating Sarah Winnemucca." Library of Congress Blog. 2 November 2017. Accessed 3 December 2018. blogs.loc.gov/loc/2017/11/native-american-heritage-month-celebrating-sarah-winnemucca/.

"Aimee Nezhukumatathil's Oceanic." The University of Mississippi, Department of English. Accessed 27 June 2019. english.olemiss.edu/aimee-nezhukumatathils-—oceanic-poetry-beauty-with-copper-canyon-press/.

Branch, Michael P. "Are You Serious? A Modest Proposal for Environmental Humor." *The Oxford Handbook of Ecocriticism*. Oxford: Oxford University Press, 2014.

Oliver, Mary. *American Primitive*. Boston: Little, Brown, 1983.

———. "At Blackwater Pond." Mary Oliver Reads Mary Oliver. Beacon Press. Accessed 1 August 2018. www.youtube.com/watch?v=M9KuLMyblfo.

———. "Mary Oliver Reads 'The Journey.'" Maria Shriver's Women's Conference 2010. Accessed 1 August 2018. www.youtube.com/watch?v=VNqSWiYWDaw.

———. "Mary Oliver Reads 'The Summer Day.'" Beacon Press. 20 June 2011. Accessed 1 August 2018. www.youtube.com/watch?v=16CL6bKVbJQ.

———. *Upstream*. New York: Penguin, 2016.

———. "Wild Geese." *Dream Work*. Boston: The Atlantic Monthly Press, 1986.

Panich, Paula. "(Still) The Land of Little Rain: Mary Austin and the Eastern Sierra." Pacific Horticulture Society. July 2008.

Paskin, Willa. "Art or Babies?" *Slate*. 3 May 2018.

Passarello, Elena. *Animals Strike Curious Poses*. Louisville: Sarabande, 2017.

———. Email correspondence with Kathryn Aalto. 29 December 2018.

———. *Let Me Clear My Throat*. Louisville: Sarabande, 2012.

Payne, David H. "John Rollin Ridge(1827–1867)." *New Georgia Encyclopedia*. 31 October 2018.

Peacock, Charlotte. Interview with Kathryn Aalto. 2 December 2018.

———. *Into the Mountain*. Cambridge: Galileo Publishers, 2016.

Pérez-Peña, Richard. "College Classes Use Art to Brace for Climate Change." *The New York Times*. 31 March 2014.

"Pesticides – DDT – Rachel Carson – Silent Spring." NV atCEPImperial. 18 April 2013. Accessed 19 September 2018. www.youtube.com/watch?v=Ipbc-6IvMQI.

"Polly Atkin on the Places of Her Poetry." Research English at Durham. Accessed 22 July 2019. readdurhamenglish.wordpress.com/2018/05/17/new-podcast-polly-atkin-on-the-places-of-her-poetry/.

Pomeroy, Elizabeth W. "Within Living Memory: Vita Sackville-West's Poems of Land and Garden." *Twentieth Century Literature*: Vol. 28, no. 3, 1982.

"Press Conference, 29 August 1962. (News Conference 42)." John F. Kennedy Presidential Library and Museum. Accessed 19 April 2018. www.jfklibrary.org/Asset-Viewer/Archives/JFKWHA-124.aspx.

Pritchett, Daniel. "Owens Valley Flora – Part I." Owens Valley Committee. Accessed 18 August 2018. owensvalley.org/2-1-ov-water-history-ltwa/flora-part-i/.

Reardon: Amy. "Becoming Her Own Cowboy: Talking with Pam Houston." *The Rumpus*. 28 Jan 2019.

"Rebecca Solnit: 2018 SF State Hall of Fame Inductee." San Francisco State University. 14 November 2018. Accessed 26 November 2018. www.youtube.com/watch?v=VN46aeykunE.

"Rebecca Solnit and John Freeman: A Conversation." 27 June 2016. Bay Area Book Festival. FORA.TV. Accessed 2 October 2018. www.youtube.com/watch?v=2Q_Djm9UYmo.

"Rebecca Solnit Speaker." PDA Speakers. 23 July 2017. Accessed 3 April 2018. www.youtube.com/watch?v=qGTTN_h32HM.

Richards, Linda. "At Play with Diane Ackerman." *January Magazine*. Accessed 22 January 2019. www.januarymagazine.com/profiles/ackerman.html.

Robinson, Marilynne. "The Nature of Love." *The Washington Post*. 24 June 2007.

Robinson, Michael. "Women Explorers." *Time to Eat the Dogs*. 17 September 2008.

Rosenberg, Tina. "What the World Needs Now is DDT." *New York Times Magazine*. 11 April 2004.

Ross, Alex. "A Walk in Willa Cather's Prairie: How Nebraska's landscape inspired the great American novelist." *The New Yorker*. 2 October 2017

Rush, Elizabeth. "Atlas with Shifting Edges." *Emergence Magazine*. Accessed 31 July 2019. emergencemagazine.org/story/atlas-with-shifting-edges/.

———. *Rising*. Minneapolis: Milkweed, 2018.

Ruskin, Zack. "The Quantum of Solnit." *SF Weekly*. 22 March 2017.

"The Silent Spring of Rachel Carson." CBS Reports. 3 April 1963.

Sackville-West, Vita. *The Garden*. London: Michael Joseph, 1946.

———. *The Illustrated Garden Book*. London: Michael Joseph, 1986.

———. *The Land*. London: William Heinemann, 1939.

———. "MCMXCII," *Poems of West and East*. West Norwood: The Complete Press, 1917.

———. *Selected Poems*. London: Hogarth press, 1941.

———. and Sarah Raven. *Vita Sackville-West's Sissinghurst*. London: Virago, 2014.

"H Is for Hawk: How a hawk helped Helen Macdonald recover from grief." *Saturday Extra with Geraldine Doogue*. 27 May 2015.

Savoy, Lauret. *The Colors of Nature*. Minneapolis: Milkweed, 2011.

———. *Trace*. Berkeley: Counterpoint, 2015.

———. Website. Accessed 4 December 2018. www.lauretsavoy.com.

Schoonover, Sydney. "Professor Carolyn Merchant reflects on legacy of ecofeminism." *The Daily Californian*. 22 April 2018.

Sehgal, Parul. "In a Raft of New Books, Motherhood from (Almost) Every Angle." *The New York Times*. 24 April 2018.

Severin, Diana. "The Thoreau of the Suburbs." *The Atlantic*. 5 February 2015.

Shepherd, Nan. *The Living Mountain*. Aberdeen: Aberdeen University Press, 1977.

———. *Wild Geese*. Cambridge: Galileo Publishers, 2018.

Shriver, Maria. "Maria Shriver Interviews Famously Private Poet Mary Oliver." *O Magazine*. 9 March 2011.

"Sightlines: A Conversation with the Natural World." *Kirkus Review*. 15 July 2013.

Silko, Leslie Marmon. *Ceremony*. New York: Viking, 1977.

Singley, Carol J. "American Literature." *American Literature*: Vol. 63, no. 2, 1991.

Smallwood, Christine. "Never Done: The impossible work of motherhood." *Harper's*. April 2018.

Snapes, Laura. "Many Addiction Memoirs End With the Writer in Rehab—But What Happens Afterwards?" *Elle*. 25 April 2017.

Solnit, Rebecca. *A Field Guide to Getting Lost*. New York: Viking Penguin, 2005.

———. "Let This Flood of Women's Stories Never Cease." *Literary Hub*. 14 November 2017.

———. "Men Explain Things to Me." *Guernica*. 20 April 2012.

———. "Rebecca Solnit, 'Men Explain Things to Me,'" BookTV. 17 June 2014. Accessed 2 April 2018. www.youtube.com/watch?v=oBASRRs6d2I.

————. *Wanderlust*. New York: Viking Penguin, 2000.

————. and Rebecca Snedeker. *Unfathomable*. Berkeley: University of California Press, 2013.

Stoll, Mark. "Rachel Carson and Silent Spring, The Book That Changed the World." Environment and Society Portal, Virtual Exhibitions 2012, no 1. Rachel Carson Center for Environment and Society. Accessed 27 April 2018. www.environmentandsociety.org/exhibitions/silent-spring/silent-spring-international-best-seller.

Stratton-Porter, Gene. *Freckles*. New York: Doubleday, Page and Company, 1904.

————. *A Girl of the Limberlost*. New York: Doubleday, Page and Company, 1909.

————. *Laddie*. New York: Doubleday, Page and Company, 1913.

————. *What I Have Done With Birds*. New York: Doubleday, Page and Company, 1917.

Taylor, Alan. "I To the Hills." *Scottish Review of Books*. 18 November 2017.

Taylor, Joanna. "Dorothy Wordsworth, Mountaineering Pioneer." The Wordsworth Trust. 1 September 2018. Accessed 17 June 2018. www.youtube.com/watch?v=reVa4SOAZa0.

Todd, Sarah. "What Mary Oliver Can Teach Us About Handling Criticism with Grace." *Quartzy*. 20 January 2019.

Updike, John. "A Sage for All Seasons." *The Guardian*. 25 June 2004.

"Vita Sackville-West reads from her poem The Land." Roger York. 8 November 2007. Accessed 1 October 2018. www.youtube.com/watch?v=AjXvkRhoXXs.

Watson, Adam. *Essays on Lone Trips, Mountain-craft, and Other Hill Topics*. Trowbridge: Paragon, 2016.

Watts, Jonathan. "We have 12 years to limit climate change catastrophe, warns UN." *The Guardian*. 8 October 2018.

White, Evelyn C. "Black Women and the Wilderness." *Names We Call Home*. New York: Routledge, 1996.

Wilentz, Gay. "Healing Narratives: Women Writers Curing Cultural Dis-Ease." *MELUS*: Vol. 30, issue 3, 2005.

Williams, Terry Tempest. "The Earth Stares Back." *Emmet Gowin: Changing the Earth*. New Haven: Yale University Art Gallery, 2002.

———. *Refuge*. New York: Pantheon, 1991.

Wilson, Frances. *The Ballad of Dorothy Wordsworth*. London: Faber and Faber, 2008.

Wood, Charlotte. "A Place on Earth: Nature Writing in Australia." 2004. Accessed 15 February 2019. www.charlottewood.com.au/nature-writing-in-australia.html.

Woof, Pamela. *Dorothy Wordsworth*. Grasmere: The Wordsworth Trust, 2013.

Wordsworth, Dorothy. *The Grasmere and Alfoxden Journals*. Edited by Pamela Woof. Oxford: Oxford World's Classics, 2002.

———. "Grasmere – A Fragment." The Wordsworth Trust.

———. Letter to William Johnson. October 1818. The Wordsworth Trust.

Wordsworth, William and Samuel Taylor Coleridge. *Lyrical Ballads, with a Few Other Poems*. London: J. and A. Arch, 1798.

Wulf, Andrea. *The Brother Gardeners*. London: William Heinemann, 2008.

———. *The Founding Gardeners*. London: William Heinemann, 2011.

———. Interview with Kathryn Aalto. 14 July 2018.

———. *The Invention of Nature*. London: John Murray, 2015.

"Yay! A girl is the winner of the 2011 Stella Shouting Contest in New Orleans!" Midori Tajiri. 27 March 2011. Accessed 19 April 2017. www.youtube.com/watch?v=r-b6BZwfahw.

SOURCES

PERMISSIONS

Excerpts from pp. 1–2, 129–130 from *The Death of Nature: Women, Ecology, and the Scientific Revolution* by Carolyn Merchant. Copyright © 1980 by Carolyn Merchant. Reprinted by permission of HarperCollins Publishers.

Excerpt from "Living Like Weasels" [pp. 66–68] from *Teaching a Stone to Talk: Expeditions and Encounters* by Annie Dillard. Copyright © 1982 by Annie Dillard. Reprinted by permission of HarperCollins Publishers.

Excerpt from *A Match to the Heart: One Woman's Story of Being Struck by Lightning* by Gretel Ehrlich, copyright © 1994 by Gretel Ehrlich. Used by permission of Pantheon Books, an imprint of the Knopf Doubleday Publishing Group, a division of Penguin Random House LLC. All rights reserved.

Excerpts from *The Solace of Open Spaces* by Gretel Ehrlich, copyright © 1985 by Gretel Ehrlich. Used by permission of Viking Books, an imprint of Penguin Publishing Group, a division of Penguin Random House LLC. All rights reserved.

Excerpts from *The Solace of Open Spaces* (Viking/Penguin Random House, 1985) and *A Match to the Heart: One Woman's Story of Being Struck by Lightning* (Penguin Books/Penguin Random House, 1994) by Gretel Ehrlich. Copyrights © 1985 and © 1994 by Gretel Ehrlich. All rights reserved. Used with permission of Penguin Random House and Darhansoff & Verrill Literary Agents.

Excerpts from *Ceremony* by Leslie Marmon Silko, copyright © 1977, 2006 by Leslie Marmon Silko. Used by permission of Viking Books, an imprint of Penguin Publishing Group a division of Penguin Random House LLC. All rights reserved.

Excerpts from *The Human Age: The World Shaped by Us* by Diane Ackerman. Copyright © 2014 by Diane Ackerman. Used by permission of W. W. Norton & Company, Inc.

Excerpts from *The Human Age: The World Shaped by Us* by Diane Ackerman. Copyright © 2015 by Diane Ackerman. Reproduced by permission of Headline Publishing Group.

Excerpt from *A Natural History of the Senses* by Diane Ackerman, copyright © 1990 by Diane Ackerman. Used by permission of Random House, an imprint and division of Penguin Random House LLC. All rights reserved.

Robin Wall Kimmerer, excerpt from "Learning the Grammar of Animacy" from *Braiding Sweetgrass: Indigenous Wisdom, Scientific Knowledge and the Teachings of Plants*. Copyright © 2013 by Robin Wall Kimmerer. Reprinted with the permission of The Permissions Company, Inc. on behalf of Milkweed Editions, www.milkweed.org.

Copyright © 2015 by Lauret Edith Savoy, from *Trace: Memory, History, Race, and the American Landscape* by Lauret Savoy. Reprinted by permission of Counterpoint Press.

Excerpt from *Storming the Gates of Paradise: Landscapes for Politics*, by Rebecca Solnit, © 2007 by the Regents of the University of California. Published by the University of California Press.

Excerpt from *Unfathomable City: A New Orleans Atlas*, by Rebecca Solnit, © 2013 by the Regents of the University of California. Published by the University of California Press.

Excerpt from *A Field Guide to Getting Lost* by Rebecca Solnit, copyright © 2005 by Rebecca Solnit. Used by permission of Viking Books, an imprint of Penguin Publishing Group, a division of Penguin Random House LLC. All rights reserved.

Excerpts from *Black Faces, White Spaces: Reimagining the Relationship of African Americans to the Great Outdoors* by Carolyn Finney. Copyright © 2014 by the University of North Carolina Press. Used by permission of the publisher. www.uncpress.org.

Excerpts from *H Is for Hawk* by Helen Macdonald. Published by Jonathan Cape. Reprinted by permission of The Random House Group Limited. © 2014.

Excerpts from *H Is for Hawk* by Helen Macdonald. Copyright © 2014 by Helen Macdonald. Used by permission of Grove/Atlantic, Inc. Any third-party use of this material, outside of this publication, is prohibited.

INDEX

KATHRYN AALTO is an American landscape designer, historian, and writer living in Exeter, England. She is the author of three books, including *Nature and Human Intervention* and *The Natural World of Winnie-the-Pooh*. Before her expat life, she renovated a turn-of-the-century farm and taught in the Pacific Northwest. You can find her online at kathrynaalto.com and on Instagram and Twitter (@kathrynaalto).

GISELA GOPPEL is an illustrator currently living on the edge of the Bavarian forest in Germany. She studied textile design at the University of Arts in Berlin and illustration in Barcelona. Since then she has been working for magazines and publishing houses around the world. She has two children, and when she's not drawing, she loves being outside with her family exploring wild nature or getting her hands dirty in the garden. Visit her at giselagoppel.de.